THE BIBLICAL CONCEPT OF POWER

by

CYRIL H. POWELL

LONDON: THE EPWORTH PRESS

FIRST PUBLISHED IN 1963

Book Steward
FRANK H. CUMBERS

SET IN MONOTYPE BASKERVILLE AND PRINTED IN
GREAT BRITAIN BY THE CAMELOT PRESS LTD
LONDON AND SOUTHAMPTON

CONTENTS

PART 2. THE INTERTESTAMENTAL PERIOD AND LATER JUDAISM

PART 3. THE NEW TESTAMENT

PREFACE

THIS Fernley-Hartley lecture represents the re-writing of a thesis originally presented to the University of Sheffield in 1957, for which the degree of Ph.D. was awarded. In its original form, and in its re-writing, it owes much to a host of writers and to the advice of a number of teachers under whom it has been my privilege to work, or from whom I have received notable help. I would especially like to mention with deep gratitude the names of Professor F. F. Bruce and Drs E. L. Allen, W. F. Lofthouse, W. F. Howard, C. R. North, and N. H. Snaith. It must, of course, be made clear that none of these is in any way to be held responsible for what follows!

Amongst the authors to whom special indebtedness must be expressed is Walter Grundmann, whose work, *Der Begriff der Kraft in der Neutestamentlicher Gedankenwelt*, and whose articles on δύναμις and ἰσχύς, etc., in Kittel's *Wörterbuch* are background influences. As is the way with theses, it is hoped that scholarly material once published may be incorporated without the necessity of asking permission. In each case I have endeavoured to make my indebtedness clear by footnote references. To all these writers and to all other scholars whose suggestions have contributed to the thought and study behind this book I would wish to pay my grateful thanks.

CYRIL H. POWELL

SUTTON, SURREY
December 1962

CHAPTER ONE

INTRODUCTION

THE word 'power' conjures up for modern man the idea of force breaking remorselessly through opposition. Primitive man thought of it somewhat similarly, though he had not abstracted the concept from the concrete situations in which he experienced it. His respect for power was animistic and spiritualistic as over against modern man's more 'materialistic' conceptions.

In order to enter the world of Hebraic thinking, both these sets of presuppositions need to be shed. The foundations of the concept here is in the personal God who has empowered every living thing. He is not to be thought of in such terms as 'the first cause', nor is He Himself force, nor just the source of power. It is His 'personhood', as Eichrodt describes it, that is the most distinctive factor about Him—'a personhood which is fully alive and a life which is fully personal'. His is the Will directing all things and making history. 'This', as Eichrodt says, 'implies a fulness of personal life which not only is different in principle from mere natural forces, but rejects as utterly alien the primitive conceptions of God attaching to the beliefs in spirits, "power", and magic.'[1]

Yahweh, the God of the Old Testament, is *qadosh* ('The Holy One'), the High God separated by the distance of His might and holiness from men and the world they live in. Yet He has revealed Himself as concerned to establish relations with men; and in these relationships He is not only to be known in His Wrath, exercising judgement in righteousness, but in grace and mercy.

Examining this concept of power, we follow the clues provided, seeking to understand God's government of the world, His intervention, when necessary, in its affairs, the way His powers are mediated, and how certain men are reinforced and enabled to serve His purposes.

Let us notice what this programme involves. First, we shall follow these clues in the Old Testament, and then into the literature of later Judaism. This background will better enable us

[1] *Old Testament Theology* (E.T.), 1961, I.211, 287.

to understand the emergence of God's 'Kingdom' in the New Testament era of fulfilment, when God's power is shared with men in the blessings of the new age.

In the New Testament we shall note our Lord's own interpretation of the Kingdom and Messiahship, and examine what 'power' and 'authority' mean in the context of His ministry. Then we come to the great New Testament 'acts of power' in Cross and Resurrection; and observe how, after this, the Spirit that has been fully upon Jesus has invaded His disciples. These men are now 'apostles', the centre of the infant church, which, though weak in men's eyes, exists and grows by the power of God.

Then we are able to sharpen our understanding of the power known in apostolic days by contrasting it, as does the New Testament, with the sorcery of the times. After inquiring into New Testament ideas concerning 'principalities and powers' and Satan and the forces of evil, we look again at the authority of the State and its rulers. Finally, we examine the kind of 'faith' which the New Testament shows to be closely allied with *dunamis*—the living link with God's Kingdom.

Here, in biblical religion, we are in the realms of the personal, learning of a God who can be intimately known, who shares His Spirit with the believer, to whom the fitting response is one of humility and obedience, love and service. No manipulation of supernatural forces avails here, but communion with God in His Being and through all He has made evident and available in His historic acts. The record of this unfolding is of the highest interest and fascination.

[Note: The version of the English Bible used, except where otherwise stated, is the Revised Version of 1901.]

Part One

THE OLD TESTAMENT

CHAPTER TWO

THE GOD OF POWER

THE God of the Bible is the God of *power*. Israel's cult is founded in this knowledge of Him. She had not come to know Him through speculation or processes of abstract thinking. He had acted in her history, making His promises to Abraham, revealing Himself to Moses, bringing the Hebrew slaves out of Egypt, and, throughout the years continuing to be this people's covenant God.

The recollection of the great historical events of the past was built into Israel's conscious and subconscious thinking. Much recent work on the Old Testament has proceeded on the assumption that behind the Hexateuch and the Psalter lie cultic festivals at which God's mighty acts were recounted in speech and song. Joshua's speech at Shechem provides the indication of a covenant-renewing festival continuing over many years.[1] On the basis of the kind of ritual carried through at the Akitu and New Year Festival of Babylonia, it can be imagined that the proceedings would involve a 'cultic drama', re-enacting the story of the first Covenant. This would account for the fact that in the credos no mention is made of the revelation at Sinai. There would be no need of mention, for at such a festival these events would form the background of all that was done.[2]

Whatever be the truth regarding this, we are certainly given the setting for one of these credal statements in Deuteronomy. At the Harvest Festival, the bearer of the first-fruits, as the priest takes the basket from his hand, is instructed to say:

A wandering Aramean was my father; and he went down into Egypt and sojourned there, few in number; and there he became a nation, great, mighty, and populous. And the Egyptians treated us harshly, and afflicted us, and laid upon us hard bondage. Then we cried to the Lord the God of our fathers, and the Lord heard our voice, and saw our affliction, our toil, and our oppression; *and the Lord brought us out of*

[1] The Qumran liturgy of their covenant-renewing festival, from a later time, enables us to conjecture what some of the elements might be (Deut 32; Ps 78, 105, 106, etc.). A. Weiser, *Psalms* (E.T.), 1962, p. 35.
[2] Cf. John Bright, *A History of Israel*, 1960, p. 115.

Egypt with a mighty hand and an outstretched arm, with great terror, with signs and wonders; and he brought us into this place and gave us this land, a land flowing with milk and honey. (Deut 26^{5-10}, R.S.V. Italics mine.)

At the back of everything to do with Israel's cultic life lay the thought of this great deliverance. The introduction to the Decalogue speaks of this: 'I am the Lord your God, who brought you out of the land of Egypt, out of the house of bondage' (Ex 20^{2}; Deut 5^{6}). As H. W. Robinson states, 'the only definition of Yahweh is the "out-of-Egypt-bringing God" as a German might say'.[3] Modern Germans (M. Noth, von Rad) have, indeed, designated the phrase 'Yahweh delivered his people from Egypt' as Israel's original confession.[4] This was the Israelite's definitive statement of God's power, made known in history. The phrase continually reminded him that Yahweh is the Living God, as present with His people contemporaneously as when He brought them out of Egypt. 'I am that I am' or 'I will be what I will be' is the One adequate for every situation, the Sovereign Lord.

These great credos, doxological statements and designations are scattered throughout the Old Testament, at every stage of its writing. In these statements the open reference to the concept of power is especially to be noted (e.g. 1 Ch 29^{10ff}; Ps 21^{13}, 59^{17}, 68^{33ff}; 2 Ch 20^{6}). Each succeeding generation learned of the *Heilsgeschichte*: 'We have heard with our ears, O God, our fathers have told us what work thou didst in their days, in the days of old' (Ps 44^{1ff}, $48^{8, 13f}$, 62^{11}, 75^{1}, 78^{3ff}, cf. 145^{4}), 'He hath made his wonderful works to be remembered . . . he hath showed his people the power of his works' (Ps $111^{4, 6}$).[5]

Whatever occurred in the actual escape from Egypt—and the events long talked over obviously become the source of various traditions by the time the Hexateuch came to be compiled—there can be no doubt as to Yahweh's intervention in power. As the ancient fragment in Ex 15^{21} reminds us concerning the pursuing Egyptians, 'He threw horse and rider into the sea'.

It is important, too, to notice that the establishing of the covenant at Sinai and the accompanying revelation of God's commandments happened against the background of events stressing the

[3] Art. 'The Religion of Israel', *Companion to Bible*, 1939, p. 290.
[4] G. von Rad, *Old Testament Theology*, (E.T.), 1962, I.176.
[5] A. Weiser, *Psalms*, p.43, W. Grundmann, *Theologisches Wörterbuch zum Neuen Testments* (hereinafter *T.W.z.N.T.*), II.295.

power and awefulness of God. The thunder and lightnings, the thick cloud upon the mountain (Ex 19^{16}), the fire, smoke and earthquake of verse 18 are folklore ideographs representing this. The God here revealed is the 'jealous God' who, though making covenant and coming into personal relationship with man, will yet brook no trifling with all He represents. As Walther Eichrodt comments, 'the terrifying power of the God, who will turn his weapons of leprosy, serpent and plague (cf. Ex 4^{1-7}; Num 21^{6ff}, 11^{33f}) against his own people, leaves men in no doubt that the covenant he has created is no safe bulwark behind which they can make cunning use of the divine power to prosecute their own interests'.[6]

From very early days it is clear that Yahweh is the only God who matters—and this because of His power. 'Who is a God like unto thee?' the Hebrew could ask, appealing to these deeds by which God had made Himself known. Before this demonstration of Yahweh's might, the gods of the heathen are as nothing. Yahweh is supreme (Ex 20^{3}), the Incomparable (Ps $89^{7, 9}$; Isa 43^{11ff}). This realization of Yahweh's power involved ascriptions of 'cosmic majesty' even at an early date. The Song of Deborah pictures how before this great and terrible One the earth trembles. the heavens drop, the mountains quake (Jdgs 5^{4f}). Even if figurative language is being used, it is impressive to be told that 'the stars in their courses' (Jdgs 5^{20}) and the sun in the heavens (Josh 10^{12f}), under God's power, come to the help of Israel.

These conceptions of Yahweh's invincible might, made known in Israel's history and guaranteeing His present ability to aid, did not pass without repeated challenge during the thousand years of her chequered career. Never was this more the case than in the events leading up to and including the Exile. Yet reflection was able to set this right. He who had allowed His people to go into Exile was the One who, through His servants the prophets, had warned them and predicted what would happen. He was as much behind these events as any other. Isaiah had, indeed, spoken of Assyria as the rod of *His* anger, and Jeremiah of Nebuchadrezzar as the servant of His purposes. The people had contributed to their own downfall. They had been faithless to the covenant. What had happened was punishment, fully deserved. It could also be a refining experience fitting them for better service in the future.

[6] *Old Testament Theology*, I.45.

It was thus in Exile that the Jew came to a deeper understanding of God's *universal* power, and began to think in terms of a great missionary purpose. In the years following 597 B.C. Judaism was born.[7] And the fact of the return from Exile provided almost as great a miracle as Yahweh's bringing of His people to the land of promise centuries beforehand.

At every point the instructed Hebrew saw evidence of God's power.

From the mid-years of Israel's history we can choose such a hymn as Psalm 29 to illustrate Yahweh's handling of what we think of as the 'natural world'. Whether this, as has been suggested, was originally a Canaanite hymn to the storm god adapted to Israelite use or not, it typifies the ancient Hebrew conception of Yahweh's Kingship and the outworking of His might. It can be dated in the tenth century, or even earlier.

The 'sons of God' (*bene elim*) are called upon to praise Him who is King among all gods. Yahweh's voice sounds over the waters, in the thunder, breaking the cedars, making the mountains dance, darting from heaven in the stroke of the lightning, shaking the wilderness, manifesting power and striking terror, making the hinds calve prematurely in fear (or, like the Baals of Canaan, making them fertile?)[8] and stripping bare the forests.[9] No wonder that in His Temple (in the first place, of course, the heavenly Temple where 'the sons of God' acclaim Him) the shout of glory is raised.

This is Yahweh who sat enthroned over the flood (or, who controls the cosmic deep?).[10] He is in control over the fiercest and most destructive of forces: the One giving strength to His people, and granting them peace. This psalm, recalling seven great kratophanies in which Yahweh reveals His power, rounds in with the typical thought that His greatness is manifested most in His blessings to Israel.

The poems in Job (*c.* fourth century B.C.) again illustrate this thought of God's complete control of all that is:

> If one wished to contend with him
> one could not answer him once in a thousand times.

[7] See John Bright, *History of Israel*, pp. 323, 328ff.
[8] So G. W. Anderson, 'Psalms' in *Peake's Commentary*, 1962.
[9] R.S.V. by a slight emendation translates verse 9: 'The voice of the Lord makes the oaks to whirl, and strips the forests bare.'
[10] The word *mabbul* is used only here and in Genesis 6[11], however.

He is wise in heart, and mighty in strength
  —who has hardened himself against him, and succeeded?—
he who removes mountains, and they know it not,
  when he overturns them in his anger;
who shakes the earth out of its place
  and its pillars tremble;
who commands the sun, and it does not rise;
  who seals up the stars;
who alone stretched out the heavens,
  and trampled the waves of the sea;
who made the Bear and Orion
  the Pleiades[11] and the chambers of the south;
who does great things beyond understanding,
  and marvellous things without number.

(Job 9^{3-10}, R.S.V.)

As in Deutero-Isaiah (e.g. Isa 40^{26}, 45^{12}), one glimpses here the God who made and rules the constellations.

In Job 26^{5ff}, after using all the myth and imagery of the Near East (Sheol, Abaddan, Rahab, the serpent, etc.) in a tremendous description of the cosmic creative force of Yahweh the poet concludes, in verse 14 (R.S.V.),

Lo, these are but the outskirts of his ways;
  and how small a whisper do we hear of him!
But the thunder of his power who can understand?

[11] The names of the constellations are our Western equivalents of Job's 'Lion', 'Fool' and 'Fat One': W. A. Irwin 'Job': *Peake's Commentary*, 1962, p. 395.

CHAPTER THREE

ASPECTS OF HIS POWER

SOME of the facets of the Old Testament God of power need to be examined in closer detail. Reference has been made to His power in the realm of 'nature' and to His holiness. These are among the concepts which must now be reviewed.

I. GOD AND 'NATURE'

Typical of Hebrew thought regarding Yahweh's relationship to 'nature' is the idea of His Kingship. He reigns over all things (Ps 93^{1}). He rules the sea, holding back the floods and keeping in check the forces of chaos (Ps 104, 107^{23ff}). He is Lord of the world of men and of animals (Ps 36^{6}), providing His creatures with food (Ps 104^{14f}, 147^{9}). Governing the earth, He sends or withholds the rain upon it (Jer 5^{24}; 1 K 17). It is Yahweh who causes the great flood of Genesis 7 and overthrows the cities of the plain (Gen 19). By contrast with the complete control He exercises, the Baals of Canaan seem to be part of the very realm of which they are 'gods'.

> But ask the beasts, and they will teach you;
>   the birds of the air, and they will tell you;
> or the plants of the earth, and they will teach you;
>   and the fish of the sea will declare to you.
> Who among all these does not know
>   that the hand of the Lord has done this?
> In his hand is the life of every living thing
>   and the breath of all mankind.
>
> If he tears down, none can rebuild;
>   if he shuts a man in, none can open.
> If he withholds the waters, they dry up;
>   If he sends them out, they overwhelm the land.
>
> (Job $12^{7-10, 14f}$, R.S.V.)

It is axiomatic that God, being who He is, has all things in His control. The beginning as well as the end is bound to belong to Him. His creative activity[1] is continued in His providential

[1] Which always evokes awe and wonder on the part of man (Ps 24^{14ff}, 104; Job 38^{4ff}; Prov 30^{4}; Isa 40^{12}).

concern over all He has made. Nehemiah 9^{6} speaks of this: 'Thou art Yahweh, even thou alone; thou hast made heaven, the heaven of heavens, with all their host, the earth, and all things that are thereon, the seas and all that is in them, and thou preservest them all. . . .' Passages such as Jeremiah 10^{13}, and Psalm 147^{16f}, 65^{9f} fill in this picture. The saga of Genesis 1 tells how an almighty God brought all things into being through His creative word, after agitating the formless chaos by a divine storm.[2]

In Jeremiah 4^{23ff} the prophet envisions what would happen if in His anger God should withdraw His presence from the world: all things utterly fail, the heavens are without light, and the earth returns to the *tohu wa-bohu* from which it came. This idea of God's possible destruction of His creation is not infrequent in prophetic thought (cf. Amos 1^{2}; Isa $13^{10, 13}$, etc.). Yahweh is not in any way bound by His creation. He can shake the heavens and the earth at any time. It is true that God gave assurance of future seed-time and harvest to Noah: but the days of the earth's remaining are under His grace, and are due to nothing else.[3]

Behind nature's handiwork, the Hebrew sees God. On the one hand, the physical world is a pledge of His steadfastness and goodness and, on the other, a perpetual reminder of His majesty, wisdom and power. It is the arena in which God fulfils His purposes for man, and in which the 'history-forming' power of God[4] is shown. 'Shall evil befall a city and Yahweh hath not done it?' asks Amos (3^{6}; cf. Is. 45^{7}). The very limitations and defects of nature, for the Hebrew, point beyond themselves to the unlimited resources of its Creator and Upholder, who shall finally be its redeemer.[5]

All nature is thus, in the sense of our modern term, 'supernatural'. God is directly in charge. Of course, He controls the weather. What we think of as 'miracle' is simply, for the Hebrew, the occasion when His command and intervention become more

[2] So von Rad for *ruach Elohim* (verse 2): see *Genesis*, p. 47.

[3] L. Köhler, *Old Testament Theology* (E.T.), 1957, pp. 91f.

[4] The phrase is W. Grundmann's in *T.W.z.N.T.*, II, p. 293. Cf. H. W. Robinson, *The Religious Ideas of the Old Testament*, pp. 72, 98. G. F. Moore (*Judaism*, I.449) quotes the Syriac Apocalypse of Baruch 14^{18}: 'that it might be known that he [man] was not made for the sake of the world, but the world for his sake.' Moore cogently remarks that in Jewish sources the proposition is more commonly expressed that the world was made for Israel! (e.g. 2 Esd. $6^{55, 59}$, 7^{11}; Ass Moses 1^{12}). All God's transforming acts in nature are for the benefit of His people (e.g. Isa 41^{17f}, 43^{20}).

[5] Cf. Rom 8^{20ff}.

obvious than usual.[6] In obedience and humility, man, realizing his creatureliness, should recognize God's power to act with decision and miracle, true to no purposes but His own.[7]

II. YAHWEH'S HOLINESS

Amongst the great titles that Deutero-Isaiah uses for God is *qadosh*. He is the 'Holy One' of Israel.[8] The root word behind this title has a history of associations with the separation of sacred places and objects. Everything withdrawn from common use because of its connexion—even by chance—with the supernatural was described by this term.[9] So far from possessing an ethical flavour originally, the word was used of the dedicated prostitute of Canaanitish sanctuaries (Deut 23^{17}).[10]

Otto has described the *mysterium tremendum* felt by man in the presence of the unknown and the divine. As the 'wholly other', God calls out this response. It is the awareness of a gulf of separation. Primitive man knew a dread containing elements of awe and 'overpoweringness'. Also involved was the recognition of energy. At the centre of the holy lay dynamic power. There was a 'livingness' behind all things so designated. Combining with these other responses in man was the 'fascination' exercised by the supernaturally-charged object. Man was both allured and repelled by it: recognizing its fascination, but afraid of its power.[11]

Holiness, resulting from the *ganz andere* nature of the supra-human, built up an accumulation of force in special places. Sinai was specifically *the* Holy Mountain of the desert-experience; the Tabernacle, *the* Holy Tent of meeting with Yahweh; then there were the wells, tombs, and stones where holy energy was active and Elohim had made themselves known. The Ark was a centre

[6] C. R. North, *Old Testament Interpretation of History*, 1946, p. 169.

[7] Cf. Job 38ff; Isa 48^{11}, 55^{8f}. (see Bultmann, *Essays Philosophical and Theological*, (E.T.), 1956, pp. 115ff.)

[8] This designation of God, according to Sellin, has no parallel outside Israel, though the general conception of *qadosh* and *qodesh*, as what is sacred or separated from the secular is general. H. W. Robinson, *Record and Revelation*, p. 323.

[9] N. H. Snaith, in a long discussion of the root meaning and origin of the root *q-d-sh* (*Distinctive Ideas of the Old Testament*, pp. 21ff), makes the point that the root stands for the difference between God and man, but that it does so positively rather than negatively. The separation, he says, is separation *to* rather than separation *from*. The root immediately suggests contact with the supra-human world.

[10] Snaith again makes the point that we should not dismiss the possibility of ethical meaning quite so brusquely. The word had no moral content in our developed sense, 'but it did involve pre-ethical restrictions, as undeveloped in content as itself' (ibid., p. 32).

[11] *The Idea of the Holy* (E.T.), pp. 12ff, 20ff, 23f, 30ff.

of such force. So strong were its associations that, for good or ill, it was a most potent source of holiness (1 Sam 5^{6}). On looking into it, the men of Beth-Shemesh asked (1 Sam 6^{20}), 'Who is able to stand before Yahweh, this holy God?'

Later, this idea became moralized, the capricious, dynamic element in holiness giving place to considerations concerning ethics and law-morality. Since *q-d-sh* has to do with what is of God, the picture of what is 'holy'[12] is filled out by further understanding of His will and of His reaction to sin.

When Yahweh, in Isaiah's phrase, came to be designated 'the Holy One of Israel', it meant the recognition that 'all the holiness of Israel is being derived from Him'. For Israel now there is only one divine being.[13] There is no *qodesh* apart from Him. And the more His character is understood as concerned with righteousness and goodness, the more does the significance of His title as Holy One change from associations of mysterious energy and 'unpredictable' power to those of judgement and righteousness.

III. THE WRATH OF GOD

Otto indicates the connexion between God's holiness and His wrath (*'aph* from *'anaph*, 'to snort', 'be angry'). As with His 'holiness', there was about it, in the early days, the element of the unpredictable. It was like 'stored-up electricity, discharging itself upon anyone who comes too near'.[14] This is illustrated in the story of Uzzah and the Ark in 2 Sam 6, when God's 'anger' was kindled against the man touching the object replete with holiness (verse 7). Many references in the older parts of the Pentateuch emphasize the fearful and incomprehensible nature of God's anger (Ex19^{22}; Num 11^{10}, 22^{22}), though the tendency increases to rationalize and explain these outbreaks (e.g. Num 12^{9ff}, 16^{20ff}, 21^{6f}, 25^{11}).

Just as the idea of holiness became moralized, so the Israelite came also to a developing understanding of God's wrath. It had always been roused by disobedience and wilfulness (Num 32^{13f}) and by the worship of other gods and by idolatry (Deut 32^{19}; 2K 17^{13ff}, 22^{17}), but the increasing insistence is that it is especially provoked by sin in His people (Ps 89 ^{30ff}; Is 47^{6}). It is impressive

[12] See e.g. *The Faith of Israel* (H. H. Rowley), p. 66. Holiness comes to be seen as the 'antithesis of all moral stain, that quality in God which is not only a rebuke to all in man which is contrary to His will, but in whose presence sin cannot live'.

[13] J. Pedersen, *Israel*, I.502. [14] *The Idea of the Holy*, p. 18.

to note that in pre-Exilic days the divine wrath is rarely shown as turned upon Gentiles. Neither the destruction of Sodom and Gomorrah, nor the Red Sea annihilation, as A. T. Hanson points out, are referred to as manifestations of it. The fact stresses the intensely personal nature of God's wrath, as then understood: it was His reaction against His own people, with whom He had personal dealings.[15]

Passages in Amos (3^{6}, 4^{6ff}) show the connexion made between this concept and the onset of adversity. A series of references in Isaiah 9^{8}, 10^{4}, indicate how various calamities—foreign invasion, destruction, fire, famine, fratricide—are all attributed to God's fierce anger, and Isaiah 10^{5} emphasizes that He uses human instruments, as well as natural forces, as channels of His wrath.[16]

The prophets observe that God's love and compassion temper His wrath, lifting it above likeness to human anger (Hos 11^{9}; cf. Amos 7^{1ff}; Jer 18^{7ff}; Dan 9^{16}). These two things in Him are not contradictory. There is, indeed, a sense in which His wrath is best conceived as His love 'in reverse'.[17] It is because His love is set on Israel, that He will not tolerate what works against this.

It is to be observed how the Chronicler, re-writing ancient stories in later days, rationalizes and moralizes some of these earlier conceptions. In 1 Chronicles 15^{13}, the fearful breaking out upon Uzzah is explained, and in 21^{1} it is Satan, and not God in His wrath, who moves David to number Israel. In these writings the Wrath, which here is most often provoked by idolatry, is referred to almost as if it were an impersonal force (1 Ch 27^{24}; 2 Ch 19^{10}, etc.), which is very much the conception that meets us in Romans 1, 12^{19}, and 13^{4}.

If then it might be said that the Chronicler prepares us for the Pauline treatment of God's wrath,[18] so, similarly, Daniel prepares us for the treatment in Revelation. Cosmic destruction attends the working out of the impersonal and majestic Wrath poured out upon the enemies of God (Dan. 8^{19}, 9^{27}).

The prophets have widened the bounds of the incidence of God's wrath. They see it now not only visited upon unfaithful Israel, but also upon Gentiles, who, by their attitude towards Israel, show themselves to be God's enemies (Jer 50^{13}; Ezek 38^{18}; Ps 79^{6f}). Amos has a series of oracles (1^{3}-2^{3}) concerning other

[15] *The Wrath of the Lamb*, 1957, p. 12. [16] Ibid., p. 7.
[17] Ezek 23 and Amos 3^{2} help to make this clear. [18] Hanson, op. cit., p. 23.

nations whose blatant acts of inhumanity constitute an offence against Yahweh's righteousness and judgement, and who are therefore objects of the Wrath. Because of their crimes and injustices, God will not 'turn away the punishment' irretrievably rolling against them.

One further development needs to be noticed: though the Wrath may be experienced at any time, the prophets associate its breaking out in power and destruction more particularly with the coming Day of the Lord. This is to be a day of judgement and of vengeance (Isa 2^{10ff}; Jer 30^{5ff}; Joel 3^{12ff}; Zeph 3^{18}). From 'being a temporary misfortune', comments Walther Eichrodt, 'the wrath of God became an *inescapable eschatological doom*'.[19]

IV. DIVINE REVELATION AND COMMUNICATION

In the earlier anthropomorphism, God's face (*panim*: cf. Peniel, the place where God is seen: Gen 32^{30})[20], His voice (*qol*: Gen 3^{8}; Ex 19^{19}), God's word (*dabar*: Gen $15^{1, 4}$) are all vehicles of His self-manifestation. Associated with His presence is also His glory (*kabod*: Ex 24^{17}, 23^{34}), which is pictured, therefore, 'like devouring fire' 'filling the tabernacle'. He was the God who walked and talked with the man He had made in the garden in the cool of the day (Gen 3^{8}), revealing Himself to the patriarchs by the sacred wells, trees, and stones of Beersheba, Mamre, and Bethel, and to Moses at the Burning Bush. Storm and fire phenomena were associated with the theophany of Sinai. These were manifestations of Yahweh. On the dark thunder-clouds, riding on the cherubim (Ps 18^{10}), He came from Seir (Jdgs 5^{4}).

Yahweh's *mal'ak*, His 'angel', is a special form of manifestation. He is, indeed, Yahweh Himself, though in some sense different. In Genesis 31^{11ff} Jacob reports: 'The angel of God spake unto me . . . and said, I am the God of Bethel' (cf. Gen 16^{7ff}; Num 22^{22ff}, etc.).[21]

[19] *Old Testament Theology* I.267.

[20] Gen. 4^{14}; Ex 33^{14}. There are other passages where the contrasting idea is quoted: that man cannot see God's face and live (Ex 33^{20}; Jdgs 6^{22}, etc.).

[21] Moore (*Judaism*, III.123, n. 133) comments that the etymology of *mal'ak* suggests the English equivalent 'agent'. Yahweh's *mal'ak* was at times obviously a human messenger (e.g. Hag 1^{13}; Mal 2^{7}). S. A. Cook (*The Old Testament: a Reinterpretation*, 1936, p. 160) says that it is possible from the Hebrew and Greek texts of some passages (e.g. Gen 21^{17f}, Jdgs 6^{13}) to discern the difficulty later editors found in dealing with what in these instances was evidently a complete manifestation of Yahweh, yet not precisely Yahweh Himself.

V. GOD AND THE UNSEEN WORLD

Part of the genius of Yahwism was to turn the manifold superhuman beings known to pre-Mosaic religion, and to the Canaanites, into servants and messengers of Yahweh.[22] In the Old Testament Yahweh is described as holding court in heaven (e.g. Job 1^{2}, where among his servants is Satan, the accuser. See also 1 K 22^{21}; Ps $103^{19, 21}$; Zech 14^{5}, etc.). 'Worship him, all ye gods', says the Psalmist (97^{7}).

S. A. Cook comments concerning 'the numerous angels of the post-Exilic period', that they 'can probably be best explained as the late representatives of the earlier gods'.[23] In the earlier stories we have heard of Yahweh's *mal'ak*. This was a temporary manifestation of Yahweh, quite different from the *mal'akim* of Exilic and post-Exilic times. These acted as God's agents, revealing His will to men (e.g. Ezek 3^{12}, 8^{2f}; Zech 1–8, etc.). With monotheism established in much more absolute fashion, and with the thought of God becoming increasingly transcendent, pressure developed for the envisaging of angelic beings as mediators between Him and the world of men. This process continued to go forward during the Greek period; paving the way for the New Testament references to angelic powers.[24] The process was much influenced by Persian thought, but the material for its development already existed in Judaism's earlier background.

References also occur to the demon inhabitants of the unseen world. Isaiah 34^{14} mentions a number of 'demons of the waste', thought to invest the bodies of certain animals: 'And the wild beast of the desert (*tsiyyim*; cf. Jer 50^{39}) shall encounter the wolves (*'iyyim*) and the *sa'ir* ("he-goat") shall meet his fellows; there in truth shall *lilith* (the fearful nocturnal demon known among the Assyrians and Babylonians) repose.' The *se'irim* of Leviticus 17^{7}, and the ghoul (*'aluqah*) of Proverbs 30^{15} also form part of the Old Testament picture.[25] It is never implied, however, that these demons are anything but subservient to Yahweh. Their abode is, typically, the desert. The *seraphim* (winged serpents) thought by

[22] M. Löhr, *A History of Religion in the Old Testament*, 1936, pp. 178f.

[23] *The Old Testament: a Reinterpretation*, p. 159.

[24] See C. H. Dodd, *The Bible and the Greeks*, 1935, pp. 17ff, and *The Parables of the Kingdom*, 1935, p. 83.

[25] For an account of Hebrew demonology, see Oesterley and Robinson, *Hebrew Religion* (2nd Ed., 1937) pp. 111ff, L. Köhler, *Hebrew Man* (London, 1956), pp. 135f, and E. Langton, *Essentials of Demonology*, 1949.

some to have once been part of the demon pantheon, are found in Yahweh's worshipping entourage.[26] In the vision of Isaiah 6, they are spirits worshipping Him (cf. 2 K 18^{4}; Num 21^{4ff}).

G. B. Caird quotes an amended version of Deuteronomy 32^{8f}, which, if accepted, sheds light on the developments that had occurred by Exilic times: 'When the Most High gave to the nations their inheritance, when he separated the sons of men, he fixed the borders of the peoples, according to the number of the sons of God.[27] For Yahweh's portion is his people; Jacob is his allotted inheritance.' As Caird points out, this is in conformity with Deuteronomy 4^{19}: 'lest thou lift up thine eyes unto heaven, and when thou seest the sun and the moon and the stars, even all the host of heaven, thou be drawn away and worship them, and serve them, which the Lord thy God hath divided (allotted) unto all the peoples under the whole heaven'.

By the time Daniel was written this conception is fully fledged. In God's heavenly court guardian angels represent each nation. In this way, influenced still further by Zoroastrianism, the 'gods of the nations' have become God's own appointed ministrants and messengers. This is the background to the conception of the ἐξουσίαι, the angelic rulers of the nations, which some commentators discern in the references in Romans 13^{1ff} and elsewhere in the New Testament.

[26] Another suggestion is that seraphim means 'burning ones', and that they are not demons, but personifications of lightning.

[27] 'Sons of God' by the reading in LXX and Qumran text (see P. W. Skehan, 'A Fragment of the "Song of Moses" (Deut 32) from Qumran', *Bulletin of American Schools of Oriental Research*, No. 136: December 1954). See also Caird's comments, *Principalities and Powers*, p. 41f.

CHAPTER FOUR

THE EMPOWERMENT OF MAN

MAN is a body vitalized by a breath-soul (e.g. Gen 2^{7}, where Yahweh, having modelled man's body out of the earth, quickens it by His breath, and man becomes *nephesh chayyah*, a 'living soul').[1] Inanimate flesh and bones are *nebelah* ('carcase'). The 'living soul' is distinguished from *nebelah* by the blood flowing in the veins, and the breath in the lungs.[2] At death, man's vitality, represented by his breath (*ruach* or *neshamah*) goes from him, and returns to God who gave it.[3]

In the later account of creation this sense of a special link with God is deepened; man, it is there stated, is made in the image (*tselem*) of God (Gen 1^{26f}). There is that in man uniquely connected with God and capable of responding to Him. Man is, therefore, peculiarly open to the invasion of divine influence, e.g. to God's *ruach*.[4]

Two other features of Hebraic thinking need to be borne in mind: (1) what A. R. Johnson calls 'the awareness of totality',[5] which means that man is thought of as a whole rather than as an assembly of separate parts. The instinct for this type of thinking goes deep, and aids in understanding the closeness of the link the Israelite felt with his family, clan and race; and (2) what H. W. Robinson refers to as the 'diffused consciousness'[6] thought to operate throughout the whole body. All the organs, bones, and flesh, in virtue of this, express psychic and moral qualities.

Not only is an individual's vital power resident in peripheral

[1] Nephesh carries general rather than specific meaning, comparable to *anima* in Latin. Normally, it is used of man. Thirty-two times in the Old Testament it is used of animal life, and twenty-one times it is used analogously of Yahweh. See A. R. Johnson, *The Vitality of the Individual in the Thought of Ancient Israel*, (Cardiff, 1949, p. 12).

[2] Cf. Gen 9^{4}; Lev $17^{11, 14}$ for this vital connexion.

[3] W. A. L. Elmslie, *How Came Our Faith*, Cambridge, 1950, p. 124.

[4] And, according to the Old Testament, to other psychic invasions, too, i.e. demonic influence, and to the power of the blessing and the curse.

[5] Ibid., p. 7.

[6] In *Record and Revelation*, p. 331. At the same time, because of the point already made about awareness of totality, many references to individual parts of the body are synedochal, not to be interpreted as if referring to their independent functioning. See A. R. Johnson, ibid., pp. 39-88, for illustrations of this.

organs, but also in other things intimately associated with his person. Something of it connects with one's name, one's word, property, offspring—all of which can be thought of as 'extensions of the personality'.[7]

I. BLESSING AND CURSING

To the Hebrew blessing and cursing are not mere words. By means of them psychic strength could be increased or diminished. J. Pedersen has laid stress on their importance in understanding Hebrew psychology.[8] Here is a clue of the first order in connexion with the concept of power.

In Genesis 1^{22} God blesses the animal life He has created, and commands the animals to be fruitful and multiply. Similarly, (1^{28}, 5^{2}) He blesses mankind, telling them to be fruitful and multiply, and to have dominion over all created things.[9] God has power to bestow good, and to promote fecundity.[10]

He is the ultimate source of this strengthening. By His blessing of Abraham, Yahweh begins the whole cycle of patriarchal blessing. Isaiah 65^{16} and Jeremiah 4^{2} use a significant phrase: individuals or nations are to 'bless themselves in Him'. Isaac is the 'blessed of the Lord'. This means, as the parallelism of two phrases indicates, that 'Yahweh is with him' (Genesis 26^{2}; cf. verse 28). Yahweh is similarly described as being 'with Samuel' (1 Sam 3^{19}) and, at the beginning, 'with Saul' (1 Sam 10^{7}). David, who took the blessing from Saul, exemplifies, at every point of his successful career, how a man fares when Yahweh is with him (cf. 1 Sam 16^{18}, $18^{12, 14}$, 20^{13}).[11]

The conferment of blessing, though essentially a gift of God, is not arbitrary. Gideon's story shows the interaction between God's blessing (e.g. in the greeting, 'Yahweh is with thee') and Gideon's response and final acceptance of his commission (Jdgs 6^{10ff}). Thus does Gideon become a *gibbor chayil* (a mighty man of valour).[12]

[7] *The Vitality of the Individual in the Thought of Ancient Israel*, p. 89. Note e.g. how Goliath's strength is associated with his sword (1 Sam 21^{9}) and the mantle of Elijah possesses something of his power (2 K 2^{14}), W. A. L. Elmslie, *How Came Our Faith*, p. 126.

[8] *Israel*, especially Vol. 1. See also Moore, *Judaism in the First Centuries of the Christian Era*, I.414ff, for a discussion on the power of the spoken word, e.g. in blessing and cursing.

[9] Note, however, Gen 2^{3}, a blessing of a different order. Even this means that the seventh day, because of its character, becomes a source of vitality and increased life.

[10] Cf. Gen 9, 12^{2}, 13^{16}, 26^{24}; Ex 23^{25f}; Lev 25^{21}, etc., for this connexion between blessing and fertility.

[11] *Israel*, I.194. [12] Ibid., p. 195.

The strength of the blessing can be estimated by a man's ability to act with power. By means of it a man can implement his own counsel. Pedersen cites Psalm 21^{12}: the wicked 'intended evil, but they could not'. Compared with this ineffectiveness, the victor, the man under blessing, 'can' (*yakol*) (Gen 30^{8}, 32$^{26, 29}$).[13]

With regard to the actual act of blessing, the stories of Isaac's blessing of Esau and Jacob and Balaam's attempt to curse Israel are instructive. Isaac needed to reinforce his strength with food before girding himself to give the blessing. Having once uttered it, it could not be retracted. Coming from the soul of him who created it, the power it sought to communicate must now go forth. Balaam possessed special powers in these matters (Num 22^{6}), but he must not act out of accord with underlying reality. So, instead of cursing Israel, Yahweh instructs him to bless them, 'for they are blessed' (Num 22^{12}).[14]

The uttering of a curse was similarly charged with psychic force. If the recipient's 'psychic armour—his measure of Divine Blessing—was adequate', a curse would fall from him harmlessly, or recoil upon the one uttering it.[15]

Behind these conceptions lie not only influences which shade off into witchcraft, but also experience of the fact that in the interchange of life a man receives strengthening and enrichment from others, and sometimes denudation and weakening. For better or worse, we in our turn influence others. Those who shared in the blessings of the Covenant people knew, especially, that a man receives much from the dispensations of God to his race.

Opposing life's positive forces working in blessing and honour[16] are those of shame, falsehood, and powerlessness. One cannot, Pedersen comments, 'sin with the whole heart, for sin is the very dissolution of the totality'.[17] These latter influences work negatively. What is false (*sheqer*) is without power. The visions of 'false' prophets have no authority. Idols are falsehood; 'there is no soul (*ruach*) in them' (Jer 10^{14}, 51^{17}). The apparent prosperity of the wicked is against nature: founded on emptiness, it will swiftly pass. The man of *beliyya'al* (negative of root *y'l*, carrying

[13] *Israel*, p. 197. [14] Ibid., p. 200.

[15] W. A. L. Elmslie, *How Came Our Faith*, p. 126.

[16] In E.T. this word often stands for *kabod* (heaviness), i.e. that which gives weight to the substance of the soul. Another word for greatness of soul is *ga'on* (height). Related words are *tiph'ereth* (glory) and *hod* and *hadar*. Pedersen, ibid., p. 237.

[17] Ibid., p. 411.

through a normal, good action) are 'empty men' (2 Ch 13^{7}).[18] Sin, as revolt and disobedience against God, involves being cut off from the flow of real life in Him. The poison of dissolution, the curse that overtakes a sinner, the Old Testament knows as *'alah*. Isaiah 24^{6ff} and Jer 23^{10} give terrifying pictures of its outworkings: everything is dying and languishing, the source of life is denied, nothing grows or germinates.[19] Starting from within the soul and working outward through all things, the dreadful nemesis operates.

II. STRENGTH FOR WARFARE

Preparation for warfare is also indicative of Hebraic ideas concerning strength and power. Yahweh to the Israelites in the desert and in Canaan was 'a man of war', the God of battles (Ex 15^{3}), with them in all their fighting (Deut 20^{1ff}). His people expected help and special endowment from Him in the day of battle.

It is difficult to discover what is primary in the concept of the 'Holy War'. As Gerhard von Rad has demonstrated in his book on the subject,[20] an ideology was built up in later generations. But behind this was something original and primitive. In particular, the Deuteronomist in the days of Josiah, faced with the stresses of his own time, found in this concept a rallying-point for his contemporaries, and seems to have embellished a good deal of primitive material.

Accordingly, we are provided with what von Rad describes as the theory of the Holy War. These are its characteristic rites and accompaniments: the summons to war, through the blowing of a trumpet (Jdgs 6^{34f}; 1 Sam 13^{3}, etc.), the setting up of the camp, and the insistence that the folk therein are specifically 'Yahweh's people' (Jdgs 5$^{11, 13}$, etc.), 'sanctified', and under sacred ordinances (Josh 3^{5}; 1 Sam 21^{6}) the emphasis that the war is Yahweh's (1 Sam 18^{17}, 25^{28}) and the enemy Yahweh's enemy (Jdgs 5^{31}; 1 Sam 30^{26}). Yahweh alone is director of the battle (Ex 14$^{4, 14, 18}$, etc.), making His will known (Jdgs 20$^{23, 27}$; 1 Sam 7^{9}), and delivering the enemy into Israel's hands (Josh 2^{24}, 6$^{2, 16}$, etc.). Here a discernible pattern has been imposed on what was original and historical.

[18] Ibid., p. 431; cf. 1 Sam 2^{12} of Eli's sons and 1 Sam 25$^{17, 25}$ of Nabal.

[19] Ibid., p. 437. The classic catalogue of cursing set against the corresponding blessings in Deut 28, (cf. Lev 26), illustrates how nothing succeeds for the sinner (ibid., p. 440).

[20] *Der Heilige Krieg im alten Israel* (Zürich, 1951).

In examining the references, von Rad points out that Deuteronomy itself is by far the richest source concerning the customs of the Holy War. Characteristically—and quite unhistorically—Israel is thought of as a unity during the times described, and the battle is also between Israel's enemies and 'the people' (6^{18}, 7^{1f}, 11^{23ff}, etc.). A passage like Deut 23^{9ff} evidences the superimposition of theology; Deuteronomy 20^{1ff} demonstrates literary arrangement and elaboration; while the typical priestly war utterance of Deuteronomy 20^{2ff} (cf. 7^{16ff}) is obviously an invention.[21]

From earlier records (e.g. the Song of Deborah, Jdgs 5) we discover the sense, real and living, of first-hand reliance upon Yahweh's personal aid. One theme of the old war narratives is that Israel is 'not to fear, but to trust' (e.g. Ex 14^{13}; Josh 8^{1}). Von Rad criticizes Pedersen for providing a predominantly magical interpretation of the facts connected with the Holy War, as if it were 'a huge, magical concatenation of power'.[22] It is true that Pedersen views God as the source from whom each separate warrior receives strength. The task of the leader of the host is to increase this through communication with its source, and he comments, 'the powers are such that, though unseen, they decide the outcome'. On the other hand, von Rad sees the decisive intervention, not in 'powers', but in the *tsideqoth yhwh*, the 'righteous acts', the saving direction of Yahweh, which Deborah's song recalls (Jdgs 5^{11}), an intervention always personal, not through mediatory powers, but because Yahweh Himself was present to thunder, or to shake the earth. The truth about Israel's warfaring is probably in a mid-position between these two views. The preparations for it, undoubtedly embedded in the fully-fledged doctrine of the Holy War, were designed to put the relation between Yahweh and the people in order. Sacrificial rites, therefore, preceded a campaign (1 Sam 7^{8ff}, 13^{9f}). The correct state of the warriors was *qodesh* (holiness). They were thought of, at least in some sense, as the 'sanctified' of Yahweh (Isa 13^{3}). These preparations find their summary in the expression to 'sanctify war' (Jer 6^{4}, 22^{7}; Mic 3^{5}, etc.).

III. SACRIFICE AND FESTIVALS

Of all the ways of renewing holiness, and of being set right with God, none was more frequently resorted to than sacrifice. This

[21] *Der Heilige Krieg im alten Israel* (Zürich, 1951), pp. 68ff.
[22] Ibid., p. 30; cf. *Israel* II.1-32.

was something man felt he could do from his side of reality. When the Israelite presented himself, together with his sacrifice, in penitence and submission, divine power cleansed him from sin, brought him into fellowship with God again, and renewed God's gifts in him. The sacrifice of the animal was both the means of his approach to God, and 'the organ of God's approach in power to bless him'.[23] Many in Israel, doubtless, thought of sacrifices as a magical means of securing God's favour: but in their true meaning, as symbolic acts, 'actualized approaches to God',[24] their efficacy depended upon the worshipper's attitude of mind, his faith and humility.[25]

Israel's ultimate sacrificial system was, without doubt, part-Canaanitish and part Israelite in origin.[26] A number of motives would thus be operating in the resulting complex system. Pedersen thinks that in the offering of the first-fruits and the first-born, the principle of giving is conceived as operating in the holy sphere just as it does among men. In return, blessing comes, the worshipper himself 'obtaining a share in the holiness created by the sacrifice'. At the close of the monarchical period, the idea of expiation was much in mind. The Temple at Jerusalem, as the central holy place, became the focal point where, through sacrifice, one might maintain oneself in holiness and receive help in the fight against evil.[27] Rightly offered, the sacrifice connected one with the realm of power. The fire, the smoke and the burning helped to carry one's needs and one's spirit towards God, bringing back from Him an answer.[28]

Doubtless, the absence of reflection on the meaning of sacrifice

[23] H. H. Rowley, 'The Meaning of Sacrifice in the Old Testament, *John Rylands Library Bulletin*, September 1950, p. 95.

[24] H. Wheeler Robinson, *Inspiration and Revelation in the Old Testament*, p. 227.

[25] No single theory of sacrifice does justice to all the facts. The following elements are all discernible at times: (1) Sacrifice provides a means of communion between God and worshipper, especially in the sacrificial meal (W. Robertson Smith, Jevons, Burnley). (2) It was a propitiatory offering meant to secure God's help (Tylor, Curtiss, Baumgartner, Eichrodt, and Westermarck think the sacrifice was meant to enable the Deity to maintain his strength. A. B. Davidson and H. W. Robinson regard the gift theory as the prevailing idea in sacrifice. (3) E. O. James, R. Dussand, Bertholet, G. F. Moore and others believe that the fundamental principle is that vital power is released by the death of the animal. (See H. H. Rowley, *John Rylands Library Bulletin*, pp. 76ff.)

[26] This latter in spite of such passages as Amos 5[25] and Jer 7[22]. Israelite sacrifice would find its origin in ancient Semitic sacrifice. The older sources of the Pentateuch clearly associate sacrifice with Moses and the wilderness period.

[27] *Israel*, II.322, 374.

[28] Rowley, *The Faith of Israel*, p. 96.

would be due to the idea of its divine appointment. As such, it was not to be questioned nor examined. The one principle which Vincent Taylor declares *was* stressed was that 'the blood is the life' (Gen 9^{4}, Lev.17^{10ff}, Deut 12^{23}).[29] He also takes issue with Behm, who in Kittel's *Wörterbuch* ascribes little more to the expression 'blood' in sacrificial language than a vivid allusion to violent death and destruction.[30] The primary intention, Taylor asserts, is in the reverse direction to that of destruction: 'The victim is slain in order that its life, in the form of blood, may be released, and its flesh burnt in order that it may be transformed or etherealized, and in both cases the aim is to make it possible for life to be presented as an offering to the Deity.'[31] Quoting Heb 9^{22} he admits that, in popular misrepresentation, the victim's shed blood might be thought of as possessing 'magical properties', but the 'instructed and thoughtful worshipper knew that it was the symbol of dedicated life and of a life with which he could identify himself.'[32]

Obviously there is a cluster of ideas variously interpreted behind Old Testament sacrifice. Of them all, this conception of a living link afforded by the animal's shed blood seems to offer the surest insight into its deepest meaning. The way through to God and the powers of God does not result from quasi-magical ritual or performance, but from identification with the offering of the animal's life (not death). Broken relationships could thus, in some measure, be put right. A channel was provided by which new life, vitality, blessing, and holiness could reach men in need.

Another great opportunity for renewal of blessing was provided by the sacred feasts. At them the leader blessed the people in the name of Yahweh (cf. 2 Sam 6^{18}; 1 K $8^{14, 55}$). At smaller, family occasions it was customary for the father or the chief to pronounce a blessing.

Knowledge recently come to light regarding the great festivals of the Near East has helped still further to stress the importance of the festivals in Israel's cultic life. Thus was the *Heilsgeschichte*

[29] *Jesus and His Sacrifice*, p. 49.
[30] Art. αἷμα, *T.W.z.N.T.*, I.172ff.
[31] *The Atonement in New Testament Teaching*, 1940, pp. 34ff.
[32] *Jesus and His Sacrifice*, p. 54. cf. von Rad; *Old Testament Theology*, Vol. I: 'Expiation therefore does not depend upon the blood, but upon the life, whose bearer the blood is' (p. 270).

kept in view. But the Hebrew festivals are not to be equated with those of her neighbours. One thing is quite clear: that the death-and-resurrection theme so common to the great Babylonian and Egyptian seasonal festivals was not finally taken over into Hebrew ritual. Mowinckel, in his *Psalmenstudien*, suggested that Psalms 47, 93 and 95–100 are enthronement psalms, to be interpreted in the light of the Babylonian Akitu festival. F. F. Hvidberg answers this succinctly: 'In the Old Testament Yahweh nowhere meets us as a dying and rising Deity. In Israelite cultic usage it was not the resurrection or renewal of Yahweh which was represented, but Yahweh's saving acts on behalf of Israel which were celebrated, and the covenant which was renewed.'[33]

A modified form of this theory has, however, much to commend it. The ritual drama of the New Year festival would bring a 'remembrance' of the events at the creation of the world, when God set chaos to nought, and by the creation of a firmament kept all antagonistic forces at bay. A. Bentzen says that 'the creation of the heavens is God's decisive act of salvation and the proof of His power over all other gods'. 'All the gods of the peoples are idols; but Yahweh made the heavens' (Ps 96^{5}, R.S.V.) In this 'remembrance' this act of salvation would be re-experienced by the people.[34]

The king, as the centre of Israel's psychic life (2 Sam 6^{13ff}; 1 K 8^{18f}), was accorded a special place in the cult. Since others received blessing from him, everything that could be done was done to make him great. Psalms 61^{71}, 63^{12}, 84^{10}, and 1 Samuel 2^{10} show the close connexion made between the cult and the king.[35]

After the Exile, it was the high priest, in place of the king, who pronounced the great Mosaic blessing (Num 6^{24ff}) over the people (Lev 9^{22f}). In the Temple, not only at feast-times, but always, the priests were to bless the people in the name of Yahweh (Deut 10^{8}, 1 Ch 23^{13}).[36]

[33] *Graed of Lather i det Gamle Testaments*, 1938, p. 118, quoted G. W. Anderson, art. 'Hebrew Religion', in *The Old Testament and Modern Study*, 1951, pp. 295f. For further discussion, see E. O. James *The Old Testament in the Light of Anthropology*, p. 54, *Myth and Ritual* (ed. S. H. Hooke).

[34] A. Bentzen, *King and Messiah* (E.T., 1955), pp. 11f. See also A. R. Johnson, *Sacral Kingship in Ancient Israel* (Cardiff, 1955).

[35] Pedersen, op. cit., pp. 429, 433, 435.

[36] Ibid., p. 448. Pedersen also notes the contrary power of a curse issuing from the Temple, quoting Deuteronomy 27^{14ff} and 1 K 8^{31f}.

IV. MEN AND *RUACH*

Because of its connotation, A. R. Johnson[37] thinks that *ruach* was used originally of anybody who, like the wind, was full of abounding energy (e.g. of Elijah in 2 K $2^{9, 15}$). Jacob (Gen 45^{27}), and Samson (Jdgs 15^{19}) have their *ruach* revived when good news comes to them. As applied to men, the term comes to be used in two ways: (1) a purely physical reference to 'breath' synonymous with *neshamah* (especially after the Exile), and (2) with special reference to life's psychical aspects, denoting men's moods and emotional changes (Isa 51^{3}; Ps 77^{4}, 143^{7}; Job 6^{4}, etc.).

Normally, however, the word refers to a man's *ruach* in its totality, as in Deuteronomy 2^{30}, when Yahweh 'hardened' Sihon's *ruach* (cf. 1 Ch 5^{26}, and 2 Ch 36^{22}). In Psalm 51^{10ff} the Psalmist prays that God will renew a right *ruach* within him (the 'willing spirit' of verse 12), taking not away His own holy *Ruach* from him. Isaiah 57^{15} tells us that God answers a prayer of this kind, dwelling 'with the contrite and lowly in *ruach*, and bringing life to the *ruach* of the lowly'. God, as the author, giver, and sustainer of life, renews in man this central necessity.

The word is seen in its full force when Isaiah states (31^{3}) that Yahweh is '*ruach* and not flesh (*basar*)'. *Ruach* can thus be given to man, but it does not belong to him whose native sphere is that of *basar*. It is God's who, in the fullness of the times, will 'pour it out' 'upon all flesh' (Joel 2^{28f}). In this gift He gives energy, inspiration, and new life.[38] It is especially God's gift enabling a man to do the work to which he is commissioned.

Through His spirit, God equips men for tasks requiring superhuman strength and daring (Jdgs 3^{10}, 6^{24}, 11^{29}; 1 Sam 2^{6}, etc.). The *gibbor chayil* ('mighty man of valour') of the period of the Judges was empowered in this way. Bezaleel received his outstanding skill as craftsman from the same source. Seer and *nabi'* (prophet) are inspired by the Spirit (1 Sam 10^{10}), and when the days of prophetic trance and excitement are over, the later prophets still know the Spirit as the source of their inspiration (e.g. Mic 3^{8}).

[37] *The Vitality of the Individual in the Thought of Ancient Israel.* His footnote 4, pp. 26f, makes clear how useful is the service he has rendered in examining the Old Testament usage of *ruach* independently of considerations to do with Yahweh and the Spirit.

[38] When *ruach* is withdrawn from man, it means the end of his power and of his life (Eccles 12^{7}; Ps. 146^{4}).

The development of religious understanding in Israel brings a change in thought concerning God's *ruach*. In the early days, the 'Spirit of God is a quasi-material energy producing results in human lives that have nothing essentially ethical or religious in their content. How materialistic this conception is', comments H. W. Robinson,[39] 'may be seen from the narrative which describes the transference to the seventy elders of a portion of the Spirit given to Moses, or from the prayer of Elisha for an eldest son's portion of Elijah's spirit (Num 11^{25}; 2 K 2$^{9, 15}$)'. By the time of the prophets of the Exile, the idea of the Spirit is ethicized and spiritualized (e.g. Ezek 11^{19}, 36^{26}, etc.). It still stands for the power of God coming upon a man to equip him for tasks otherwise impossible, but there is a filling out of the conception at other points, bringing it into harmony with a developing understanding both of God's nature and of His ways with men.

V. THE USE OF MAGIC

By use of magical procedures, man has attempted a short-cut to power in an exploitation of the psychic and the supernatural. Magic is always an endeavour engineered from the human end, without reference to the will of God. It seeks, rather, to compel divine forces.

References to this and injunctions against it meet us in Scripture. 'Thou shalt not learn to do after the abominations of those nations', says Deuteronomy 18^{9}, and the verse that follows lists child-sacrifice, divination, soothsaying, augury, sorcery, the uttering of charms, spiritualism, wizardry, and necromancy as amongst the proscribed practices. Echoes of these are found in such texts as 2 Chronicles 33^{6} and (1) Genesis 22, Exodus 22^{29}, 34^{20} (cf. Mic 6^{7}), (2) Leviticus 8^{5ff}, 1 Samuel 15^{23}, (3) Joshua 13^{22} and Numbers 23, Micah 5^{12}, (4) 2 Kings 21^{6}, (5) Malachi 3^{5}, (6) Ezekiel 13^{18}, Psalms 64^{3f}, 140, (7/9) 1 Samuel 28^{3ff}, Isaiah 8^{19}, 19^{3}. And references to recourse to amulets, charms, the use of figurines, etc., meet us in Genesis 30^{14ff}, 35^{4}, Judges 8^{21}, and Isaiah 3^{18f}, etc.

In these matters the influence of Egypt, as well as of Canaan, was very strong. Later, Babylonia and Persia were to exert a suasion equally potent.

The brazen serpent of the wilderness (Num 21^{8f}), exteriorizing

[39] *The Religious Ideas of the Old Testament*, p. 111.

the troubles by which the people were afflicted, witnesses to the use of sympathetic magic (cf. 2 K 18^{4}): the serpent itself was worshipped by eastern peoples (cf. the caduceus of Aesculapius, and the Canaanite symbol of Eshnun). Psalm 58^{4f} and Jeremiah 8^{17} speak of serpent-charming as a means of controlling demonic powers thought to reside in them.

Elijah's actions on Mount Carmel have similarities to typical rain-making ceremonies, and the symbolic actions of some of the prophets seem related, also, to mimetic magic (e.g. 1 K 11^{29ff}; Isa 20^{3ff}; Jer 13^{1ff}, 19^{1f}; Ezek 4^{5}). The relation is, however, much more to the Word of Yahweh; and the initial impetus towards the symbolic act is not from the human will of the prophet, but from what he knows of Yahweh's revealed intentions.

In such stories as those of the wonder-working rod of Moses (Ex 4^{2ff}, 7^{9}), the budding of Aaron's rod (Num 17^{1ff}), the mantle of Elijah (2 K 2^{8ff}) and the floating iron axehead (2 K 6^{2ff}) the border-line between magic and religion is difficult to define.

Israel must have been greatly influenced towards the 'abominable practices of the nations' for Isaiah to declare (2^{6}): 'Thou hast rejected thy people, the house of Jacob, because they are full of diviners from the east and of soothsayers like the Philistines.' Notice, too, that the diviner of Isaiah 3^{2} is evidently a man of importance, listed among judges, prophets, and elders! Later, it is related with relish concerning Daniel (e.g. 1^{20}, 2^{2}, 5^{11f}) that he possesses gifts superior to those of the Babylonian soothsayers and magicians at the courts of Nebuchadnezzar and Belshazar. Daniel was evidently a great adept in the occult!

What triumphs in Israel, however, is the experience of Yahweh's personal relationship with His people; this supersedes any merely magical element in religion. His prophets come to know the drive and power of His Word (*dabar*: Isa 1^{2}, 6^{8}; Ezek 3^{1ff}; Amos 3^{8}; Mic 6^{1f}). It was like a blazing fire in Jeremiah, or a hammer crushing the rocks (Jer 20^{9}; cf. also 1^{5ff}, 15^{16}).[40]

VI. FAITH AND OBEDIENCE

The essence of man's relationship with God, by which his life is sustained at all levels and, in particular, his *nephesh* and *ruach* renewed, is the attitude of trust and obedience. Abraham was a

[40] Art. 'Old Testament Prophets', J. Muilenburg; *Peake's Commentary*, 1962, p. 481.

standing witness to all his descendants that this trust should be unconditional (Gen 15^{6}). This fundamental assurance (*he'emim* from *'aman*, which in the *hiphil* means 'to be sure', 'to trust in') received emphasis from priest (Lev 26^{13}), prophet (Hos 13^{4}) and psalmist (Ps 81^{7}).[41] It is this insistence on faith as an inward attitude that prepared the way for Israel's unique contribution to religion, and for all that was to flower in New Testament days.

It is important, too, to notice something which becomes clearer in New Testament times. Faith is the means to the reception of power.[42] In the text which became so prominent both in Judaism and Christianity (Gen 15^{6}), attention is concentrated upon God's promise. Here *he'emin* involves the recognition of the promise, certainly in God's power to fulfil it, and the honouring of God as the mighty Lord.[43] In Isaiah 7^{9}, the prophet asks from Ahaz the recognition of God's truth and power and for the confidence to go forward, secure and established in this.[44] As opposed to mere political expediency, 'faith' brings in a higher range of possibilities. This great guiding principle is emphasized again in 8^{13}, and in 28^{16}: 'he that believeth shall not make haste',[45] and in 30^{15}, 'in returning and rest shall ye be saved; in quietness and confidence shall be your strength'. The prophet coveted for his people the kind of faith resulting from first-hand knowledge of God: this kind of believing does not fuss, nor become impatient (28^{16}). It awaits God's action and is sure of it.

Otto Proksch, writing of Isaiah, says that 'Faith is not a leap into the void, but into the bosom of God'. On 30^{15} he comments that faith is rooted in humility, which receives all from God and has nothing of its own to bring. It can be analysed as including (*a*) repentance (returning), (*b*) rest, the abandonment of oneself to God which a man needs to make even when he is putting forth all his powers; quiet waiting as was asked of Ahaz (7^{4}), when a man can do no more, and must be content to leave the issue to God, and (*c*) confidence, the trust in God which is mentioned often in the

[41] B. D. Eerdmans, *The Religion of Israel* (Leiden, 1947), p. 330.

[42] W. Grundmann, *Der Begriff der Kraft*, p. 116 (see footnote).

[43] A. Weiser, *T.W.z.N.T.*, VI.187.

[44] 'If ye will not believe (*ta'aminu*), ye shall not be established (*te'amenu*).' G. A. Smith endeavours to reproduce this paranomasia with the help of a North-Country word: 'If ye have not *faith*, ye cannot have *staith*.'

[45] Cheyne, by a slight emendation, favours 'shall not give way'. The LXX has 'shall not be ashamed'.

poetical books. In this attitude is man's liberation ('saved') and true strength. Proksch goes on to point out that Isaiah's own attitude in face of the Syro-Ephraimite coalition and Assyria was an instance of the faith for which he calls.[46]

Complementary to this quality of trust was the needful humility of the creature and the redeemed before the Creator and Redeemer. So deep is the insistence upon this that in the Psalms, for example, 'the humble' is an equivalent for 'the religious man'.[47]

Because of the emphasis upon Yahweh's power, His foreknowledge and control, it would seem, at times, that there was little place for human freedom. Before Yahweh men are as nothing. They are but dust and ashes.[48] In His presence, none is righteous (Job 4^{17f}; Ps 143^{2}). The only fitting attitude is that 'fear of the Lord' which is the beginning of wisdom (Prov 1^{7}; cf. Ps 111^{10}; Job 28^{28}).[49] It is not true, however, that man has no choice before God (as, for example, the analogy of the potter in Jeremiah 18 might seem to suggest). 'Choose life, that thou mayest live' is the advice given in Deuteronomy 30^{19} when the blessing and the curse are set before Israel. Though, as Deutero-Isaiah asserts, God knows the future, yet the prophet invites men to obedience (58^{3}). As H. W. Robinson states: on the one hand, 'Israel will have no limitation of the divine power', nor, on the other, any 'mechanical determination of the human will. . . . The one would destroy religion and the other morality.'[50]

The fact, however, is that the sphere of power, the centre of initiative, the seat of wisdom is not with men upon earth, but with God in Heaven. By trust and obedience, one linked one's own life

[46] *Theologie des Alten Testaments*, (1950), pp. 181ff.

[47] Max Löhr, *A History of Religion in the Old Testament*, p. 161.

[48] This theme occurs in the Qumran Thanksgiving Psalms: e.g. 'As for me I am but dust and ashes. What can I devise except Thou hast desired it?' (see T. H. Gaster *The Scriptures of the Dead Sea Sect*. 1957, p. 171).

[49] Pedersen, *Israel*, pp. 623ff. Proksch comments concerning the relationship with God that there is both a centrifugal and a centripetal tendency in it (*Theologie des Alten Testaments*, pp. 610, 615). The 'fear of God' is the centrifugal element, and the 'knowledge of God' the centripetal: both together hold man in balance and enable him to find his right relationship to God, his everlasting source and centre. Proverbs 1^{7} speaks for the whole of the Old Testament when it says that 'the fear of God' is the 'beginning of knowledge'. God reveals Himself to those who fear Him (cf. Gen 22^{12}, 20^{11}; Isa 11^{2}). Because of who He is, God is to be feared: but He has revealed Himself as the God of the Covenant, and He is therefore to be loved and trusted. The fear of God thus exiles other fears (Ps 27^{1}) and leads to the relationship of trust.

[50] Art: The Theology of the Old Testament' in *Record and Revelation*, p. 320.

with God, in the context of His covenant relation with the people.[51]

H. H. Rowley quotes the Psalmist for a picture of the attitude most to be coveted in one's relationship with God: 'Teach me thy way, O Yahweh; I will walk in thy truth (*'emeth*—which J. M. P. Smith translates here as 'in fidelity to thee'—the perfect response to God's *'emeth* and *'emunah*): 'Let my heart rejoice (R.V.: "unite my heart") to fear thy name. I will praise thee, Yahweh my God, with my whole heart; And I will glorify thy name for ever.'[52]

VII. MAN AND GOD'S RIGHTEOUSNESS

The background to man's life is God's righteousness (*tsedaqah*). This is not an abstract standard, but rather His will in action, His personal power and design. Man must align himself with this. We make a mistake in identifying *tsedaqah* with law and juridical standards and processes. Since it concerns personal relationships, there is a sense in which it is law's very opposite. It is 'God's character in His dealings with men'.[53] Prophets and Psalmists depict this as involving a concern for man's salvation and wholeness: it is a kind of sharing after the manner of New Testament ἀγαπή.

When man acts in conformity with this spirit, i.e. in brotherliness, kindness, and goodness, he can count on God's supporting might, His *kraft* and δύναμις (cf. Ps 1).

God's righteousness is displayed in His great acts and in His covenant relation. The tension resulting from man's waywardness and failure to live by God's standards has two outcomes: (1) God cannot let wickedness go unpunished. Says Ludwig Köhler: 'The same God who defends and maintains His fellowship with man exercises judgement on those who are disloyal to the relationship and those who oppose it.'[54] And (2), equally, God is merciful

[51] The idea of faith as *belief*, e.g. in the existence of God or some credal statement, is not Jewish. 'The world of Israel grew out of covenants with God.' Jewish Emunah, comments M. Buber, is in the history of a nation, and for the Israelite was thus not something to be argued about: it was assumed. In this it differs from Christian πίστις. The kind of separation against which the prophets inveigh does not come about through negative 'unbelief', but through being false to what is known, or failing to make this relationship effective (*Two Types of Faith* (E.T.), 1951, pp. 40, 170f).

[52] *The Faith of Israel*, p. 135 (the reference is to J. M. P. Smith's *The Old Testament: an American Translation* (Ps 86^{11f}).

[53] S. H. Hooke, 'Genesis', *Peake's Commentary*, 1962, p. 190.

[54] *Old Testament Theology*, p. 35.

and 'slow to anger', desiring, and working for, the reclamation of the sinner (Isa 45^{26}). Psalm 143 depicts the man who, knowing that no man can be righteous before God, fears His judgement (verse 2), and who yet knows that this very righteousness of God will deliver him from trouble (verse 11)! (cf. Mic 7^{9}).

God, in His judgements, is not so much *judex*, declaring what is right, as the great *arbiter*, helping to put matters right. His power is at work in the struggle for righteousness. His judgement is therefore always with *tsedaqah* (cf. Ps 98^{9}), i.e. according to His own character and sovereignty. For this reason *mishpat* (judgement) and *tsedaqah* are often found in closest association in the Old Testament.

'Righteousness', as A. Deschamps states, 'is found under the sign of power',[55] and therefore shares in the diverse aspects of that power. Sometimes it shows itself in terribleness, sometimes in benignity and grace. Part of the key to the theology of the Old Testament is to be found in this somewhat enigmatic concept of *tsedaqah*.

VIII. PRAYER AND POWER

By means of prayer man comes into communion with God and himself becomes a sharer in God's purposes. It is not just a cry wrung from man in *extremis*. Throughout the Old Testament there is certainty that God hears and answers prayer. He responds in terms of power.

Primitive prayer has unquestioned affinity with the uttering of spells. It might be said, too, that the use of prayer as 'magic' is to be observed in all centuries down to this day and hour. Through prayer man tries to secure the answer to purely selfish desires.

In 1 Kings $17^{20, 21}$ (two of the most primitive forms of prayer in the Bible), Ludwig Köhler notes[56] the brevity, awkwardness—and objectivity—of the prayers: 'Yahweh, my God', is how they begin. All true prayer necessitates a similar appeal and 'tuning in' to the One addressed. Here is the confession of a relationship which provides the key to the act of praying itself.

The background to all Hebrew prayer is the thought of God's covenant relation with His people. It is everywhere assumed, and notably so in the Psalms, which contain prayers of great intimacy and audacity. They were uttered by men determined to be heard:

[55] Quoted, E. Jacob, *Theology of the Old Testament* (E.T.) 1958, p. 96.
[56] *Old Testament Theology*, p. 243, n. 58.

they cry aloud, and even roar, to God. L. Köhler again comments that one of the striking facts about Old Testament prayer is that it is neither fixed in pattern nor content.[57] It is living and real—emerging out of the pressure of circumstance and need. In the Psalms men ask God for help in connexion with material needs, for long life and its maintenance, for relief from distress and sickness, and for vindication from persecution and misrepresentation, as also for deliverance from guilt before Him.

Intercession is much more the act of the great leaders in the Old Testament than of the commonalty. Moses' prayers are especially noteworthy (e.g. Ex $32^{11ff, 31f}$, 33^{12ff}, 34^{9}; Num 11^{11ff}, 14^{13ff}, 21^{7}; Deut 9^{18ff}, $10^{10, 33}$), as is Abraham's intercession for Sodom (Gen 18^{22ff}). The prophets continue in this heritage, interceding for Israel.

Prayer is often linked with sacrifice (Ps 66^{13ff}, 54^{6}). Originally, no doubt, ideas of propitiation and magic would be at work here. Later, this combination probably operated conversely: safeguarding sacrifice from being regarded as a magical act, because prayer accompanied it, and the sacrifice itself helping prayer to be truly objective.[58]

What illuminates Old Testament praying, keeping it clear of magical connotations is the background conception of the nature of Yahweh. He is 'my God', 'our God', who brought His people out of Egypt and with whom the whole people are in covenant relationship. One can therefore appeal, as is often the case in the Old Testament, to His nature and His promises (e.g. Ps 44, 79; Dan 9^{11ff}, etc.). This is informed prayer, intimate and often arguing with God.

What emerges has often been characterized as 'prophetic' rather than mystical prayer.[59] The gulf between man and his Creator is recognized, but faith discovers an attitude which bridges the gulf. The true object of this kind of praying is not selfish. The concern is to further God's purposes and the object is harmony with His will. The picture of Moses, communing with God and in the ensuing dialogue finding his objections overruled, Hannah's prayer

[57] Ibid., p. 251, n. 153.

[58] A. Maillot, art. 'Prayer', *Vocabulary of the Bible*, ed. von Allmen (E.T.), 1958, p. 331.

[59] Otto Procksch, *Theologie des Alten Testaments*, p. 625. See also chapter 3, T. R. Hughes, *Prophetic Prayer*, 1947, pp. 13ff, and F. Heiler, *Prayer* (E.T.), New York, 1958, Chapters VI and IX, for an important distinction between mystical and prophetic prayer.

for a son, Elijah's strong praying, Jeremiah's outpourings in Chapters 11–20 of his book, all illustrate 'prophetic prayer'.

'Israelite prayer,' says Fernand Ménégoz, 'tends to make the believer an energetic co-operator and not a beatified enjoyer of God.'[60] The consummation of this type of praying comes in New Testament days, when men learn to pray in Christ's name, and in the power of the Holy Spirit, for the purposes of the Kingdom.

IX. RULERSHIP

Chieftain and King needed Yahweh's blessing so that they might be strong in counsel.[61] By this strengthening of soul they emerged to leadership, and through it they were sustained.[62] The *gibbor chayil* ('mighty man of valour') in ancient Israel was the man full of blessing and honour. In cunning of counsel, uprightness of heart, boldness of spirit, and with power to succeed, it was evident that Yahweh had blessed him and designated him for leadership.

The roots of Israel's life are in the family, and all the developments of social life within the nation are expansions from this model.[63] Israel's leaders serve her best when they conform closest to the patriarchal standard, living in the midst of the people, representing them, both 'blessing' them and being 'blessed' by them, under Yahweh. They are all part of the one 'house'.

The emergence of 'elders' and 'judges' was an inevitable process in Mosaic times, a devolution of the supreme power invested in Moses, as the father of the people[64] (see Ex 18^{25f}). The Covenant under which the nation now existed emphasizes its close unity and interdependence, and the peculiar relationship of those specially entrusted with tasks of leadership.

The founding of the hereditary monarchy represents a break between old Israel and the new. The *gibbor chayil* raised up by

[60] Quoted, E. Jacob, *Theology of the Old Testament*, p. 176.

[61] See Pedersen, *Israel*, I.183. The ideal King of Isa 9 is 'Wonderful Counsellor'; cf. Isa 11^2.

[62] The blessing first came to Israel through Abraham. His story is punctuated with the promise of God's blessing upon him and his descendants. He showed these powers of leadership, and 'wealth grew up around him', Pedersen, ibid, p. 190.

[63] Note how in Ex 6^{14}; Num 3^{24ff} 'father's house' is a natural term for the clan. All the tribes together become 'the house of Israel'. Ewald, *Antiquities of Israel* (E.T.), 1876, p. 242.

[64] Moses himself is the ideal leader: one in whom obedience to God is pre-eminent. His strength and confidence, his sense of mission, all derive from God. Joshua, his successor, is bidden to be strong and courageous, faithful, as Moses was, to God's law (Josh 1^7): 'as I was with Moses, so I will be with thee'. In this he will find strength for leadership.

God in time of crisis, and filled with His *ruach* to do exploits, recedes before the permanent figure of the monarch. Part of the genius of David was that he wedded so much of the ancient traditions to his conception of kingship. This was to be no Oriental despotism, but was based on a covenant (2 Sam 5^3) involving a threefold relationship between King, people, and God. David was to be the father of his people (2 Sam 5^1), thus looking for the strength of soul that resided in the blessing of the entire community;[65] and the same time he fostered the idea that the King was in a special relationship to Yahweh,[66] needing the endowment of His spirit, not for occasional exploits, but as a permanent reinforcement.

In other lands the ruler was in a privileged position.[67] Deuteronomy 17^{14ff} indicates that in Israel the king himself is under the code, with his powers restricted. Verse 20 of this passage emphasizes that his heart is not to be 'lifted up above his brethren'.[68] Unqualified powers are *not* his right (cf. 1 K 21). The revolt under Rehoboam took place on this very issue.

Even with these safeguards, however, it seems evident that the institution of the monarchy was a retrograde step in theocratic Israel. There is an inner contradiction between a people thinking of itself as God's people and the acceptance of the domination of a king and his officials.[69] The entanglements of foreign alliances, the duplicities of court life, the need for an army, for taxes and the array of officialdom, detract from the character of a theocracy. The State organized after this pattern, as Bultmann comments, is an instrument of power, involved in power politics; and its absorption in this, and in the consciousness of power, so easily leads to forgetfulness of God's overriding providence.[70]

[65] Pedersen, ibid., p. 83.

[66] Note how this idea develops, e.g. Ps 2^7, 45^7: see A. R. Johnson, *Sacral Kingship*.

[67] The idea of the divine right of kings was widespread throughout the ancient world. It gave them an unbounded and indisputable authority. The kings of Egypt and Syria were regarded as incarnate gods. See art., 'Pagan Religion at the Coming of Christianity', Gilbert Murray (Peake's *Commentary*, 1929, p. 630), James Fraser *Golden Bough* (Abridged Ed., 1932, pp. 104f, 162f).

[68] cf. Jer 22^{13}, 'The Sovereign does not belong to a different species, he is no semi-divine being, as most Oriental kings claimed to be; he has a special position with peculiar privileges, but he is only *primus inter pares*, and his privileges are limited in themselves and balanced by responsibilities' (T. H. Robinson, *History of Israel*, I.229).

[69] Bultmann, *Essays*, p. 201. Our documents provide us with two contrasting views regarding the monarchy; cf. 1 Sam 8^{4ff} and 1 Sam $24^{6, 10}$.

[70] After the Exile, Israel implements the idea of the theocracy, but then no longer as a state (Bultmann, *Essays, Philosophical and Theological*, p. 202). The pious turn from the Hasmoneans as soon as they involve themselves in statecraft.

Ethelbert Stauffer, in his *New Testament Theology*,[71] quotes texts from Egypt, Assyria, and Babylonia revealing 'the beginnings of a theology of civil power'. The ruler is a bulwark against chaos and the forces of disruption. A number of Iranian pictures and texts similarly illustrate the conception that the whole fabric of Persian law and government, with the Emperor at its head, is the one protection against the forces of chaos and confusion.[72]

In the centuries when Israel was dominated by one of these imperial forces after another, she had to learn to submit to the authority of the ruler and to recognize that this was of divine appointment (Dan 4^{25}; Jer 27^{5ff}). Joseph in Egypt, himself an ideal administrator, is portrayed as Pharaoh's loyal servant (Gen 41^{39ff}).[73] 'Seek the welfare of the city whither I have caused you to be carried away captive', is the oracle Jeremiah passes on to the Israelites in Babylon, 'and pray unto the Lord for it; for in its welfare shall ye have welfare.'[74]

Texts such as Daniel 2^{21}, 4^{17}, 5^{20}; Job 12^{18} demonstrate the view that God brings kings to power, and can dethrone them at His will.[75] Nebuchadnezzar is His 'servant' (Jer 27^{6}), and Cyrus His 'anointed' (Isa 45^{1}).

Two strains are to be observed towards the close of the Old Testament era: one concerns the ideal 'Prince' of Israel. Haggai and Zechariah had looked to Zerubbabel hoping that he, as scion of the house of David, would usher in the Messianic days (e.g. Hag 2^{22}; Zech 3^{8}, 4^{6ff}, 6^{12f}). With the fading of these hopes, the idea of the theocracy in Israel came to be emphasized more and more.[76] Fanned by the Apocalyptists of the era immediately preceding the New Testament, Messianic expectation once more flamed into life. Through the person of His 'anointed', God's sovereignty was fully to be made known. The source of Messiah's strength would be where Zechariah expected to find his: 'not by might nor by

[71] pp. 81^{ff}, e.g. 'The whole land is ruined.... Asiatics have come down to Egypt... one man takes the life of another... a king will come from the south. Justice will once more come into her own, and injustice will be driven out' (A. Erman *Die Lit. der Ägypter*, 1923, pp. 151ff).

[72] Stauffer, p. 82, who refers (p. 272, n. 205) to some of these pictures.

[73] Cf. Jub 40^{9}, 46^{2}: 'The land of Egypt was at peace... and Pharaoh's kingdom was well ordered, and there was no Satan and no evil person therein.'

[74] Jer 29^{7} (changing 'peace' to 'welfare'), cf. Baruch 1^{11f}.

[75] Note the Apocalyptists' special standpoint that all the kingdoms (full of bloodshed and violence as they may be—Sir 10^{8}) will continue until the End, when the Son of Man appears and takes over 'all authority and rule'.

[76] W. O. E. Oesterley, *A History of Israel*, II.99ff.

power, but by my Spirit, saith the Lord of hosts' (Zech 4^6).

The other strain which passes over into the New Testament concerns the relationship of God's people to heathen overlordship. However brightly hopes for the ruler's overthrow might burn amongst the populace or in the ranks of the zealots, the doctrine of orthodox Jewry was submission to the ruler, as God's agent set to maintain order in society. One obeyed the ruler as best one could, provided that he did not usurp the prerogatives of the One alone to be worshipped, the true God, source of all power and might.

Conceivably, in the background theology there is a connexion between the power of an earthly ruler and that of the heavenly guardian, or 'watcher' of each nation. We have noted earlier[77] Deuteronomic texts recognizing the appointment of the 'gods' of other nations by Yahweh, and their possession, therefore, of derivative authority. In the visions of the Apocalyptists the idea of the merging of earthly powers and their heavenly counterparts occurs frequently.[78] Isaiah 24^{21} and $34^{2, 4}$, depicting the approaching doom of evil rulers, clearly set in parallel 'the kings of the earth on earth' and 'the host of the high ones (or "height") on high', and the 'nations' and their 'hosts'.[79] When we pass to the consideration of rulership in the New Testament, all this is of utmost importance.

[77] See p. 17.

[78] The vision of the Apocalyptists encompasses heaven and earth in an all-embracing sweep, and envisages the destruction of the powers in all realms that are in rebellion against God. Dan 7 and 8 provide a typical picture, merging events on earth with events in heaven.

[79] G. B. Caird, *Principalities and Powers*, p. 10.

Part Two

THE INTERTESTAMENTAL PERIOD AND LATER JUDAISM

CHAPTER FIVE

THE SEPTUAGINT

THE Greek translation of the Hebrew Scriptures represents an important stage in the history of the concept of power, for not only did Hebrew words have to be translated into Greek, but, amongst the Diaspora, Graecized terms inevitably opened the way to Graecized concepts. *Chayil*, *geburah*, *'oz*, etc., the Hebrew words for power, were translated into what are now familiar New Testament terms δύναμις, ἐξουσία, ἴσχυς, κράτος, etc. In using these expressions in their Greek dress, some of their Greek associations affected their subsequent use. But by far the most potent influence came with the translation of the divine names of the Old Testament.

We have not stressed in earlier sections the evidence provided by the divine names in Hebrew, for, in spite of the best authority,[1] their etymology is largely a matter of conjecture. It is impressive, however, that in general they connect with ideas of majesty and power, e.g. the generic El, with its plural forms Eloach and Elohim, may be derived from the root *'ul*, to be strong; Yhwh may be a 'plain noun' formed from *hyh*, 'to be', (Köhler), thus emphasizing God's sovereignty and living power, or in the form Yahu it may be an onomatopoeia of the rolling thunder, the fire that comes from heaven (Eerdmans); Shadday may have been formed from the Accadian *šadū*, 'mountain'. When these names are dealt with by the LXX translators, however, we are able to observe the nuances which now attach to them. Their meaning is revealed by the way they are translated.

One thing immediately becomes evident: that by this time, *circa* 250 B.C., the thought of God's transcendence made the use of personal names for God quite distasteful, if not blasphemous.

How long the practice went back into history by which Yahweh's personal name was read in the forms Elohim or Adonay, it is difficult to conjecture. This was one of the ways in which what was read (*Qere*) differed from what was written (*Kethib*). The Massoretic text represents this tradition by providing the

[1] See e.g. the *Old Testament Theologies* of Jacob, Köhler, and Eichrodt.

consonants *Yhwh* with vowel points from these other two names for God. The LXX takes this sensitivity a stage further by the complete excision of Yahweh's name and the substitution of κύριος.[2]

The choice of κύριος is illuminative. Deriving from κύρος, 'supreme power', 'authority' (Liddell and Scott), the word indicates the rightful might and authority of God.[3] He is the 'sovereign Lord'.

The etymological interpretation of Yahweh given in Exodus 3[14], 'I am that I am', is rendered in the form ἐγώ εἰμι ὁ ὤν (ἔσομαι ὅς ἐσομαι in Aquila and Theodotion.) Hellenistic Judaism was thus provided with a designation for God which was most congenial. The Self-existent was a term already in use by the philosophers.

'Adonay, similarly, became κύριος. This translation occurs in all but nine instances, where, instead, ὁ δεσπότης is used.

Apart from κύριος, the other great LXX expression for God is ὁ θεός. This is used to translate *Elohim* and *El*. In Job and occasionally elsewhere (e.g. Num 24[4]; Neh 1[5], 9[31f]; Ps 7[12], 41[3], etc.) some translators used ὁ ἰσχυρὸς or ὁ ὑψηλός.

When *El*, *Eloach*, and *Elohim* are used in ways not now consonant with the idea of the one God, ἄγγελος appears.[4] Where the gods of other peoples are meant, θεός is used in its ordinary Greek sense of 'a god', or some such word as εἴδωλον is substituted.

Shadday is variously translated. θεός and κύριος, and a transliteration all are used. In Ruth 1[20f], Job 21[15], 31[2], 39[22], and Ezekiel 1[24] the translation ἱκανός again provides Hellenistic Judaism with an expression with suitable philosophical connotations. 'He who suffices' was the contemporary (and quite erroneous) Rabbinic explanation of the etymology of *shadday*.[5]

Elyon became ὕψιστος and, again, by this translation the Hellenistic Jew drew near to his neighbour.

Tseba'oth is often transliterated. In other instances (e.g.

[2] In the Hebrew and Samaritan texts of the Pentateuch, agreement occurs in the form of the divine names in over 300 cases, differences occurring in only eight or nine (J. Skinner, *The Divine Names in Genesis*, 1914, pp. 38, 116). Going back to an era prior to the LXX, this enables us with some confidence to conclude that the forms of the divine names in the Massoretic text are, in all likelihood, exactly those the LXX translators had before them.

[3] Cf. Foerster, *T.W.z.N.T.*, III. 1,043: κύριος is 'one who can dispose of something or somebody'. The title points to the personal, lawful, comprehensive might of God (ibid, p. 1,087).

[4] C. H. Dodd, *The Bible and the Greeks*, p. 21. The Hellenistic use of ἄγγελος for the Hebrew *malak* prepared for this usage. (In the Hebrew Bible Jacob's assailant in Hos 12[4] is *Elohim* and in Gen 32[29] *Malak*).

[5] Ibid., p. 16.

1 Chronicles, Hosea, Amos, Micah, etc.) it is translated παντοκράτωρ (-των in Zech. $8^{2, 6}$)[6] and in Psalms, Jeremiah, and some other places it is actually translated as κύριος τῶν δυνάμεων.[7]

One further point of importance is that in two places (Isa 14^{13} and Job 22^{26}), the periphrasis 'Heaven' is used where *El* and *Eloach* occur in the Hebrew.[8]

We can thus state quite categorically that by the time the LXX began to be translated, anthropomorphic conceptions of the Deity were out of favour, belief was completely monotheistic, and the God of Israel was recognized as the one supreme ruler of the universe, so far above man that mention of His name must be avoided.[9]

[6] παντοκράτωρ, as C. H. Dodd points out (ibid, p. 19), is not the same thing as παντοδύναμος. The equivalence of παντοκράτων and παντοκράτωρ, he argues, indicates that the meaning of the word is to be discovered in the verb κρατεῖν, 'to exercise κράτος, power or might' and so 'to rule, control'. Thus παντοκράτωρ = 'one who has power of control over the world'. Since God controls, especially, all the cosmic powers (δυνάμεις), it becomes the equivalent, as a paraphrase, of ἡ κύριος τῶν δυνάμεων.

[7] Eissfeldt's suggestion (*Misc. Acad. Berolinensis*, 1950, pp. 130ff) is that *tseba'oth* was originally a cult name for God, but there is little doubt that, long before the time of the LXX, the apparent connexion with the root *tsb'* began to dominate interpretation. *Tsabo'*, where it obviously means 'host' or 'army', is translated either as στρατία or δύναμις : yet in translating *yhwh tseba'oth*, though δύναμις is sometimes used, στρατία never appears.

[8] This periphrasis becomes typical in later Judaism (e.g. 1 Macc $3^{18f, 50}$, $4^{10, 24}$, etc.). The tendency is to avoid mentioning God directly at all, e.g. Tobit 3^{16}, 12^{12}, where God becomes ὁ μεγάς, ὁ ἁγίος, etc. 1 Maccabees sometimes uses the second or third person simply instead of mentioning God. W. O. E. Oesterley, *Introduction to Books of the Apocalypse*, 1935, p. 78.

[9] Here we are merely noting a change of emphasis. The picture of the merciful God full of compassion is, of course, carried over into the LXX. There are, also, the other names for God not mentioned here: King, Father, etc.

CHAPTER SIX

THE APOCRYPHA AND PSEUDEPIGRAPHA

THOUGH this literature covers a period of many centuries, some books dating from well into the Christian era, it is useful to survey its assumptions in broad outline as indicative of the period just prior to the New Testament.

I. THE POWER OF GOD

The conception of God is completely consonant with what we have noted in connexion with the LXX. The personal name Yahweh has disappeared; and in the Greek books, or in Greek translations of books originally Hebrew or Aramaic, ὁ θεός and κύριος are the two major terms. The title παντοκράτωρ, whether used singly (e.g. 1 Esd 9[46]; 2 Macc 5[20], 7[38]; 3 Macc 2[2]; 3 Bar 1[3], etc.) or with κύριος (1 Bar 3[14]; Jud 4[13], P. Man 1, etc.), or θεός (2 Macc 7[35], 8[18]; 3 Macc 6[2]; Arist [18f], etc.), is a familiar usage.

There are many variants on these themes: Lord of lords (1 En 9[4]), the God of gods (Apoc Abr 8), 'the lord of Spirits' (1 En 37[2])[1], 'Almighty living God of heaven' (3 Macc 6[28]), etc.

ὕψιστος ('the Most High') also occurs frequently. Other appellations concern God's holiness, or refer to 'heaven' ('Lord God of heaven' Jud 6[19]), similarly removing God into the highest, away from men.

Linked with the title κύριος, which, as noted above, suggests God's sovereign authority, are numerous expressions emphasizing His Kingship: ὁ βασιλεὺς τῶν βασιλέων (2 Macc 13[4]), etc. (see 3 Macc 2[13]; 1 En 91[1, 3]; Sir 50[15]; Tob 13[6]).

God is frequently addressed as κτίστης (Jub 7[20], 10[8], etc.), the 'One who created all things' (2 Macc 1[24]; Sir 24[8]; Jub 2[31f], etc.). He is the 'ruler and Lord of the universe' (Arist [16]) who 'does everything upon the earth' (Jub 12[4]), 'doing everything easily by a nod' (2 Bar 54[2]).

[1] Cf. 'The Prince of the gods and the King of the venerable ones, and the Lord of every spirit, and the Master of every work' (*Qumran Thanksgiving Psalms*, X).

Another revealing reference is the translation of the phrase 'Living God' and the widening of these references: He is θεὸς ζῶν in Bel and the Dragon $^{5, 25}$ and Jubilees 1^{25}, 21^{4}, the 'Living One' (Ah 1^{1}, Arab), 'All life is from before His face' (Jub 12^{4}), He is 'Lord of Life and Spirit' (Adam and Eve 28^{2}), 'He who is life and deathless endless light' (Sib Frag 3^{34}), 'through whom all things are endowed with life' (Arist ^{16}).

The Book of Adam and Eve (28^{2}) uses δύναμις as an appellation: 'Thou art the true light gleaming above all light(s), the living life, infinite mighty Power (δύναμις). To thee the spiritual powers (δυνάμεις) give honour and praise.' The fact of God's power is made clear in one of these titles after another. He is 'God of all power and might' (Jud 9^{14}). 'There is one God, sole sovereign, excellent in power, unbegotten, almighty, invisible, yet seeing all himself' (Sib Frag 1^{7f}).

Sirach (Ecclesiasticus), written originally in Jerusalem by Jesus ben Sira about 180 B.C. and translated into Greek by his grandson in the year 132, mirrors the orthodoxy of a Palestinian Jew in the era just preceding the Maccabean. Here are no traces, as in the 'Wisdom of Solomon' of Hellenistic influences.[2] God is One, Everlasting, Almighty (36^{1-5}, 42^{21}), Creator (16^{26ff}, etc.), 'He is mighty in power and beholdeth all things' (15^{18}). In 43^{27} it is not an expression of pantheism which leads the writer to say, τὸ πᾶν ἐστιν αὐτός ('He is all'). The following verses make this clear. He is beyond description, great beyond all His works, His power is marvellous (θαυμαστὴ ἡ δυναστεία αὐτοῦ).[3]

II. GOD'S TRANSCENDENCE AND THE ROLE OF 'WISDOM'

Though anthropomorphisms occur in the Apocrypha and Pseudepigrapha (and particularly in apocalyptic books), they are poetic and metaphorical in character. All writers are equally sure

[2] Not until 174-171 B.C. do the 'height of Greek fashions and the influx of foreign customs' (2 Macc 4^{13}) appear in Jerusalem. R. H. Pfeiffer, *A History of New Testament Times: With an Introduction to the Apocrypha*, 1949, p. 371.

[3] In the heart of Judith's prayer, in Chapter 9 of the book bearing her name, there is an interesting reference to the relationship between God's power and His foreknowledge. Verses 5 and 6 read: 'For thou wroughtest the things that were before those things, and those things, and such as ensued after; and thou didst devise the things which are now, and the things which are to come; and the things which you didst devise came to pass; yea the things which you didst determine stood before thee, and said, Lo, we are here: for all thy ways are prepared, and thy judgement is with foreknowledge.' The vision of things, previously existent in God's mind, becoming actual and reporting, 'Look, we're here!' is a very engaging one!

of the spirituality of God.[4] The increasing sensitivity concerning His transcendence had to adjust itself to the thought of His creatorship and of His contact with our world. There is thus to be noted the development of a series of conceptions implicit in earlier Israel involving the idea of mediatorship and even of the 'hypostatization' of God. His *ruach*, His word (*memera*) His presence (*shekinah*) His glory (*kabod*) and His wisdom (*chokmah*) are concepts lending themselves to this process. It is not only the pressure of ideas from the Persian-Babylonian background to which the Jews in Exile were subjected, but also the accent on God's transcendence that in the same period encouraged the belief in angels.

In Sirach we meet with a developed picture of Wisdom,[5] behind which undoubtedly lies Proverbs 8. 'Wisdom', who has been with the Lord for ever (1^{1}), was created by Him (1^{8}). 'She is with all flesh according to his gift; and he gave freely to them that love him' (1^{10}), which means to those 'who keep the commandments' (1^{26}).

The Wisdom of Solomon, which may be dated within the first century B.C., shows the feelings of a Diaspora Jew regarding the pressure of the disintegrating forces amongst which he lives, and, at the same time, gives evidence of the way in which certain of the ideas from this environment have already invaded his religious thinking. Its background is Alexandrian, in the period before Philo. The answer that Alexandrian Judaism gives to the wisdom of this world is a setting forth of the divine Wisdom (σοφία), which fulfils all that the Old Testament Scriptures meant by *chokmah*, as well as all a true Jew could feel was honouring to this conception in current Greek philosophy.

As well as conforming to the LXX of Exodus 3^{14}, we are in the world of Platonism in 13^{1} (God is 'He that is' ὁ ὤν)[6] and 11^{17}, in which we are told that the Almighty hand made the world out of formless matter. Plato's 'soul of the universe' which 'ordains the whole world' and which in Philo becomes the immanent logos, is

[4] The poetic character of the anthropomorphisms is illustrated in the contrast between 2 En 39^{3ff}: 'I am one who has seen the Lord's face', even, in verse 4, 'I have seen the Lord's eyes', and 48^{5}: 'From the invisible He made all things visible, Himself being invisible.' T. H. Walker, *The Teaching of Jesus and the Jewish Teaching of His Age*, 1923, p. 39.

[5] R. Smend, declaring the book's fundamental Jewishness, says succinctly, Wisdom is 'subjectively, the fear of God, objectively, the law book of Moses': *Die Weishert des Jesus Sirach eklärt*, Berlin, 1906, p. xxiii.

[6] See p. 42, above, and *Timaeus*, 270.

fulfilled completely in the picture of Wisdom's activities ($7^{22, 27}$, $8^{1, 5}$).[7] In much of this language, Wisdom is akin to the Stoic 'seminal reason' (λόγος σπερματικός). The part Wisdom plays in Creation needs, however, to be strictly noted. It is God who is Creator (1^{14}, 6^{7}, 9^{1}, 11^{17}, etc.). He created 'all things with His word' (9^{1}). Wisdom, who existed with God, was present with Him when he made the world (9^{9}) and becomes, thenceforward, the architect and the power behind all things (7^{27}, $8^{1, 5}$, etc.).

In 8^{4} the writer says of Wisdom: 'She is initiated into the knowledge of God, and she chooseth out (for him) his works.' Expressions of this order lead to the charge of 'hypostasis'. As Grundmann says in Kittel's *Wörterbuch*: 'In some measure Wisdom assumes the place of a female element beside the Godhead.' 8^{3} makes this even clearer: 'She glorifieth her noble birth in that it is given her to live with God, and the Sovereign of all loved her.'

Wisdom is in a special relationship with men. It is she who 'in all ages entering into holy souls, maketh them friends of God, and prophets' (7^{27}). Taught by Wisdom, 'Solomon' develops in all manner of knowledge, inspiration and artistic possibilities (7^{16-22}). She 'teaches temperance and prudence, justice and fortitude':[8] all that makes for righteousness is her gift (8^{7}; cf. 1^{4ff}). She is 'found of them that seek her' (6^{12}). This, however, is by God's grace. 8^{21} reminds us that she is God's gift, given especially in answer to prayer (cf. 9^{4}).[9]

In writing of Wisdom in 7^{25f}, the author says: 'She is a breath of the power of God . . . an effulgence from everlasting light, and an unspotted mirror of the working of God, and an image of His goodness.' This is the Greek notion of God's radiance manifested as the λόγος, considered here in the form of Wisdom.[10] All streams from God's essential power.

The full force of God's wrath against His enemies is also pictured in these chapters, and in Chapter 12, referring to God's righteous judgement on the wicked, the character of His power is declared in verse 18: 'But thou, being sovereign over thy strength, judgest in gentleness, and with great forbearance dost thou govern us; for the power is thine whensoever thou hast the will.'

[7] See *Phaedrus*, 246c, *Laws*, 896E, R. H. Pfeiffer, op. cit., p. 343.
[8] The four cardinal Stoic virtues. [9] Cf. Jas. 1^{5}.
[10] Here the logos is a unit: in plural form, as in Philo, the radiance is manifested as δυνάμεις. Art., 'Wolfson's Philo', E. R. Goodenough, *J.B.L.*, LXVII (Philadelphia, 1948), p. 105.

III. ANGELS AND DEMONS

Just as the Wisdom teaching of this era helped to bridge the gap in thought between the transcendent God and His universe, so the doctrine of angels explained the possibility of God's acting in providential ways without disturbing His transcendence.

After the Exile, with God's monotheism established, there are no direct theophanies. Angels now bring God's message (Zech 1–8; Ezek 3^{12}, 8^{2f}, etc.). It is still true, however, that the angel's presence was a mediation of the presence of God (Jub 16^{1}; Tob 5^{17}; Ep Jer 7).[11]

The angelology of post-exilic Judaism bears undoubted marks of Persian influence.[12] In Daniel, each people has its guardian angel, its prince (*sar*), that of Israel being Michael (Dan 12^{1}).[13] The names given to angels[14] during this period generally terminate in '-el',[15] showing that they are subordinate to El, and in some sense manifestations of Him.

The Apocalyptic books are full of descriptions of heaven, and of the hierarchy of angels.[16] The Book of Enoch abounds in pictures of this kind (see, e.g., Chapter 71). 61^{10} sets forth the various orders of angelic beings: 'And he will summon all the host of heavens, and all the holy ones above, and the host of God, the Cherubin, Seraphin, and Ophannin, and all the angels of power, and all the angels of principalities, and the Elect One, and the other powers on the earth [and] over the water.' In comparison with the great figures of Cherubin, Seraphin, and Ophannin, 'the other powers on the earth' would seem to be lower angel-powers over nature.[17] Uriel (in 82^{8}), to whom the Lord of the whole

[11] 'There was a natural disinclination to bring the Godhead down into human conditions, and for supernatural conversations angels formed a convenient substitute for God. Such a use was quite compatible with a full sense of personal communion with God in everyday life.' C. F. Montefiore, *Origin and Growth of Religion as illustrated by the Religion of the Ancient Hebrews*, p. 430.

[12] Jer. Rosh ha-Shanah, 56d, states that 'the names of the angels were brought up from Babylon' (Moore, *Judaism*, I.402). For a discussion concerning Persian influence on Judaism, see, e.g., W. O. E. Oesterley, *Jews and Judaism during the Greek Period*, 1941, pp. 85ff, W. F. Albright, *From the Stone Age to Christianity*, pp. 275ff.

[13] In this way the 'watchers' replace the old tribal gods of each people.

[14] Josephus, *Jewish War*, ii, 7.7, recounting the nature of the Essenses initiatory oath says that they promise to preserve the names of the angels (or 'messengers').

[15] E.g. Michael, Uriel, Raphael, Gabriel, etc.

[16] C. Guignebert, *The Jewish World in Time of Jesus* (E.T.), 1939, pp. 96f., says that the description in Daniel 7^{10} is exactly that of an Oriental court, such as that of the King of Persia, thronged with an immense train of servants and courtiers.

[17] *Ophannin* = 'wheels', obviously originating in Ezek 1^{15}. The Talmud sets them in this same company.'

creation has subjected the hosts of heaven, 'has power over night and day in the heaven to cause the light to men—sun, moon, and stars, and all the powers of the heaven which revolve in their circular chariots'.

The functions of the angels are (1) existing to bless and praise God continually (En 39^{12f}); (2) carrying God's messages to men, revealing things that are 'hidden', and generally acting as agents of His providence (Bel 33ff, 2 Esd 2^{44}; En 60^{8}; 2 Macc 5^{1ff}, etc.); (3) bringing men's needs and prayers before God, and responding to these (En 15^{2}, 99^{3}, 100^{4}; Jub 31^{14}); (4) keeping the wheel of nature turning by exercising power at all points of the creation.[18]

C. H. Dodd says that it is possible in Hellenistic Judaism to trace a tendency 'to rationalize the angels of popular mythology in terms of δυνάμεις, as divine agencies'.[19] He quotes Testament of Judah 25^{2} where 'the powers' (αἱ δυνάμεις) 'of glory' are listed together with the Angel of the Presence, heaven and earth, the sun, the moon, and the stars. The use of this expression here (αἱ δυνάμεις) lights up such a New Testament text as Col 1^{16}.

In 3 Baruch 1^{8} occurs the phrase 'angel of the powers', already noted in Enoch 61^{10}. In Testament of Abraham 14, Michael is ἀρχιστράτηγος τῶν ἄνω δυνάμεων.[20] Maybe the powers are thought of here in the sense in which Philo interprets them.[21] Whether that be so or not, they are certainly intermediaries between God and man, ruling over the kingdom between heaven and earth.[22]

Clearly, too, there is a fusion of ideas concerning the δυνάμεις and the stars. Job 38^{7} and Psalm 89^{5ff} point to this (cf. Isa. 34^{4}; Dan 8^{10}). Psalm 148^{2} in the LXX reads: Αἰνεῖτε αὐτον πάντες οἱ ἄγγελοι αὐτοῦ αἰνεῖτε αὐτον πᾶσαι αἱ δυνάμεις αὐτου. Δυνάμεις here is for *tseba'oth* in the sense of 'hosts', and is parallel to 'angels' in the first part of the verse.[23]

The Book of Enoch is also our source for information concerning the demonology of this period.[24] We are told of the origin of the

[18] In the Book of Jubilees, God is depicted creating the angel of the spirit of fire, wind, snow, hail, etc. (2^{2ff}). En 65^{8} tells of the angel controlling the fountain that produces lead and tin! 60^{16ff}, 'the spirit of the sea, the hoar-frost, hail, snow and mist', etc. 'Six great angels watch over the universe, having Paradise, Tartarus, and the world under their government' (10^{4}).

[19] *The Bible and the Greeks*, pp. 17ff.

[20] Cf. 2 Thess 1^{7}.

[21] see pp. 61f, later.

[22] *T.W.z.N.T.*, II.297.

[23] This fusion of ideas is also illustrated in Pray Man 15; En 61^{10}, etc.

[24] It is noteworthy that the Qumran scrolls have no special term for demons: the word 'angel' is applied to them, e.g. 'angel(s) of darkness' (frequently in *Manual of Discipline* and *Damascus Document*).

demons, and their names are as confidently listed as those of the corresponding angels (Chapter 6). There are 200: they are fallen angels (cf. Gen 6^{2ff}) gathered in groups of ten, under leaders (whose names, with the exception of Samjaza, their supreme leader, also end in '-el'). Amidst all the evil wrought by them, the demons also teach men much useful knowledge, such as the working of metals, etc. (8^{1}), and various forms of magic (8^{3}). Samjaza (Satan)[25] is to be bound and his kingdom destroyed (10^{11}). The day of consummation and judgement will bring about the complete destruction of the demons (16^{1}). Chapters 54, 56 and 64 fill in the details of this picture. 65^{6} mentions those on the earth whose 'ruin is accomplished because they have learnt all the secrets of the angels, and all the violence of the Satans, and all their powers—the most secret ones—and all the power of those who practise sorcery', etc. Satan, as a name in the singular, occurs in 53^{3} (cf. 40^{7}: a voice 'fending off the Satans'). Here, then, is a kingdom of evil, organized as over against the good, darkness against light.[26]

The idea of the opposition of Ahura-Mazda and Angra-mainyu has now passed beyond the bounds of Persia. Judaism as it assimilates these ideas (e.g. in Tobit, a book which demonstrates the force of Persian influences on angelic and demonic conceptions), manages—sometimes almost perilously—to avoid a thoroughgoing dualism. At all times, God is omnipotent and in control. The power of the demons is under His rulership (Jub 10^{9ff}). The scene is set, however, for the 'eschatological unfolding of God's might',[27] when Satan's kingdom will be overthrown.

IV. THE MESSIAH

Against the general Messianic picture already provided by the prophets—wherein already was foretold the Day of the Lord and, in Ezekiel, even stranger matters, such as the war with Gog and Magog—the 'new dreamers' of this changeful era painted 'the

[25] Also known as Belial, Beliar, Mastema, Sammael, Malkira, and Azazel in this literature.

[26] J. M. Allegro, in his book on the *Dead Sea Scrolls* (Pelican, 1956), pp. 121, 124, 128, comments that the Qumran community saw the world as a battle-ground between the forces of Good and Evil, Light and Darkness. The spirits of Good and Evil are, however, both under God's supreme rule. After 'a prolonged cosmic battle', God will eventually give the battle to Good.

[27] The phrase is Grundmann's in *T.W.z.N.T.*, II. 296f.

designs of their imaginations'. Within the bounds of the Old Testament Daniel provides a thoroughgoing exhibition of what is possible with this material. Thus, says J. Klausner, was forged 'the *complete* Messianic chain whose separate links are: the signs of the Messiah, the birth pangs of Messiah, the coming of Elijah, the trumpet of Messiah, the ingathering of the exiles, the reception of proselytes, the war with Gog and Magog, the Days of Messiah, the renovation of the world, the Day of Judgement, the resurrection of the dead, the World to Come'. Not all these links are found in every book in the Apocrypha and Pseudepigrapha, but they are there throughout the collection, and in that order.[28] They reappear, as he says, in the Talmudic-Midrashic literature, as also in the Apocalypse and many other references in the New Testament.

God will thus, in this Messianic picture, set Israel on high over her oppressors (2 Bar 82^{2ff}; 4 Ezra 13^{46ff}, etc.). Judith pronounces (16^{17}): 'Woe to the nations that rise up against my race: the Lord Almighty will take vengeance on them in the day of judgement. . . .'

The Psalms of Solomon have God's special relationship with Israel typically in view. He is Israel's God 'from the beginning' (8^{37}). They are His Covenant people (9^{16ff}). God's Messiah, Son of David reigning over Israel, is especially the agent of God's Kingdom, by which He will shatter unrighteous rulers, destroying the pride of 'sinners' as a potter's vessel, and 'with a rod of iron' rule the nations. Psalms of Solomon 17^{23ff}, from which these statements are taken, is a great Christological psalm. In all that He does, the Messiah will 'glorify the Lord' (17^{32ff}). His strength is in God(17^{38}) 'For God will make him mighty by means of His Holy Spirit' (17^{42}).[29]

Practically all the items in the 'Messianic chain' are found scattered throughout the Qumran documents. 'In the Day of Judgement God will destroy all the worshippers of idols and the wicked from the earth.'[30] Two Messiahs ('of Aaron' and 'of Israel') are expected, and would seem to represent the ideal High

[28] *The Messianic Idea in Israel* (E.T.), 1956, pp. 384ff.

[29] A note to be rediscovered in the New Testament picture of the power of Jesus, particularly in Luke's presentation.

[30] See *Commentary on Habakkuk*, at $2^{2, 3, 19}$ (tr. Millar Burrows, *The Dead Sea Scrolls*, 1956, pp. 368ff).

Priest and King of the coming Great Age.[31] The sufferings of the present era are linked with the thought of the 'End'. The Judgement and its execution will be in the hands of 'his elect' (*Commentary on Habakkuk.*) The *Damascus Document* speaks of the period of wrath, of wickedness, of the 'office of the sons of Zadok', of the destruction of the land, of 'the first visitation', of Israel's transgression. The fate of the wicked is destruction in fire.

V. MAN AND HIS EMPOWERMENT

Man is still the breath-soul of the Old Testament, as, e.g., in Sirach 36^{10}, created out of the dust, and (17^{1}) returning thereto. In life (17^{31}) he is flesh and blood, and in death $(10^{9}, 17^{32})$, dust, and ashes. He is, however, considered much more as an individual now than as a unit in the family of Israel. Greek ideas of the immortality of the soul, and growing appreciation of the prospect of immortality, tended to develop the idea of a soul implanted in a body (Test Naph 2^{2ff}) and it is even stated, in Wisdom 9^{15}, 'A corruptible body weigheth down the soul'.[32] What continues in the life beyond is the soul of man (2 En 23^{5}, 49^{2}).

In fulfilment of the Genesis picture, man created in God's image (Apoc Mos 35^{2}) has authority (ἐξουσία) over all the things of the earth (Sir 17^{2f}). God, says 2 Enoch 30^{12} 'appointed him as ruler to rule the earth and to have His wisdom'.

VI. STRENGTH FOR WARFARE: THE MACCABEAN BOOKS

The background detail of the 'Holy War' is to be found in the Book of Judith, written in Maccabean days to nerve its readers for the fight.[33] The High-priest takes the lead in the preparations,

[31] Balaam's prophecy from Num 24^{17} is applied to the military leader in the *War Document* (11^{6}), which ascribes the power in the war to God (Bruce, *Second Thoughts on the Dead Sea Scrolls*, 1956, p. 81). 'Thine is the battle, and from thee is the power, and it is not ours; nor has our strength or the might of our hand done valiantly, but it is by thy strength and by the power of thy great might, as thou didst make known to us of old, saying, "A star shall come forth out of Jacob. . . ." ' etc. Tr. Millar Burrows, op. cit., p. 397.

[32] One writer described the author of Wisdom as using language like 'a poet rather than a scientist' (R. H. Pfeiffer, op. cit., p. 336). He has three terms, which he appears to use indiscriminately for the spiritual part of man: πνεῦμα, ψυχή and νοῦς $(9^{15}, 15^{11}, 16^{14}$ exhibit this use in parallelism).

[33] For the 'Holy War', see above, pp. 21f. This figures also in the Qumran literature. See the *War Document* for the part played by the Chief Priest (ii, 1), the use of trumpets, phrases such as 'the gathering of God': 'One priest shall go before the men of the rank to strengthen their hands in the battle' (vii, 11); 'thou art in the midst of us, a great and terrible God, to despoil all our enemies before us', therefore they must be 'on guard against every indecent, evil thing' (x, 11f). A writer has suggested that this scroll is based on Roman military manuals. It is based far more on the 'Holy War' of Deuteronomic conception, and is completely devoid of any real military significance.

and his directions are followed (4^{6ff}). Judith cries in her prayer (9^{7f}): 'Thou art the Lord that breaketh the battles: the Lord is thy name. Dash thou down their strength in thy power, and bring down their force in thy wrath.' God's people, 'sanctified unto Him' (6^{19}, 9^{14}, 13^{17}, etc.), look for such an answer.

1 Maccabees sets out to recount history, and therefore is in slightly different vein. All here, however, is in keeping with the doctrine of the 'Holy War', which must have formed part of the inspiration behind the revolt. The book, belonging to the period between 135 and 63 B.C.,[34] reflects a strongly anti-Hellenist spirit. The 'law and ordinances' (2^{21}) are paramount, and are in vivid contrast to heathen presumptions (1^{21}) and blasphemies (7^{38}). Israel is the divinely chosen people of God, and her enemies are, therefore, His enemies. At every point, the writer sees the overruling power of the Almighty. The disaster coming upon Israel through Epiphanes is due to God's 'wrath' (1^{64}). Equally, the deliverance is due to God (2^{61}, 3^{18}), though it is to be noted these victories come not through prodigies and miracles,[35] but through the courage, skill, and wisdom of men dedicated to Him.

It would seem almost that 2 Maccabees was written to offset 1 Maccabees, as it differs from the teaching of the former book at almost every point.[36] The austerity of 1 Maccabees is replaced by a fulsomeness almost equally remarkable:[37] the indirect references to God's action behind the Maccabean struggle are replaced by accounts of divine wonders and miraculous help to aid the faithful (2^{21}, 3^{24ff}, 5^{4}, etc.). Its standpoint, however, is orthodox without any traceable influence of Greek philosophy. In 15^{21} the expression 'the Lord that worketh wonders' reveals the standpoint of 2 Maccabees. In his prayer, Maccabeus asks God 'to send a good angel before us to bring terror and trembling: through the greatness of thine arm let them be stricken with dismay that with

[34] C. C. Torrey thinks that the writer was certainly contemporary with the events he describes, and gives a date, *circa* 125 (*The Apocryphal Literature: a Brief Introduction*, Yale, 1945, pp. 72, 74). 16^{23f}, however, suggests that John Hyrcanus is dead, which would bring the date this side of 104 B.C.

[35] There are no prodigies, nor miracles, in Judith either.

[36] It is not possible that the author of 2 Macc can have read 1 Macc with any care, however: the discrepancies between their historical allusions are too great. It is true that the Sadducean standpoint of the first book is answered by the Pharisaic outlook of the second. (The reference in 2^{23} to Jason's five-volume work is probably nothing more than a literary device to add a touch of distinction to the narrative.)

[37] Note, e.g., how the avoidance of the divine name characteristic of 1 Macc is contrasted by the frequent use in 2 Macc of such titles as 'the All-seeing Lord, the God of Israel' (9^{5}), 'the great Sovereign of the World' (12^{15}), 'King of Kings' (13^{4}), etc.

blasphemy are come against thy holy people' (15^{23f}). The latter verse is in the style of the 'Holy War', and the former introduces the angelology of the book. 3^{34ff}, 10^{29ff}, 11^{6ff} provide pictures of angelic visitants, riding on horses, dealing swift and terrible vengeance.

In the highly romantic book, 3 Maccabees,[38] God intervenes in one prodigy after another to save His people. 4 Maccabees is a product of Hellenistic Judaism, in which Stoic conceptions rub shoulders with Jewish Pharisaism. Using the martyrdoms under Seleucus and Antiochus Epiphanes as illustrations, the writer demonstrates the essential reasonableness of the requirements of the Jewish Torah, and lauds the martyrdoms of those who were faithful to it unto death.[39]

VII. THE SPIRIT, WISDOM, AND MESSIAH

God's Spirit is now identified as the source of life breathed into all men: e.g. Test Naph 10^{9}; 'Blessed[40] is the man who does not defile the holy spirit of God which has been put and breathed into him.' The heroes of old, Abraham (Zad 4^{2}), Isaiah (Mart Is 5^{14}), were strengthened by the Spirit. 'Now Joseph was a good man', says Testament of Simeon 4^{4}, 'and had the spirit of God within him'; 'He had no defilement in his heart, because the spirit of God rests upon him' (Test Ben 8^{2}, cf. Test Jos 9^{2}). The *πνεῦμα* of these books is not the same thing, however, as the *ruach*, the 'force', of the Old Testament. It is the spirit inspiring to good conduct: assimilating far more to the *yetser tob*, the inclination to good within man, as contrasted with the *yetser ra'*, the impulse to evil.[41] God thus strengthens man 'to do righteousness' (Jub 22^{10}). The Lord of

[38] The product of an Alexandrian Jew who uses historical invention as a vehicle for encouraging his contemporaries to faithfulness in the time of trial. It was written before the destruction of the Temple (1^{8ff}), probably towards the end of the last century B.C. (Torrey, op. cit., p. 82).

[39] Note the uses of the word *δύναμις* in this book. 14^{10} uses the word in quite an ordinary connotation, i.e. of the 'power of fire'; but Antiochus, taunting Eleazar in 5^{13} to give up his 'foolish notions', says, *εἰ καὶ τίς ἐστιν τῇδε τῆς θρησκείας ἐποπτικὴ δύναμις συγγνωμονήσειεν σοι ἐπὶ πᾶσιν δι' ἀνάγκην παρανομία γεινομένῃ*. Here speaks the Hellenist, in this vague way, of any *δύναμις* which might have some interest in this religion!

[40] Something of the pristine strength has gone out of this word as we meet it in this literature. Note, e.g., Sir 25^{7ff} for the rather innocuous picture of the ten types of men who are blessed (*μακάριος*). 'Blessed', says 2 En 42^{13}, 'is the man in whose mouth is mercy and gentleness'. The term now means 'fortunate', 'honoured of God'.

[41] For a discussion of the meaning and importance of the conception of the *yetser*, see T. Walker, *The Teaching of Jesus and the Jewish Teaching of His Age*, pp. 202ff.

Spirits 'strengthened the spirits of the righteous, in the name of his righteousness' (En 41^{8}).[42]

The picture of Wisdom provided in Proverbs, Sirach, and Wisdom has close affinities with that of the Holy Spirit in the New Testament (e.g. Wis 7^{25ff}). The Old Testament has no doctrine of personal distinctions within the Deity; and the tendency to hypostasize and differentiate did not make its way easily. Much that emerges in the New Testament in the conception both of the Son and the Spirit is to be seen, however, in embryo in the figure of 'Wisdom' (cf. Wis 1^{16ff}; Sir 9^{15}, 37^{16}; Wis 8^{17}: Wisdom is God's agent in creation, the power by which He upholds all things, His spirit immanent in the universe, and in man).

It is the Messiah who is specially to be equipped with the Spirit (e.g. Ps Sol 17^{42}). 'The spirit of understanding and sanctification shall rest upon him' (Test Levi 18^{7}; cf. Test Jud 24^{2}, and Jud 62^{2}). Through the Messiah, the people will come to experience the Holy Spirit: he 'shall make them know his holy spirit' (Zad 2^{10}). It will be the 'eschatological gift'.[43]

VIII. HOLINESS: AND MAN'S ATTITUDE TO GOD

By this time, 'holiness' and 'righteousness' can be equated (e.g. En 39^{4}: 'holy' in the first line is parallel to 'righteous' in the second). As God's elect, His people are to be 'righteous and holy' (En 25^{5}). Concerning the distinction between the two terms, it has been said that righteousness was 'the ethical, holiness the ceremonial aspect of the acceptable life'.[44]

The idea of 'separation' originally involved in holiness now implies separation from heathen nations, and from their depravity and wickedness. This was to be safeguarded by honouring the ceremonies and rites which distinguished the Jew from his fellows. By the Sabbath observance, circumcision, the avoidance of

[42] Cf. in the Qumran *Thanksgiving Psalm*, VII^{6}, 'I thank thee O Lord, because thou hast sustained me with thy strength and hast shed abroad thy Holy Spirit in me; I shall not be moved.' IX^{32}: 'With thy Holy Spirit thou dost delight me, and to this day thou dost lead me.' There is an assimilation to the doctrine of the two *yetsers* also. Test Abr 1^{2} says: 'Two ways has God given to the sons of men, and two inclinations. . . .' The Qumran Covenanters taught that God 'made for man two spirits, that he might walk by them until the appointed time of his visitation'. These are 'the spirits of truth and perversion' (quoted, M. Burrows, op. cit., pp. 257f, from the *Manual of Discipline*.) This doctrine seems to owe its origin to Zoroastrianism.

[43] The *Manual of Discipline* says that at the end of this age God will cleanse man by sprinkling upon him 'the spirit of truth' (M. Burrows, ibid., p. 329).

[44] T. Walker, ibid., p. 227.

unclean foods, and the distinction between what was clean and unclean, inculcated in the Torah, the Jew was set apart. In 1 Maccabees 2^{32ff} we are told of the 1,000 extremists who preferred death to the profanation of the Sabbath by fighting (cf. 2 Macc 5^{25f}, 6^{11}, 15^{1ff}). Mattathias and his sons wisely decided that, in their immediate circumstances, it was right to fight on the sacred day (1 Macc 2^{40f}), but it is worthy of note that this meant only the modicum (cf. 2 Macc 8^{26ff}). These rites, keeping the Jew separate, were part of His service, done in what he described as 'the fear of the Lord' (Sir 19^{20}).

Sins against holiness were rigorously condemned. 'Impious deeds' (3 Macc 6^{10}) needed atonement. The daily sacrifices were thus a perpetual seeking of forgiveness on behalf of the people 'with blood before the altar' (Jub 6^{14}). The ritual of the Day of Atonement made it possible for God to 'forgive all their transgressions and pardon all their sins'. These ideas were not purely magical, however: it is important to note that sacrifice was unacceptable unless it proceeded from a right intention (Sir 7^{8f}, 34^{18f}; 2 En 45^{3}).

Fasting (Ps Sol 3^{9}; 1 Macc 3^{46f}), and almsgiving (Sir 3^{30}; Tob 4^{10}, 12^{9}) were now regarded as most meritorious. Yet, our writers tell us, these spiritual exercises needed to be done with humility and sincerity (Test Jos 10^{2}; Test Abr 2^{6f}).

The Qumran community afford an excellent example of a group endeavouring to live the life of 'holiness'. They called themselves by such titles as the *chasidim* of the Most High, the *maskilim* (wise), the elect of God, the holy people of the Covenant, the sons of light, and thought of themselves as 'volunteers for holiness'. Great importance was attached by them to ritual cleansing. By their discipline they hoped to make expiation for Israel (thus fulfilling the role of the Suffering Servant of Isa 52^{13ff}?). Their leader, the 'Teacher of Righteousness', had 'marked out the path of holiness for them'.[45] This included Sabbatarianism of the strictest kind.[46] Man's littleness and creatureliness before God is as much taken for granted by the intertestamental writers as by those represented in the Old Testament. So much is this the case that the recurring phrase 'the fear of the

[45] F. F. Bruce, *Second Thoughts on the Dead Sea Scrolls*, pp. 101f.

[46] See the twenty-five Sabbath regulations listed in the Zadokite *Laws*, which are now considered to belong to the Qumran community, and the regulations in the *Damascus Document*, xiii.

Lord' covers very much what others might think of as love for Him.[47] These writers, too, are able to couple the thought of God's omnipotence with that of man's freedom.[48] In Judith verses which stress God's almighty power (8^{11ff}, 16^{13ff}) are balanced by others which underline, as certainly, the fact of human self-determination before Him ($8^{22, 34}$, 10^{9}, 15^{9f}). Human freedom is 'everywhere taken for granted'[49] in this literature (cf. En 5^{2ff}; Ps Sol 9^{7}).

The cardinal qualities required of man before God are obedience and trust. Obedience, now, is seen almost entirely on the lines of fulfilment of the Torah, in which God has made His will known (Ps Sol 10^{5}; 2 Bar 19^{3}; Wis 18^{4}). God's Covenant requirements are here made explicit.[50] Throughout these books, the same kind of faithful loyalty to God is encouraged as is commended in the Old Testament. To describe this, the words πίστις and πιστεύειν begin to be used, with a meaning nearer to the Old Testament Emunah, however, than to New Testament 'faith'.

IX. PRAYER AND POWER

References to prayer abound in these books, and much of it is of the type Otto Proksch describes as 'prophetic prayer'.[51] It is uttered in accordance with what is known of the will of God, and is answered by God's creative power. The examples of the patriarchs as men of prayer is especially noted and commended, and their stories embellished by showing its importance in their deliverances and successes (Jub 11^{17}, 12^{20}, 22^{7ff}; Test Jos 3^{3}, etc.). The story of

[47] Notice the parallelism between these two phrases in Sir 2^{15f}; cf. also Test Zeb 10^{5}; Test Dan 6^{1}; Test Jos 11^{1}.

[48] Not so the Qumran sectaries. Their words speak of a deterministic theology (so L. Rost). The *Damascus Document* describes men as divided into four assigned groups which settle their destinies. This document and the *Manual of Discipline* make frequent use of the phrase 'the lot', e.g. 'men of the lot of God', or 'of Belial'. No attempt is made to resolve this doctrine with exhortations and commands which, equally, imply man's freedom of choice (M. Burrows, op. cit., pp. 262f, 336).

[49] T. Walker, *Hebrew Religion between the Testaments*, 1937, p. 81.

[50] The two terms 'covenant' and 'Torah' are almost interchangeable (e.g. Jub 1^{10}, 24^{11}; Ass Mos 1^{14}; Zad 7^{12}). 'The law is life' (2 Bar 38^{2}) makes clear how obedience to the Torah was regarded.

[51] In *Theologie des Alten Testaments*, p. 625; see p. 33, above. T. R. Hughes, *Prophetic Prayer*, pp. 29ff, issues the caveat, however, that 'the tendency in this period is for prayer to be formal, and free spontaneous utterances are replaced by ritual'. As an instance of the idea of prayer as inspired by the activity of God in the heart of man he quotes Baruch 3^{7}, 'For Thou hast put Thy fear in our hearts to the intent that we should call upon Thy name', and also refers to Sirach 8^{21}, 9^{6}, where the wisdom essential to the moral life is represented as a gift from God. This, he says, 'is the nearest approach to the Apocrypha' to the belief that prayer is divinely inspired (ibid, p. 32).

Tobit hinges on the conception of answered prayer ($3^{1ff, 13ff}$, 4^{19}, $8^{4f, 13}$). Sirach speaks of prayer as a means to developing certain virtues (23^{3ff}, 51^{14}) and to recovery of health (38^{9ff}). His book is full of personal prayers. Judith and the people alike, in the book under her name, seek help from God in prayer, and receive it ($4^{9, 13}$, 6^{18f}, 7^{19}, 9, 12^{6ff}). It is noteworthy in 1 Maccabees that every time the enemy faces the Israelites, 'whether Gorgias (4^{10}), or Lysias (4^{30}; cf. 2 Macc 11^{6}, 13^{10}), or Nicanor (7^{40}; cf. 2 Macc $8^{2, 29}$), he is confronted by people who have just prayed', and their subsequent triumph is always ascribed to God, who gives help in response to prayer.[52]

A man, however poor, can be sure that God will hear him (Ps Sol 18^{3}): 'the Lord hears the prayer of everyone that fears God, and every request of the soul that hopes for Him the Lord accomplishes' (Ps Sol 6^{8}). He receives 'every single prayer of man' (Apoc Abr 25).[53]

X. RULERSHIP

Chapter 10 of Sirach begins by referring to the way that people take their tone from their rulers: 'As is the judge of his people, so are his ministers; and as is the ruler of the city, such are all they that dwell therein. An uninstructed king will destroy his people; and a city will be established through the understanding of the powerful.' Verses 4 and 5 continue by enunciating the principle we have noted already as the Biblical idea of rulership: 'In the hand of the Lord is the authority (*ἐξουσία*) of the earth; and in due time he will raise up over it one that is profitable. In the hand of the Lord is the prosperity of a man; and upon the person of the scribe shall he lay his honour.'

The Psalms of Solomon contrast the man swollen with a sense of power (the reference here is plainly to Pompey),[54] who becomes

[52] T. Walker, *The Teaching of Jesus and the Jewish Teaching of His Age*, p. 58.

[53] Occasionally we have references to intermediaries who carry prayers to God, or of heavenly intercessors (e.g. Moses in Ass Mos 11^{17}), but, as T. Walker comments, 'Books which countenance mediation are not less emphatic on direct approach to God' (*The Teaching of Jesus and the Jewish Teaching of His Age*, p. 55).

[54] References in $2^{1f, 30f}$, $8^{18f, 22ff}$, and $17^{6, 14}$ seem to point to happenings involving Pompey. Langen, Hilgenfield, Drummond, Schürer, Ryle, and James concur in relating 2^{20} to Pompey's death in Egypt. It would seem that these psalms, originally written in Hebrew, were used at one time in the public worship of a synagogue (the inscription implies this). Note that in the psalms the sense of God's judgement is implicit (e.g. $2^{12, 16, 36ff}$, 3^{3}, 5^{1}, 8^{7ff}, etc.). The problem of man's free will also finds expression here: all are in the hands of God (5^{4ff}), yet each exercises the freedom of his own choice.

insolent before God, and God Himself, in whose hands alone is all true power. The offence of the impious man is thus described in $2^{33\mathrm{ff}}$.

> He said: I will be lord of land and sea;
> And he recognized not that it is God who is great,
> Mighty in his great strength.
> He is King over the Kingdoms.
> (It is he) who setteth me up in glory,
> And bringeth down the proud to eternal destruction and dishonour,
> Because they knew Him not.[55]

Insolence before God is bound to bring ruin.

[55] Tr. G. Buchanan Gray, *The Apocrypha and Pseudepigrapha of the Old Testament*, II, ed. R. H. Charles.

CHAPTER SEVEN

PHILO

THE finest example of the attempt to marry Hellenistic philosophy to Judaism is afforded by Philo of Alexandria. Judaism demanded an implicit acceptance of the Torah, God's direct revelation to man. All that Philo, or any other Hellenistic Jew, might wish to carry into his total philosophy must, accordingly, be found therein—either by inference or in some embryonic form. In virtue of this, the doctrine was evolved that Greek philosophy had derived its truths from Moses![1] To discover these truths in the Pentateuch needed an allegorical method of the most inventive kind. Philo proved himself a master in this field.

What dominates Philo's system is the conception of the mediation between God, utterly transcendent—man cannot name Him, nor claim to know Him in any real sense—and the world of men and material things.[2] It is true that he uses a number of terms by which to give God a title. Of them all, that provided by the LXX of Exodus 3^{14} was the most congenial, harmonizing exactly with Greek philosophical conceptions. God was ὁ ὤν, or τὸ ὄν, or ὁ ὄντος ὤν.[3] These were scarcely names: rather, they were assertions that 'God alone has veritable being'[4] As Philo hastens to make clear, this group of appellations is different from the variety of other divine names which he uses: the latter are no more than means by which he can refer to the unnameable, and also, in this way, single out for attention some partial aspect of His total perfection.

The centre of Philo's mediatoral system is the λόγος. The LXX, again, had prepared the way for this. Psalm 32^{6}, 147^{18}, 148^{8} and Wisdom 9^{1} speak of ὁ λόγος τοῦ κυρίου as the creative

[1] Clement of Alexandria and Eusebius quote Aristobulus (*c.* 200-150 B.C.) for this. His work was known as *An Explanation of the Mosaic Law*. A Greek version of the Pentateuch made prior to 525 B.C. would need to have been at the disposal of the earlier Greek writers!

[2] See Moore, *Judaism*, II.416.

[3] Drummond, *Philo Judaeus*, 1888, II.63n., gives ὁ ὤν, 29x, τὸ ὄν, 38x, and ὁ ὄντος ὤν as occurring very frequently in Philo; τὸ θεῖον, 12, τὸ ἄιτιον, 23, etc.

[4] *Quod Deterius Potiori Insidiari Soleat*, 160.

agent by which the heavens were made and all things sustained according to God's purposes.[5] Wisdom 9^{1f} affords a bridge between the conception of Wisdom[6] and the Logos: in parallel passages we are told of the λόγος, by which all things were made, and of God's Wisdom (σοφία), by which He 'ordained', or 'prepared' man.[7] The Logos, the very Thought of God, is source and origin of the entire Cosmos—and, in the first place, of that Cosmos which exists in archetypal pattern in the Mind of God. As well as this, the Logos is the executive power by which what is in the Mind of God takes shape, assumes power, and is actually manifested and continues in being.[8] The invisible, seminal artificer is the divine Word.[9] Under Him exist a hierarchy of other powers.

The clearest statement of this philosophy is found in *Quaestiones et Solutiones in Exodum* at Exodus 25^{22}:

The first of all is He who is elder than the One, the Monad, and the Beginning. Next is the Logos of the Self-Existent, the seminal essence of all beings. And from the divine Logos, as from a fountain, the two powers are separated. The Creative power (ἡ ποιητική), by virtue of which the Creator rules that which has come into being is named κύριος. The other great power is the Governing Power.[10]

Under this hierarchy exists an infinite number of δυνάμεις, forces which undergird and underlie all that is. Behind all known physical forces, e.g. the four elements of 'fire, air, earth and water', 'sun, moon, heaven', behind all mental faculties, are these δυνάμεις of God, vivifying and unifying all things, existing in and through Him. It is because of these forces that we can, in any measure at all, come to understand the Self-existent; just as Moses, not able to see God's face could yet see His 'back parts' (Ex 33^{12ff}).[11] Even these ministering powers of God,

[5] It is the λόγος equally that is revealed in the Torah (Ex 34^{27f}; Deut 10^4), and that speaks to the prophets, and, in turn, is spoken by them (Isa 2^1; Jer 1^2; Ezek 3^{16}, etc).

[6] Discussed above, pp. 46f.

[7] Note Wis $7^{22, 24}$. It was a common Greek conception that there emanated from God's self that which, considered as a unit, might be spoken of as the λόγος or σοφία, and thought of in its manifestation in plurality, as δυνάμεις (Goodenough, art., 'Wolfson's Philo', *Journal of Biblical Literature*, lxvii, 1948, p. 105.

[8] This agrees, in some sense, with the Stoic conceptions of the 'inward' and 'uttered' λόγος, cf. amongst many passages in Philo, *Somn.* ii, 6, *Opif.* 3, 5.

[9] *Quis Rerum Divinarum Heres*, 119.

[10] ἡ βασιλική, by which He governs all which has come into being (*Fug.* 94ff). High amongst the powers, too, is the legislative (ἡ νομοθετική)—this is a completely Jewish conception injected into this system!

[11] *De Mutatione Nominum*, 9, 28, 29.

however, partake of the quality of the infinite and unknowable.[12]

'When out of that confused matter, God produced all things', Philo comments in *De Specialibus Legibus*, 329, 'He did not do so with His own handiwork, since His nature, happy and blessed as it was, forbade that He should touch the limitless chaotic matter (πεφυρμένης ὕλης). Instead, He made full use of the incorporeal powers well denoted by their name of Forms, to enable each kind to take its own appropriate shape.' These Forms are Plato's ἰδέαι: which are thus both 'patterns' and 'causes',[13] emanating from God, and forming His 'glory'.

The powers together form the 'intelligible world' (κόσμος νοητός), which in turn is nothing else than the λόγος of God,[14] the archetypal idea, or seal, of the 'perceptible world' (κόσμος αἰσθητός).[15]

Zeller, in his great work on Philo, suggests that he borrowed the conception of four kinds of intermediaries from various sources: (1) the doctrine of 'forms' or 'ideas' from the Platonic philosophy, (2) the doctrine of efficient causes from Stoicism, and then (3) the angels, of Jewish-Persian origin, and (4) the demons of Greek mythology.[16]

Yahweh tseba'oth thus becomes the 'Lord of Powers'.[17] Especially is this phrase interpreted as Lord of the host of stars, or of the heavenly host, of angels.[18] The army of the heavenly host, God's lieutenants (ὑπάρχοι), as Philo calls them, form a closely marshalled organization. Each has his special function, and his place in the heavenly contingents.[19] As in the post-Exilic literature, Philo knows of archangels.[20] Also, as elsewhere in this literature, the angels carry messages from 'the Father to His children', and 'report their need' to Him.[21] The angels are not, however,

[12] Just as Jacob's assailant at Peniel refused to disclose his identity. *De Mutatione Nominum*, 2; cf. *De Vita Mosis* 1, 14; *De Somnis*, 1, 39f.

[13] as indeed for Plato: e.g. *Sophist* 247 D-E where 'ideas are conceived not only as patterns, but also as causes (αἰτίαι) in which sense he describes them as possessing power.' H. A. Wolfson, *Philo*, Harvard, 1948, p. 217.

[14] *De Opificio Mundi*, 6.

[15] *De Opificio Mundi*, 6, *De Mutatione Nominum*, 23.

[16] III.2:4, p. 407. Note regarding 'demons' (e.g. Plato's *Phaedrus*, 246A) that Philo equates the philosophers' 'demons' with Scripture 'angels' *De Gigantibus*, 2, *De Somnis*, 222.

[17] 'An identification already known to his [Philo's] readers': Wolfson, ibid., p. 219.

[18] Cf. Pseudepigraphal *Prayer of Manasses*, En 61[10], etc. Note in Philo *Abr.*, 23 and 28, the interchange from δυνάμεις to ἄγγελοι.

[19] *De Confusione Linguarum*, 174.

[20] E.g. *Quis Rerum Divinarum Heres*, 42, *De Confusione Linguarum*, 146, *De Somnis*, 1, 25.

[21] *De Somnis*, 1, 22; cf. *De Abrahamo*, 23.

δυνάμεις of the same order as the great powers who framed the 'intelligible world' and the 'perceptible world'. Neither are they 'ideas' or 'logoi'. If they are δυνάμεις at all, in the full Philonian sense, it is as 'immanent powers', participating in the divine service, embodying God's thought, and used to mediate His special providence to men.

According to his allegorical method, Philo finds symbolism in all the Old Testament miracles, but at the same time he is in doubt about their historicity. His way of dealing with the subject has quite a modern ring; and at the same time it enables us to understand his conception of the creatorship and power of God. To anyone bothered about such things, he recommends an examination of the universe itself. It is far more wonderful than any individual wonder. To the God of creation, nothing is impossible.[22] The powers which God has implanted in the world, though acting with certainty and unalterably, according to law, are not at the same time independent (αὐτοκρατεῖς) powers. 'Like a charioteer grasping the reins or a pilot the tiller, He guides all things in what direction He pleases as law and right demand, standing in need of no one besides: for all things are possible to God[23] (πάντα γὰρ θεῷ δυνατά)'[24]

Man was made 'after the image of God' (Gen 1[27]). The archetypal man was what was patterned on the image of God, the Logos (τῷ ἑαυτοῦ λόγῳ: *De Opificio Mundi*, 139). Possessing kinship with the man into whom God breathed the Divine Breath, every man is thus allied to the divine logos in respect of his mind; and, in his body, is allied 'to all the world, for he is compounded of the same things, earth, water, air, and fire'.[25] Since the nature of man is thus composite, made of earthly substance and Divine Breath, he represents the borderland between mortal and immortal nature.[26]

These strange, metaphysical, and allegorical documents of the Alexandrian philosopher, so different from the main line of biblical writing, nevertheless are at one with them in certain essential matters regarding the conception of power. Of all that we know of Him who must forever be largely unknowable, the fact of His power and volition is supreme and certain: 'For it is

[22] *De Vita Mosis* I, 38 and II, 48; see Wolfson, ibid., I.354f.
[23] *De Opificio Mundi*, 14; quoted Wolfson.
[24] Cf. πάντα γὰρ δυνατὰ παρὰ τῷ θεῷ, Mk 10[27].
[25] *De Opificio Mundi*, 145. [26] *De Opificio Mundi*, 135.

the property of God to act' (ἴδιον μὲν δὴ θεοῦ τὸ ποιεῖν).[27] Of Him it is true that He is 'always working'.[28] This ceaseless activity is part of His unchangeableness.[29] It is this property in Him which Philo asserts is the source of all action in the world.[30]

[27] *De Cherubim*, 24.
[28] *Legum Allegoria*, 1, 3; cf. Jn 5[17].
[29] *Legum Allegoria*, 2, 9.
[30] *Legum Allegoria*, 1, 3; see Wolfson, ibid., II.134.

CHAPTER EIGHT

CONTEMPORARY BELIEF IN THE NEW TESTAMENT ERA

BEFORE turning to the New Testament, it is important to assess something of the background belief in both Judaistic and Hellenistic worlds, and to note its relevance to the theme of power.

Rabbinic and Hellenistic Judaism continued the Old Testament stress on God's unity, venerating Him as sole Creator and Lord. The Targum of Isaiah 48^{13} provides a sufficient example of how God's power is thought of as the origin of all, while it stresses at the same time the idea of Creation through the Word of God: 'With my Word I have created the earth, and with my power hung up the heavens.' Rabbi Shela expounds the doxology of 1 Chronicles 29^{11f} in characteristic fashion, in tune with the *Heilsgeschichte* of Old Testament days: 'Thine Yahweh is the greatness'—here he refers to the act of creation, quoting Job 9^{10}, 'which doeth great things past finding out and wonders without number'—'and the power', and here the reference is to the Exodus from Egypt, quoting Exodus 14^{31}, 'Israel saw that great hand [work] which the Lord did upon the Egyptians'.[1]

In these post-Biblical times the idea of the supremacy of the Torah developed still further. Not only was it the vehicle by which God's will was made known to men, but also that by which His grace reached them.[2] The words of the Law are thus 'life' and 'salvation'. The Mekilta on Exodus 15^{13} joins together Torah and '*oz* ('strength'), setting Psalm 29^{11} against this text as an exegetical parallel. The idea that 'Power equals Torah'[3] became the basis of the Rabbinical exegesis of such texts. The Torah is God's great agent of salvation.[4]

[1] b Ber. 58a, quoted *T.W.z.N.T.*, II.296.

[2] Torah 'must be taken to include the whole of revelation—all that God has made known of His nature, character and purpose and of what he would have man be and do' (Moore, *Judaism in the First Centuries of the Christian Era*, I.263.)

[3] E.g. Pesikt 148^a (see also M Ex 15^2, 18^1) *T.W.z.N.T.*, II.299.

[4] All that this conception of the Torah included is transferred by the Christian to Christ (see, e.g., W. D. Davies, *Paul and Rabbinic Judaism*, p. 222). Note Jacob Jocz's description of the Torah in *The Jewish People and Jesus Christ*. It is 'the greatest and most perfect gift that God has bestowed upon Israel'.

The concept of Power was also dominant in Greek philosophy, and was connected with the thought of God. Hellenistic philosophy, as we have seen in our discussion on Philo, had inherited the conception of power as the ultimate world principle. In ancient Egypt we can observe something of a pantheistic identification of the Godhead (Ra) with the Life-force.[5] With the development of the idea of differentiated powers of nature proceeding from it, controlling and moving the Cosmos, we have discovered the source of the Greek concept of 'powers' proceeding from the one central source of power. Its foundation goes deep into primitive religious beliefs.[6]

Aristotle wrote of 'the power pervading everything that is, having created the whole world'.[7] To the Stoics this Power was the efficient cause of all that appears.[8] Poseidonius in his philosophy outlined a system of powers, through whom it is declared the world was fashioned. At the heart of this system is the power of life (δύναμις ζωτική), the foundational power of all. In this way we can trace the development of the Greek concept of God. Philosophically speaking, as Grundmann comments, 'world principle' and 'Godhead' are identical.[9] This was understood among the Stoics in pantheistic fashion, whilst in Aristotelian and Platonic philosophy a more transcendent view of Godhead was established.

Whether popular thought was much affected by these philosophical currents is debatable. What is certain, however, is that all sections of the community were influenced by the astrological superstition of these times. The Zodiac, placed above the earth, was the world's archetype, where correspondences were discovered to whatever happens here. Many thought of the Zodiac as man's guide, mentor, and protector.[10] The observance of the movements of the heavenly bodies and their position at specific times of the year, suggested an association between them and the times and

[5] Grundmann, *Der Begriff der Kraft in der Neutestamentlicher Gedankenwelt*, p. 29. He refers to Friedrich Preisigke (*Vom göttlichen Fluidum nach ägyptischen Anschauung*, 1922) for this identification.

[6] *T.W.z.N.T.*, II.291f. [7] *De Mundo.* [8] E.g. Simplicius, III.49.12.

[9] Grundmann *T.W.z.N.T.*, II.289.

[10] The Qumran documents contain a number of works, says J. M. Allegro, referring to the movements of the heavenly bodies, and 'not all their study', he comments, 'was of purely academic interest'. It would seem that these ideas had infiltrated deep into Judaism in New Testament times. One of Qumran esoteric documents describes the characteristics of men born under the influence of certain sections of the Zodiac (*Dead Sea Scrolls*, p. 112).

seasons of agricultural life, and, eventually, with all seasonal institutions. This led in turn to their identification with the gods which were thought to influence such matters. Babylonia and Chaldea had gone far with this process. Egypt, too, had its own form of astrology. The Greeks, who had always thought of the stars as supernatural beings, were still further affected by the beliefs with which they made contact through Alexander's conquests. By New Testament days star-worship and astrology had penetrated the whole of the Roman world.[11] These, inevitably, encouraged the cult of Mithraism and of sun-worship. The heaven's central force, source of the world's light and heat, naturally suggested a deity all-pervasive and omnipotent.[12] Astrology also, through its very nature, fostered a fatalistic philosophy. Destiny was written in the stars And without doubt, too, it influenced the eschatology of this era.[13]

Popular belief throughout the Roman world was a strange amalgam of ideas assimilated from astrology, philosophy, and the Oriental mystery religions. The theological items in this 'paganism' could be represented thus:

the adoration of the elements, especially the cosmic bodies; the reign of one God, eternal and omnipotent, with messenger attendants; spiritual interpretation of the gross rites yet surviving from primitive times; the assurance of eternal felicity to the faithful; belief that the soul was on earth to be proved before its final return to the universal spirit, of which it was a spark; the existence of an abysmal abode for the evil, against whom the faithful must keep up an unceasing struggle; the destruction of the universe, the death of the wicked and the eternal happiness of the good in a reconstructed world.[14]

This was the period of apocalyptic thought and eschatology. Though outside Judaism the expectation was of a different character, the futility and pessimism of the pagan world expressed itself in convictions concerning the catastrophic end of the age.[15]

[11] R. Bultmann, *Primitive Christianity*, p. 146.

[12] F. Cumont, *The Oriental Religion in Roman Paganism* (E.T.), Chicago, 1911, p. 134.

[13] Time itself was deified in Iranian mythology (the Zervan Akarana of the Avesta), F. Cumont, ibid., p. 150. The time divisions of astrology provided fertile suggestions for eschatologists.

[14] G. Showerman's summary of the final chapter, 'The Transformation of Roman Paganism', in his Introduction to F. Cumont's *The Oriental Religions in Roman Paganism*, pp. viiif.

[15] Cf. Plato, *Tim.*, 32d: planetary disturbances, at long intervals, causing vast cosmic catastrophes; 39d: the Great Year. Lucan, *Phars.*, 1. 172ff, speaks of contemporary interpretation of Plato's warnings. Stoicism (*Or Sib.*, 5. 512ff) can picture a final conflagration. (W. L. Knox, *St Paul and the Church of the Gentiles*, pp. 4, 10, 15.)

Messianic hopes were, indeed, expressed in pagan literature, as in Virgil's Fourth Eclogue, and were much in evidence at the deification of Augustus. In confirmation of these hopes, a new star appeared, identified by Virgil with Apollo.

In this age of universal pessimism, the Jew, whose nation had survived centuries of persecution and calamity, found the language of apocalyptic most satisfying. From the Old Testament he inherited the teaching of the Day of Yahweh (Isa 2^{12ff}; Amos 5^{18}; Joel 1^{15}, etc.). His God was the God who moulded history, who was bound to vindicate His covenant people. . . . His scriptures brought to mind many pictures of God's shaking of the world and of nations.[16]

This is the background against which the gospel of the New Testament is set. God, source of all things, possessing final authority over the most recalcitrant members of His creation, is now, in the person of His Son, about to unfold the drama of the coming of His Kingdom in power, resulting in the salvation of men and the final defeat of Satan and all his powers.

[16] The picture of the final conflagration appears in the hymns of the Dead Sea scrolls, as well as in the more familiar apocalyptic literature. The common source of much of this material is probably to be found in Persia.

Part Three

THE NEW TESTAMENT

CHAPTER NINE

INTRODUCTORY

NO one has faced the full implications of the New Testament who has not realized that it is a series of documents witnessing to the inbreaking of power. The men who write the records and the people they describe, or to whom they write, were alive in an era of δύναμις. What they are experiencing is in the continuing heritage we have been examining. But when we come to these documents we have not only to note what continues in the vein of the Old Testament and Apocrypha, but also how the ancient biblical conceptions are amplified and clarified, and how, at times, a new element altogether is introduced, going beyond the Old Testament understanding.

We begin by emphasizing some of the factors which form the basic assumptions of the New Testament as of the Old. Primary among these is the all-encompassing fact of the Living God and His almighty power. He is the world's Creator and Governor, to be known in His mighty acts. His holiness and wrath are also everywhere assumed. As the liturgical addition to the Lord's Prayer (Mat 6^{13}) expresses it, in a doxology typical of both testaments, His is the Kingdom, the Power, and the Glory. These concepts are fundamental and axiomatic, and unless they are realized and accepted, we become false interpreters of the New Testament gospel. For the writers of the New Testament, then, as for the Old, God is Almighty Creator and Lord, source and origin of life and energy.[1] He 'created all things' (Eph 3^{9}). He rules and controls the Universe and the destinies of men. Expressing this another way, the fundamental datum of New Testament theology, as Ethelbert Stauffer declares,[2] is the absolute priority of the divine. All other 'powers' are exercised under His authority.

John, in his Prologue, ventures into metaphysics in a way not

[1] 'God and power are one and the same': Fronmüller in Zeller's *Bib. Wörterbuch*, II. 87, quoted Cremer, p. 121.

[2] *New Testament Theology* (E.T.), p. 51. The New Testament is rooted in the 'old biblical tradition': 'I am the first' (Isa 41^{4}, 44^{6}, 48^{12}; cf. Rev 1^{8}, 21^{6}). Stauffer quotes Aristobulus (*Eus. Praep. Ev.*, 13. 12. 6) as representative of Hellenistic Judaism: 'Let us begin with God.'

typical of New Testament writing, but his assumptions are those forming the substratum of all New Testament theology. It may be that he is purposely writing in a way meant to recommend itself to Hellenists, but it is not from them that he borrows as he writes of Creation and God's creative Word: 'In the beginning was the Word, and the Word was with God, and the Word was God. The same was in the beginning with God. All things were made by him; and without him was not anything made that hath been made.'[3]

Paul, addressing the Romans, appeals to the universal appreciation of God's originative power: 'For the invisible things of him since the creation of the world are clearly seen, being perceived through the things that are made, (even) his everlasting power and divinity.'[4]

God is *παντοκράτωρ*, the Almighty,[5] the ruler of all that is[6] (see 2 Cor 6^{18}; Rev 1^{8}, 4^{8}, 11^{17}, etc.). The LXX rendering for Yahweh, *κύριος*, is brought into use in the New Testament in connexion with Christ, but it is also used of God himself (e.g. Mt 5^{33}; Mk 5^{19}; Lk 1^{6}; Acts 7^{33}; Heb 8^{2}; Jas 4^{15}, etc.). In Revelations 4^{8}, we find 'The Lord God the Almighty'. Foerster in *T.W.z.N.T.* states that the title 'Lord' points to the 'personal, lawful, comprehensive might of God'.[7]

Again, following LXX usage,[8] *δεσπότης* is used of God (Lk 2^{29}; Acts 4^{24}; Rev 6^{10}); and *δυνάστης*, similarly applied to Him in the Apocrypha, occurs also in the New Testament (1 Tim 6^{15}—note the phrase: 'the blessed and only Potentate, the King of kings, and Lord of lords'). In the Magnificat, so thoroughly Hebraic in language and outlook, Mary speaks of God in His act of blessing her as *ὁ δυνατός*.[9] The periphrasis for God employed in Matthew

[3] The connexion between Jn 1^{1} and Gen 1^{1} is an obvious one.

[4] Rom 1^{20}; cf. Ps 19^{1-6}; Jer 5^{21f}. Sanday and Headlam, *Romans*, p. 43, point out that this argument, taking the beholder back from the created world to the character of the Creator 'is common to Greek thought as well as Jewish'; see, e.g., Aristotle, *De Mundo*, 6, and cf. Philo, *Legum Allegoria*, iii. 97, *Op. Mund.*, 7.

[5] *κύριος παντοκράτωρ*, representing *El shadday* in the LXX, and *π.* also being used to translate *yhwh tseba'oth* (see above, pp. 42f). As to the real meaning of almightiness, Paul Tillich (*Love, Power, and Justice*, p. 110) writes: it 'is that God is the power of being in everything that is, transcending every special power infinitely but acting at the same time as its creative ground'.

[6] Cf. with the Emperor (and the devil), who is only *cosmocrator* (P. Carrington, *The Early Christian Church*, I.223).

[7] *T.W.z.N.T.*, III.1,087. Thus, when the title comes to be applied to Christ, it 'powerfully describes His all-inclusive divine lordship'.

[8] Where it equals *'adon.*

[9] Cf. Ps 119^{4}; Zech 3^{17}.

26[64] ('the right hand of *power*') also adds its testimony to this identification of God with power. It is in conformity with Rabbinic usage, by which *geburah* provided a substitute for His Name.[10] God is thus, Himself, ἡ δύναμις.

Throughout the New Testament God is envisaged in similar terms. Jesus addresses Him as 'Lord of heaven and earth' (Mt 11[25]). The forces of nature obey His will (Mt 5[45]). 'All things are possible (δυνατά) with God' (Mk 10[27]). He is the direct source of the providential and upholding powers in nature (Mt 6[26, 30]).[11]

Equally true to the Old Testament tradition is the instinct looking for manifestations of God's power in great historic acts. We have noted repeatedly that the exodus from Egypt, the deliverance at the Red Sea, and the covenant at Sinai were regulative for all Hebraic thinking concerning the power of God. These were signs of His 'mighty hand and outstretched arm'. Now, in Christ *the* long-awaited historical event, fulfilling the promises and expectation of the Old Testament, has burst upon the world. This new deliverance exceeds the old in power, meaning, and depth: 'It is the power of God unto salvation to every one that believeth; to the Jew first, and also to the Greek' (Rom 1[16]). By means of this, man is restored to fullness of life and power in God at the same time as the forces of evil are defeated throughout the cosmos. 'In the things to do with Christ', comments W. Grundmann, 'God's power to produce history and to direct it to its end is effective in eschatalogical happening'.[12] Everything to do with Christ looks forward, and moves forward, to the great End of all things in Him (1 Cor 15[23ff]).

Bultmann notes that the title παντοκράτωρ, which occurs nine times in the Book of Revelation,[13] is descriptive of God's complete ordering of the eschatalogical drama. Though Satan and his

[10] See Strack-Billerbeck *in loc* and Dalman, *The Words of Jesus* (E.T.), p. 200. For the sake of his Gentile readers, Luke adds τοῦ θεοῦ to ἡ δύναμις by way of explanation (22[69]).

[11] But, as Bultmann comments, the New Testament view is not the same as the concept of providence in Stoicism. The latter teaches that nothing is without significance—everything has its place in the whole. The New Testament, however, says that God's will is inscrutable (Rom 11[23]); we find God's providence not through reason, but through faith. (*Essays Philosophical and Theological* (E.T.), p. 76.) 'God shows Himself, not in what is intelligible, but in miracles, in what is incomprehensible' (ibid., p. 116).

[12] *T.W.z.N.T.*, II. 307.

[13] And only once elsewhere (as noted: 2 Cor 6[18]) *Theology of the New Testament* (E.T.), I.149.

demons bring calamity and disaster upon the earth, it is under God's control and by His appointment.

'By a heavenly act like the opening of the book of fate (6^{1ff}), the blowing of the seven trumpets (8^{7ff}), the emptying of the seven bowls (16^{1ff}), by the call "Come" (6^{1}), by the command of an angel (7^{2}, 10^{1ff}, $14^{15, 18}$, 19^{17}), the demonic powers are given the signal, so to speak, to begin their raging; and their lack of independent action is repeatedly marked by saying "and power (*ἐξουσία*) was given them (or him)" (6^{8}, 9^{3}, $13^{5,7,14f}$).'

The Apocalypse, in all this indirect and unconscious reference to the divine sovereignty, conforms to the view general in the New Testament. In Revelation 16^{9}, after the angels have poured out the seven bowls resulting in hideous plagues upon the earth, the final responsibility is clearly allocated to God. It is He that has *τὴν ἐξουσίαν* over all these forces.

To the One who acts as Lord and Christ in His Kingdom, God grants His 'authority'. As the Son, Jesus possesses no merely limited commission. His authority is, in itself, a manifestation of His unity with the Father in will and action, implemented at the same time in complete freedom. How he accomplishes this it will be our concern to note in later chapters. Meantime, we can say that behind all that 'he began to do and to teach', and all that the Church has continued in His name, is the will and power of God, the Almighty. The ruler of all is manifesting His 'Kingdom'. Thus, Christ can Himself be designated 'the power of God' (1 Cor 1^{24}), the revelation and the mediator of Him who is power, known in His mighty acts.

It should be stated, too, at this point that the New Testament has far more to say about the outworkings of God's wrath than is currently recognized, and much that is not said is assumed. It is true that stress is not laid here on the awful nature of God's holiness and power, but Romans 1 and 2, and passages in Hebrews, remind us that the conception is in the background. It is impossible to excise references to doom, judgement, Gehenna, and punishment from the teaching of Jesus. We are told to 'fear him which, after he has killed, hath power to cast into hell.'[14] In the

[14] Lk 12^{5} (Matthew's parallel in 10^{28} uses the participle *ὁ δυνάμενος* in place of Luke's reference to having *ἐξουσία* here). The One who possesses this power is, of course, God, not Satan. In Rabbinical literature it is God who pronounces sentence to Gehenna. See Strack-Billerbeck.

New Testament, God's holiness comes to mean something quite different from earlier Old Testament usage. Rather than something separating and dividing Him from man and man from Him, God's holiness is especially associated with His delight in sharing with men. This is particularly noticeable in regard to the adjective customarily linked with the Spirit in the New Testament. God shares Himself in the intimate and wonderful gift of His *Holy* Spirit. Similarly, a change has overtaken the Old Testament designation, 'the Living God'. At the trial of Jesus, the High Priest uses the title in typical Old Testament style: 'I adjure thee by the living God', appealing, as Otto comments, to the God of terror and dread. But, apart from Hebrews 10^{31}, the fourteen other New Testament references are not of this order. It is the 'livingness' of God that is most in mind. He is the superabundant fountain of life whom we may know now in Christ (cf. Jn 3^{16}, $4^{10, 14}$, 10^{10}, etc.). That is rather the New Testament accent.

The 'little apocalypse' of Mark 13 stands as a continual challenge and difficulty to those who concentrate entirely on the gracious and upbuilding aspect of God's power. The fall of Jerusalem in A.D. 70, like the previous fall of the same city, was an act *in history*. Just as God's prophets had spoken in advance of the turn that events were taking, so our Lord, with prophetic insight, saw what lay ahead, and also quite clearly associated this doom, and disasters like it, with God's judgement, when 'the Son of Man is rejected'. Matthew 25 speaks of the doom coming on those failing to know 'the day of visitation'. In events like these, as well as in healing and miracle, the Kingdom comes 'with power' (cf. Mt 16^{28}; Lk 9^{27}, 21^{31}).

We have noted the treatment accorded to the wrath of God by the Chronicler in the Old Testament, who moralized and rationalized a concept which before had been crude and anthropomorphic. This treatment prepares the way for what is in the Pauline letters. The regulative conception is of a force working against all that denies the love of God. No longer is it directly suggested that God is angry: nor that His wrath is to be, or can be, appeased or placated. Much more the idea now is of a judgement of Nemesis, by which what is contrary to God is bound to work out in destruction. This process goes forward, unless God's love and power is able to reverse it, in the realm of history, appearing in final form in the Judgement at the End of all things.

The coming of Christ, in other words, does not signal the disappearance of God's wrath. Rather, it sharpens our knowledge of its workings. Part of Paul's concern at the beginning of Romans is to make this clear. Neither Jew nor Gentile can excuse their disobedience. They are all under sin, and therefore subject to the Wrath (cf. Eph 2^{3}, 5^{6}). Both the forces of nature (as in the earlier catastrophies pictured in the Book of Revelation) and human agents (as in the later pictures of the overthrow of the Empire; cf. Rev 17^{16f}) are used as its instruments. Paul's reference to 'vessels of wrath fitted unto destruction' in Romans 9^{22} carries these same overtones: unbelievers are caught up in the operations of God's wrath, becoming recipients, as well as acting as agents, of its destructive power.

There is a truth lying at the heart of the paradoxical description of 'the wrath of the Lamb'. He who came not to condemn the world, but to save it, is yet God's agent in events having to do with destruction just as surely as in the more positive aspects of the coming of the Kingdom. The Cross helps to clarify this: not only is it the picture of God's Love and Mercy; Wrath is revealed here, too. The Cross—in what it demonstrates of the rejection of God in Christ—itself crystalizes the judgement that concludes God's enemies under the Wrath. It is (Rom 1^{18}; cf. 2 Cor 5^{21}) the revelation of the wrath of God against all ungodliness and unrighteousness of man. In the picture of Revelation 19^{15}, based on Isaiah 63^{3}, the Lord is envisaged as treading 'the winepress of the fury of the wrath of God the Almighty'—through His sacrifice and identification with the needs of man, Christ becomes our means of circumventing what else is due to us.

Here, then, are some of the elements connecting immediately with Old Testament conceptions of power. We turn now to consider the account of the ministry of Jesus, and to observe how, in God's greatest act in history, so much that was previously hoped regarding God's power was demonstrated, made real and concrete. The powers of the Kingdom are at hand.

CHAPTER TEN

'DAYS OF GOD'S POWER'

ST MARK'S Gospel, largely dependent upon the preaching of Peter,[1] is most valuable in that it affords a first-hand impression of the 'days of God's power' that came with the coming of Jesus of Nazareth. Not only does it record the facts themselves, but it witnesses to the faith in which the remembrance of them glowed and burned. These are the facts, and this is what they meant to the Early Church.

These New Testament 'believers' had been introduced to a range of power which they described as 'the gospel'.[2] By means of it, a new life pulsed in them, flowing from an unimpaired relationship with God. It was a salvation-energy, experienced now, and carrying them forward in hope and certainty to the final End in God's purposes: providing confidence for this life and for that which is to come. At the centre of this 'gospel' there was power to deal with maladjustment and disease at all levels, physical, mental, and spiritual. These early disciples had witnessed, and some shared in, cases of healing and 'miracle'; they had seen men with twisted minds brought to sanity, and guilty and defeated people made new by the grace of forgiveness. By means of this 'gospel', many of them had been able to pass through persecution, or through meaningless pain, in a way that transformed these experiences. They found, too, that this salvation-energy was communicable to others through preaching and witnessing. It had a direct relationship, also, with the fellowship of the Church, to which it introduced them, becoming power, not only building up the individual Christian in the ways of God, but developing the community of believers as well. It was the power of a new life, enabling men to triumph over all manner of difficulty and disaster, and to face even death and what lies beyond it with a sense of victory.

This good news of 'power' was centred in Jesus of Nazareth. He had lived a life of which 'power' and 'authority' was characteristic. This was evidenced, not only in His words and deeds, but

[1] So Papias in the famous quotation in Eusebius *Hist. Eccl.*, iii, 39.
[2] Cf. Rom 1^{16}.

also in His presence and bearing, even in His silences.[3] But it was after His Death, with its outward circumstance of weakness and degradation, that it was realized that this occurrence itself was a tremendous moment of God's power. The Cross and the Resurrection that followed opened up new possibilities for those who, by faith, identified themselves with all that these events involved and offer. 'Believers' after this order have continued to witness to the power resident in the living and timeless Christ, to 'glory in the Cross' and 'know the power of His Resurrection'. We go back now to the outset of the story.

As is his manner, Mark bursts abruptly into the heart of what he has to say, announcing that this is 'The beginning of the gospel of Jesus Christ, the Son of God'. As he will tell us in the ninth verse, it begins with Jesus's coming to John for baptism.[4] The latter had already declared: 'There cometh after me he that is mightier than I'. The mightier One is now here.[5] Jesus rising from the water sees the heavens torn asunder and the Spirit 'like a dove' plunging into Him.[6] A voice sounds from the heavens: 'Thou art my beloved Son, in thee I am well pleased.' The beginning of the 'gospel' is in this commissioning, so similar in the details of voice and vision to the typical Old Testament prophet's commissioning,[7] yet coming to Jesus in far greater terms than to any of them. He is, indeed, the One to whom the prophets have

[3] Benjamin Kidd, in his *Science of Power*, has a passage in which he pictures Christ's silence before Pilate. Kidd says that Pilate would not have understood this silence (the Gospel accounts tell us, however, that Pilate 'marvelled' at it). He did not know, said Kidd, that in that silent man before him was 'the greatest power centre in all history'.

[4] 'Jesus's acceptance of John's baptism meant that he was moving in the same circle of prophetic and eschatological concepts as the Baptist' (C. K. Barrett, *The Holy Spirit and the Gospel Tradition*, p. 35).

[5] 'Does the name "The Mighty" reflect the El Gibhor of the Messianic passage, Isa 9^{5}, where some of the LXX texts have the reading, *ἰσχυρὸς ἐξουσιάστες*?' asks W. Manson. 'And against whom is He to measure His strength? In the Psalms and Prophets God's Reign is set to overthrow His "enemies". Does not everything about these early verses of St Mark (cf. 1^{15}) refer to a heroic battle against Satan's forces? The first exercise of the Lord's "authority" is in the expulsion of a demon' (Art., 'Principalities and Powers' in *New Testament Studies*, 1952, III.10f).

[6] It is the lightning-flash of power, but it is power 'as a dove'—linked with all that is beneficent, peaceful, good. Clearly behind this statement, as behind the Temptation narrative in Mt 4^{17ff} and Lk 4^{1ff}, is the Lord's own pictorialization of what happened. Later writers made of this intensely personal experience a sign to the Baptist of what happened. E. J. Goodspeed (*Introduction to the New Testament*, Chicago, 1937, p. 32) says that Mark's portrayal of the Spirit entering Jesus is so extreme that even translators (much less Matthew and Luke in their redactions) soften it down. It is, comments Goodspeed, probably the key, however, to Mark's understanding of Jesus (cf. B. W. Bacon, *Beginnings of the Gospel Story*, New York, 1909, p. 33).

[7] Cf. Isa 6^{1ff}; Jer $1^{4, 11}$; Ezek $1^{1, 4ff}$ (see A. H. Curtis, *The Vision and Mission of Jesus*, Edinburgh, 1954, pp. 12ff).

pointed, in whom all God's promises will be consummated.[8] Jesus now knows His destiny: to fulfil the age-long Messianic expectation, and to do this in terms of the Servant of God, whose mission is not to glorify himself, but to take upon him the sin and suffering of other people.[9]

A further point needs to be noted in connexion with Mark's account of the gospel's beginnings. Verses 12 and 13 summarize the story of the Temptation in these words: 'And straightway the Spirit driveth him forth into the wilderness. And he was in the wilderness forty days tempted of Satan; and he was with the wild beasts; and the angels ministered unto him.' Jesus needed to face His destiny and consider His future plans and methods.[10] In this way His commissioning is put to the proof. What needs especially to find right direction and control is the fund of available power, of which He is conscious.

Mark pictures this testing as at the hands of Satan, God's traditional adversary; and the place of testing is 'the wilderness', where Jesus, like Adam in Eden, is in touch with elemental things, living side by side with wild beasts, cared for by angels.[11] Significantly, also, according to Mark, Jesus is driven to this experience by the 'Spirit'.[12] Power has come upon Him, demanding the utmost faithfulness in its future use. Through Him, this power is to be passed on to others. It is the work of the Spirit to inaugurate the new era, to empower and commission the Messiah, and carry His work forward.[13]

The One so commissioned and tested commences His lifework

[8] The sentence in Mk 1^{11} is so obviously compounded of phrases from the Messianic Psalm (2^{7}) and the Servant Song of Isa 42^{1}.

[9] 'The Messiahship, since it underlies the office of Jesus as the Servant of the Lord, his status as Son of God and the descent upon him of the Spirit, is the key to the understanding of the baptism narrative, and apart from it the whole event as it is recorded in the Gospels, is meaningless' (C. K. Barrett, ibid., p. 44).

[10] This is brought out in the fuller accounts of Matthew and Luke, e.g. 'If thou art the Son of God . . .'.

[11] Cf. Ps 91^{11ff} for phrases reminiscent of these things. Do the 'wild beasts', however, symbolize the powers of darkness, and the picture become one of the conflict between the Holy Spirit—with attendant angels—and the dark powers? (cf. Ps 91^{13}). See J. A. Findlay, *The Way, the Truth and the Life*, p. 90.

[12] So 1^{8} in the best MS. We are in the Old Testament tradition here, which links the Spirit with 'power'.

[13] 'Here, as in the Birth narratives, the Spirit is the creative activity of God which calls into being the condition of the Messianic era' (C. K. Barrett, ibid., p. 45). Notice, again, the roughness of the terms Mark uses to describe the way the Spirit drives or throws Him into the desert (Goodspeed, ibid., p. 136).

with the bold announcement of verses 14 and 15: '... Jesus came into Galilee, preaching the gospel of God, and saying, The time is fulfilled, and the kingdom of God is at hand: repent ye, and believe in the gospel.'

In the rush and torrent of Mark's opening, we are thus introduced to a set of ideas—the Kingdom of God, the Son of Man, Salvation, the Holy Spirit—which concern the in-breaking of God's power into the affairs of men. The writer to the Hebrews can appeal to this background. He speaks of those who have 'tasted the good word of God, and the powers of the age to come'.[14] New Testament Christians are living in the realm of power belonging to the Coming Aeon.

Some of these background concepts need to be examined in closer detail.

I. THE KINGDOM OF GOD

The announcement in Mark 1^{15},[15] sets the scene for all that is to follow. The Messianic era is here, and it is here in Jesus. The New Age has already dawned. By the manner of the announcement itself a contrast is made with the Baptist's introductory ministry. All that he had proclaimed as imminent is at hand (ἤγγικεν), and the 'mightier than I' is declaring Himself; the possibility of a Spirit-baptism, instead of a water-baptism is here. The kingdom, the rule of grace, has come and is to be 'believed in', accepted, received.[16]

The concrete starting-point for the announcement made both

[14] Heb 6^5; cf. 2^4, where, similarly, in somewhat indefinite fashion, the 'great salvation' of the previous verse is evidenced 'both by signs and wonders, and by manifold powers, and by gifts of the Holy Ghost'.

[15] C. H. Dodd (*According to the Scriptures*, p. 69) points out the striking similarities between this 'summary of the gospel' in Mk 1^{15} and Dan 7^{22} in Theodotion's version: ὁ καιρὸς ἔφθασεν καὶ τὴν βασιλείαν κατέσχον οἱ ἅγιοι. The parallel is very striking, even if one does not hold to Dodd's suggestion of the approximation of ἤγγικεν and ἔφθασεν through the Aramaic *meta*' (Lk 12^{32} uses the second verb directly). Dodd would translate the phrase in Mk 1^{15} as 'the Kingdom of God has come' (*The Parables of the Kingdom*, 1935, pp. 43f). On the basis of this and other texts, Dodd has built up his theory of 'realized eschatalogy'. Many other scholars—particularly Continental scholars—take up the opposite view, thinking of the preaching of Jesus as preparation for the Kingdom yet to come (see, e.g., A Richardson, *An Introduction to the Theology of the New Testament*, 1958, pp. 85ff).

[16] As Keim says (*Jesu von Nazara*, II.77), 'when heaven and earth move towards each other, as in Christ's preaching of the kingdom, then on the part of God and man must the Nay give place to the Yea, anger to love, fear to joy, shame to right action; and in festive attire, not in mourning weeds, all that has affinity for the Divine goes out to meet the approaching God, proved to be or to become like Him'. This involves, on the part of man, repentance and faith.

by John and Jesus is found in the contemporary Jewish expectation.[17] By New Testament times it was a familiar concept that God's rule would be evidenced in power at the coming great Day.

Something of a fusion had occurred in the popular mind between the two Old Testament views of the Kingdom, i.e. that of the 'sovereignty of God as the eternal background of all human life'—the 'priestly' conception as E. L. Allen defines it—and the 'prophetic', 'the divine intervention that brings victory in its appointed time'. The fusion is to be noted in the Psalms, where the constant theme is that 'the Lord reigneth', and yet that He has to be fully vindicated.[18] Dalman thinks that in the days of Jesus emphasis was far more upon the 'life of the future age' than upon the *malekuth shamaim*. It was an eschatological entity, 'of which the present can be predicated only because "the end" is already approaching'.[19]

Neither Jesus nor the Baptist, when they spoke of the Kingdom, was introducing a new term. All they needed to announce was that it was at hand.[20]

The power of the Kingdom is to be observed, thenceforward, as Jesus moves to defeat God's enemies, acting in and securing the divine sovereignty at all points. The temptation narrative is explicit in its references to Satan's power over this world. It is he who offers Christ 'all the kingdoms of this world' (Mt 4^{8}: 'of the inhabited earth' Lk 4^{5}, marg.), for the world has allowed itself to be leagued with the forces that are against God rather than with Him. The old aeon, of the world under the dominion of Satan, is coming to an end. He who is the world's real ruler is asserting His decisive sovereignty. All this is by God's power and initiative alone, not by the will nor desire of man.[21]

[17] K. Schmidt, Art. *βασιλεία τ. θ.*, *T.W.z.N.T.*, I.585.

[18] E. L. Allen, *The Purpose of Jesus*, 1951, p. 23.

[19] Dalman, *Words of Jesus* (E.T.), Edinburgh, 1902, p. 135.

[20] 'Neither Jesus nor the Baptist ever explain this expression; therefore they must have been content to have it understood in its known and customary sense' (Schweitzer, *The Quest of the Historical Jesus*, p. 16). It is, of course, only Matthew who quotes John as announcing 'the Kingdom is at hand' (Mt 3^{2}). In Mark and Luke the announcement is of the 'Coming One'.

[21] In this sense, it is 'a miraculous event, which will be brought about by God alone without the help of man'. 'Reign of God is an eschatological concept. It means the régime of God which will destroy the present course of this world, wipe out all the contra-divine, Satanic power under which the world groans—and thereby, terminating all pain and sorrow, bring in salvation for the people of God which awaits the fulfilment of the prophets' "promises" ' (R. Bultmann, *Theology of the New Testament*, I4).

This is what is announced in Mark 1^{14}, and all the future preaching of Christ and His apostles follows from this. 'The time is fulfilled' indicates the entry of the new aeon. All that prophets and righteous men had desired to see is now present (Mt 13^{16f}; Lk 10^{23f}). It is 'fulfilled'. Therefore Jesus can say to those who are following Him, 'Blessed are the eyes which see the things that ye see' (Lk 10^{23}) and 'Blessed are ye poor: for yours is the Kingdom of God' (Lk 6^{20};) 'Fear not, little flock; for it is your Father's good pleasure to give you the Kingdom' (Lk 12^{32}).

Luke 11^{20} indicates that Jesus considered Himself endued with all its powers: 'But if I by the finger of God cast out devils, then is the Kingdom of God come upon you'. With the parallel in mind of Daniel 7^{22} in Theodotion's version (already noted by C. H. Dodd),[22] ἔφθασεν here would mean 'actually arrived'. Luce, in his Commentary on Luke, reports that ἔφθασα is the modern Greek waiter's equivalent for 'Just coming'. By this word, the waiter conveys that he is just at hand with service!

'In the power of the divine victory over the armed strong man, Jesus now works "by the finger of God", or by "the Spirit of God", i.e. with dynamis, exousia, charis, charisma'. This is how Rudolph Otto comments on the section from which this verse is taken (Mt 12^{25ff}; Lk 11^{17ff}). 'This dynamis of his is nothing other than the dynamis of the kingdom, the kingdom as dynamis. And this charisma and charismatic activity of his is nothing less than the coming of the kingdom itself.' A little later, Otto says that the Kingdom 'comes chiefly, not as claim and decision, but as saving dynamis, as redeeming power, to set free a world lying in the clutches of Satan, threatened by the devil and by demons, tormented, possessed, demon-ridden; and to capture the spoil from the strong one: i.e. it comes chiefly as saving dynamis, as redeeming might.'[23]

We would follow Otto, also, in his interpretation of the logion in Matthew 11^{12} and Luke 16^{16}. The Kingdom is no static entity. It is the inbreaking of divine sovereignty in power. Following Melanchthon, Zahn, Harnack and others, Otto takes βιάζεται in the Matthaean passage to be, as in Lk 16^{16} a verb in the

[22] See above, p. 80, n. 15.
[23] *The Kingdom of God and the Son of Man* (E.T.), pp. 104f.

middle voice. It is thus the kingdom that rushes forcefully on its way.[24]

Confirmation of our Lord's certainty regarding the imminence of the Kingdom in Himself, and of its association with saving *dunamis*, is to be observed in the affirmation with which He concluded His reading of Isaiah 61[1f] in the synagogue at Nazareth, 'This day is this scripture fulfilled in your ears' (Lk 4[16ff]). And the association of the Kingdom with the Lord becomes so close that texts like Matthew 13[41], 16[28]; Luke 1[33], 22[30], 23[32] provide equivalents in personal terms to the general phrase 'the kingdom of God'. Just as surely it is the Kingdom of Christ (cf. Eph 5[5]).[25] Devotion to Christ and to the Kingdom can be equated, as in the transposition of Mark 10[29] (cf. Mt 19[29]) to Luke 18[29]. 'Till they have seen the kingdom of God come with power' in Mark 9[1] becomes 'till they see the Son of Man coming in his kingdom' in Matthew 16[28].[26] 'In the

[24] In Lk 16[16] the verb is recognized as a deponent middle conforming to a usage frequent in Greek writers: πᾶς εἰς αὐτήν βιάζεται thus means 'everybody presses into it [the kingdom] violently' (so Harnack, Dalman, Zahn, Windisch, Bauer and Schrenk in *T.W.z.N.T.*, I.611). Commentators have been loth to grant the same meaning to the verb in Mt 11[12]. Schrenk favours the idea that the verb is passive, and thinks the sentence designates the enemies of God's Kingdom as the cause of the violence suffered. It is attacked, persecuted, or hemmed in by warlike opponents (so Merx, Dalman, Schlatter, M. Dibelius—who thinks, *Joh. de T.*, II.20ff, that the enemies are opposing spirits in the heavenly spheres). Bauer quotes B. Weiss, J. Weiss, and H. Windisch for the idea that the violence suffered is 'through the attempt of the unbidden to force themselves in'. Schweitzer interprets the violence done to the Kingdom as done either by Jesus Himself or the recipients of His message.

Following Otto's interpretation, and taking the verb as middle, the saying contrasts the time when men were still awaiting the news that the Kingdom had come, with the time of its inbreaking, the era of John the Baptist representing the dividing line between the two. The saying also pictures the kind of men who seize what the Kingdom offers (the βιασταί). 'On the one hand', writes Otto, 'the kingdom exercised force, on the other, those who exercise force seize it. This combination of contrasts sums up the whole of Jesus's preaching and its characteristic bi-polarity of thought. For on the one side, the kingdom comes and works and affects and seizes and grows of itself, without man's being able to do anything to help. And yet on the other side, only by summoning all one's power, and with the most strenuous determination, does one press into it' (*Kingdom of God and Son of Man*, p. 111).

[25] Cullmann in *The Early Church*, 1956, distinguishes between the Regnum Christi (β. τοῦ υἱοῦ) and the β. τοῦ θεοῦ. But there is not the clear distinction he would trace in the New Testament itself; 1 Cor 15[13] would support this, but the other references point to a complete parallel (see Bultmann, *Essays*, p. 283f.)

[26] In Mt 16[28], with its reference to the Parousia, Matthew is obviously expanding what is nearer the original in Mark. The use of the perfect ἐληλυθυῖαν in Mark points to something immediate, literally fulfilled, when, as in early Acts, 'some of them that were standing by' entered, by faith, into the use of the same powers that Jesus was now knowing. 'Until they have seen that the Kingdom of God *has come* with power' is a translation which brings home the point of the actual incidence of the powers of the Messianic Age. Vincent Taylor, in his discussion of Mk 9[1] (Comm. *ad loc*), quotes C. H. Dodd for the translation 'until they have seen the Kingdom of God has come

gospel', as Marcion said, 'the kingdom of God is Christ Himself.'[27]

So the power of Satan over the human heart is challenged and broken. The misery his reign has brought to human affairs (cf. e.g. Lk 13[16]) is righted. In the Gospels, neither sin nor the senseless suffering of human beings is viewed as part of God's order. They are alien. Christ's miracles performed on the sick, as Karl Heim suggests, are not to be thought of as an interruption of nature, but as a 'binding of the strong man', a victory over the will-powers which lie behind man's suffering, over the 'spirit of sickness'. The whole of Jesus' miraculous activity rests on the assumption that the world has an inner side, accessible by the force of the will, and that 'we can strive with this inner world of Nature by faith, as we strive with some living power'.[28] When the Seventy return triumphantly from their journey, armed as they had been with the Lord's commission to heal the sick and proclaim the nearness of the Kingdom (Lk 10[9]), they report, 'Lord, even the devils are subject unto us in thy name', and He replies, 'I beheld Satan fallen as lightning from heaven' (Lk 10[17f]).[29] 'Miracle is the victory of God in this strife of spiritual powers.'[30]

There are thus two strands of reference regarding the Kingdom: (1) that it is here; (2) that it is to come. Some of the sayings referring to the immediate presence of the Kingdom, evidenced

with power', but feels that this 'realized eschatology' strains the meaning of the saying. 'It is much more probable', he says, 'that it means "until they see the Kingdom of God come": that is to say, the Kingdom is not present at the moment of speaking, except proleptically in the mighty works, but it is imminent, very shortly it will be seen to have come.' We prefer our own interpretation, however. (H. A. Guy gets rid of the difficulties of this verse by suggesting that it is one of the verses in Mark's Gospel which carries the comment of the narrator. It can be thus understood as the remark of a preacher of the gospel expressing the eschatological hope of the early Church, and incorporated in this way into the story, e.g. as if it were from Jesus's lips: *Origins of Gospel of Mark*, p. 85.)

[27] Tertullian, *adv. Marc*, 4. 33. Hebert (*Throne of David*, p. 138n.) also quotes a scholion attributed to Origen on Mt 11[11ff] (Cod. 238 of the Gospels—Gregory): 'The Kingdom of Heaven is Christ Jesus exhorting all men to repentance and drawing them to Himself by His grace.'

[28] K. Heim, *The New Divine Order* (E.T.), p. 45.

[29] The comment of M. van Rhijn (*Een blik in het onderwijs van Jesus*, Amsterdam, 1927), quoted in J. Jeremias, *The Parables of Jesus* (E.T), 1954, p. 98n., should give us pause here, however. He regards Lk 10[18], as ironical. This accords with verse 20, and may be intended to damp the over-confidence of the disciples a little. For the figure concerning the fall of Satan from Heaven, see Is 14[12] and Rev 12[8f]. Strack-Billerbeck (II, p. 167f.) make clear that the final overthrow of Satan was an integral part of the Jewish expectation of the Coming Aeon, but that there were differing opinions as to who would be the agent: God Himself, or His angels, or the Messiah. See T. W. Manson, *Sayings of Jesus*, p. 258.

[30] K. Heim, ibid., p. 50.

by Jesus's deeds as well as by His claims, are these: the phrase concerning the casting out of devils by the finger of God (Lk 11^{20} 'by the Spirit of God', Mt 12^{28}); the declaration, 'Blessed are the eyes which see what you see' (Lk10^{23f} = Mt 13^{16}); the parables in Mark 4 which 'have a common object, to confirm the glad tidings of the coming kingdom as a power of God already at work',[31] and those of the leaven (Lk 13^{20f} = Mt 13^{35}), the treasure hidden in the field (Mt 13^{44}) and the Pearl (Mt 13^{45f}); and the statements in Luke 16^{16} and Matthew 11^{12f} concerning the Kingdom exercising its force.[32] There is also the logion of Luke 17^{20f}, ἡ βασιλεία τοῦ θεοῦ ἐντὸς ὑπῶν ἐστιν, which, whatever else it means, means that the Kingdom is here 'in the human midst'.[33] Contrasted with these sayings are those which picture the coming of the Kingdom as yet in the future, e.g. Matthew 8^{11} (Lk 13^{29}), referring to the Messianic feast with Abraham, Isaac and Jacob; and of the hope of drinking wine anew in the Kingdom (Mk 14^{25}).[34] There is also the phrase in the Lord's prayer ἐλθάτω ἡ βασιλεία σου (Mt 6^{10}; Lk 11^{2}).[35] The final consummation of God's dominion is still ahead.[36] All that will be explicit in this final realization, is however, with us now. It has come near in Jesus, and He brings its imminence to the notice of men. He is, indeed, the 'King of the Eschaton'.[37]

[31] B. W. Bacon, *The Story of Jesus and the Beginnings of the Church*, New York, 1929, p. 212.

[32] See above, pp. 82f and n. 24.

[33] The division of opinion among scholars concerning the meaning of ἐντὸς ὑμῶν goes back to very early days, when Origen favoured the idea of the Kingdom being 'within you', and Ephraim Syrus preferred the rendering 'in the midst of you' (T. W. Manson, *Sayings of Jesus*, p. 303). C. H. Roberts finds evidence in the papyri for the use of ἐντὸς with the meaning 'in (your) possession' or 'in (your) control' (see *Expository Times*, October, 1951, p. 30, and *Harvard Theological Review*, XLI.1–8). The question that is being asked concerns the date of the coming of the Kingdom. Our Lord's reply is that it is not to be observed outwardly. The cry 'Lo, here' or 'There' is quite out of place. It is not that kind of kingdom at all, and, in any case, it is here already, and its powers are open to your co-operation. It is 'within your grasp'. 'They could enter and accept it, if they were willing to' (J. N. Sanders, *Foundations of the Christian Faith*, 1950, p. 87).

[34] Vincent Taylor, *The Life and Ministry of Jesus*, 1954, p. 67.

[35] 'May he establish His Kingdom during your life and during the life of all the house of Israel' (*ba'agala' ubibeman qaribh*). This Kaddish prayer can be found in the *Jewish Authorized Daily Prayer Book* (ed., Singer), p. 37. In its Aramaic form, Dalman declares, the prayer is of great antiquity. It is typical of other ancient prayers and contemporary Rabbinic references (e.g. Ass Mos 10^{1}; Midrash on Cant 2^{12}; Sopher 14^{12};—*Words of Jesus*, pp. 96ff.

[36] Cf. Mk 4^{26ff}, the parable of the seed growing secretly—till harvest. The final consummation is connected with the Parousia.

[37] The phrase is Bultmann's (*Essays Philosophical and Theological*, p. 276).

The Kingdom is, first of all, then, God's Sovereignty.[38] It is thus the realm of spiritual energy and life and love, where God's Will is being done, and where man is in living touch with the Father, Creator, and Lord of all things. In this form, it is God's gift (Lk 12^{32}; Mt 16^{19}). The Jews, because of their lack of response, will find that it is 'taken' from them, and 'given to a nation bringing forth the fruits thereof' (Mt 21^{43}). The link with the Kingdom is the living one of 'faith', synonymous with 'receiving' (e.g. Mk $9^{37, 42}$, 10^{14f}). It is noteworthy that the believer must thus receive the kingdom 'as a little child' (Mk 10^{15}=Lk 18^{17}). It is promised to children (Mt 18^{14}). As Mark 1^{15} indicates, it must be accepted in repentance. Many parables and sayings (e.g. Mt 13^{14ff}, 5^{29}, 19^{12}, 22^{1ff}) show the decisive character of the acceptance. Nothing must be allowed to supersede its claims. Thus, though typically the Kingdom is something we accept, or into which we enter (Mt 5^{20}, 7^{21}, 21^{31}, etc.), it can be striven for. We should seek and ask for it (Lk 12^{31}; Mt 7^{7f}, 13^{45f}).[39]

What happened to this phrase that was of such importance at the beginning? There is great significance in the fact that the term itself was soon displaced in the teaching of the early Church, and this with no sense of disloyalty to Jesus, and in spite of the fact that it was in association with it that He was put to death. The inwardness of His teaching concerning it, the universality of its application, and the identification of His own person with its message, altered the shape of the idea completely. John (though he uses the expression kingdom of God in $3^{3, 5}$; cf. 18^{36}), replaced it with the conception of '(Eternal) Life',[40] and Paul found it fulfilled in the conception of the Lordship of Christ (see, e.g., 1 Cor 15^{20ff}). There are texts in which we find the kingdom referred to by Paul (e.g. Rom 14^{17}; 1 Cor 6^{9f}, 15^{20}; Gal 5^{21}; Eph 5^{5}; 2 Thess 1^{5}), much in the way that the term is used in the Synoptic Gospels. 1 Corinthians 4^{20} magnificently illustrates the link we have traced between the Kingdom and God's power: 'For the Kingdom

[38] It must never be forgotten, however, when isolating the thought of the 'Kingdom' from the rest of the teaching of Jesus, that our Lord's typical word for God is not 'King', but 'Father'. Even in the prayer that teaches men to pray for the Kingdom, God is addressed as 'Our Father'.

[39] Schmidt, *T.W.z.N.T.*, pp. 588f.

[40] A. Richardson (art, 'Kingdom of God', in *Theological Word Book*, 1950, p. 121) points out 'that this equation of "life" with the "Kingdom of God" is possible even in St Mark (and perhaps therefore in the teaching of Jesus Himself) is proved by a comparison of Mk $9^{43, 45}$ with 9^{47}'.

of God is not in word, but in power.' And Colossians 1 13ff reminds us of our share, as Christians, in the life of the New Aeon: writing of the Father, Paul continues: 'who made us meet to be partakers of the inheritance of the saints in light; who delivered us out of the power of darkness, and translated us into the kingdom of the Son of his love . . .'.[41] The theocracy of the Jews has passed beyond all barriers. The Messianic era has come, and is being fulfilled in the salvation now possible to all in Jesus's name, in the deliverance from the power of the demon-forces that lord it over human life, and in the power of the Spirit available to 'believers'. The Apocalyptic element remained in the conception of the Parousia.[42] And the term βασιλεία itself, though so central in the teaching of the Lord Himself, passed from general use.[43] The gospel had become a gospel realized entirely in Christ Himself. In Origen's phrase, it was αὐτοβασιλεία. It is all fulfilled in Him.

II. THE MESSIAH

From the standpoint of the authors of the Gospels, Jesus is the King-Messiah, in whom the Kingdom comes. He invites men to accept the kingdom of God, to enter into it: but He does not merely proclaim it. He inaugurates it. It is here in Him. Just as it is not given to all to understand the 'mystery' of the Kingdom (Mk 4 11), so, during His earthly life there is a hidden quality about His Messiahship.[44] No one is forced, by any kind of pressure, spiritual or material, to acknowledge either. Since the gospel came from a community which, from the far side of Christ's death and Resurrection, worships Him as Lord, it is

[41] Bultmann (*Theology of the New Testament*, II.234, 150) believes that Col 1 15ff is a pre-Christian hymn that had already received a Christian editing before its use here. It seeks to 'combine the cosmological terminology with traditional Christian terminology'. (But it need not be assumed that it was necessarily a Gnostic hymn in honour of the παντοκράτωρ.)

[42] Note the clear avowal of Rev 11 15ff, when the climax of the conflict means that 'the kingdom of the world is become the kingdom of our Lord, and of His Christ; and He shall reign for ever and ever'.

[43] In part because of its liability to grave political misunderstanding, e.g. Acts 17 7f, where the use of the term did precipitate trouble.

[44] Not only is Jesus's claim kept secret. The greater 'secret' by far is our Lord's consciousness of what it means to be 'Messiah'; cf. T. W. Manson, art., 'Realized Eschatology and the Messianic Secret' (*Studies in the Gospels*, ed. Nineham, pp. 209ff: 'The messianic secret, which undoubtedly exists in the Gospels, is not concerned with the identity of the Messiah, but with the nature of his task. . . . The essence of the matter is that the Ministry *is* the Kingdom and the power and the glory' (ibid., pp. 220f).

remarkable how the first three Gospels preserve the remembrance of the stages of Christ's self-revelation. Mark's Gospel, indeed, seems to be built up on a framework of declarations of the Messiahship.[45] It is as King Messiah that, finally, He comes to Jerusalem and is brought to trial and Crucifixion.[46]

The title which our Lord seems deliberately to have used concerning Himself is 'Son of Man' (some 10 times in John, and 70 times in the Synoptics). It is a title with a wide background of reference. For instance, in Ezekiel the prophet uses the term some 90 times of himself. God addressed him in this way, and it was as Son of Man that he was commissioned as God's prophet and servant.[47] The Book of Enoch uses the term of its strange apocalyptic figure (e.g. 48^{2} and 46^{1ff}, 'One, who had a head of days, and His head was white like wool, and with Him was another being whose countenance had the appearance of a man. . . . This is the Son of Man who hath righteousness . . . who shall raise up the kings and the mighty from their seats').

There are some significant uses of the phrase in the Psalms. Psalm 80^{17} is concerned that God's endowment of power shall rest upon His future hero: 'Let thy hand be upon the man of thy right hand, Upon the son of man whom thou madest strong for thyself.' Of all the Old Testament references echoed in the New Testament concerning the 'Son of Man', Psalm 8^{4-6} seems, however, to have occurred most readily to many New Testament writers (e.g. 1 Cor 15^{27}; Phil 3^{21}; Eph 1^{22}; Heb 2^{6ff}; 1 Pet 3^{22}).[48] The reference in this Psalm is usually taken to be a general one to mankind, 'Son of Man' being parallel to 'man' in the strophe:

> What is man, that thou art mindful of him?
> And the son of man, that thou visitest him?[49]

Mowinckel and other Scandinavians have put this matter in a new light,[50] shed by the theory concerning the Enthronement

[45] See C. K. Barrett, *Holy Spirit and the Gospel Tradition*, p. 118.

[46] e.g. the Triumphal Entry, Mk 11^{1ff}, fulfilling Zech 9^{9}; Lk 23^{2}, etc.

[47] G. S. Duncan, *Jesus, Son of Man*, p. 118.

[48] 'There are three passages in the Scripture containing the term "Son of Man", and three only, which can be proved to have been employed for testimonies (that is by New Testament writers): Ps 8, Ps 80 and Dan 7' (C. H. Dodd, *According to the Scriptures*, p. 117).

[49] E.g. C. H. Dodd, ibid.: 'In Ps 8 the "son of man" (in parallelism with "man") is simply man as such, man in his weakness and insignificance, yet "visited" by God, and by his merciful ordinance "crowned with glory and honour".'

[50] See above, p. 25, and also A. R. Johnson, *Sacral Kingship in Ancient Israel*.

Psalms. It is thought that at the New Year Festival a ritual remembrance of the events of Creation was enacted. Psalm 8 is seen to be connected with this circle of ideas, in that the heavens, the work of God's fingers, is pictured as the defence set by God against all His enemies. 'This work of Yahweh is greater than any other work of His, even greater than the First Man, who was created to be King of God's World.'[51] Mowinckel thus explains the origin of the 'Son of Man' conception in the Gospels, as well as that in the Ethiopic Enoch, and 4 Ezra, as coming from the cycle of ideas concerning creation and the 'Son of God', who should effectively rule it.[52] The early chapters of Genesis provide this conception, Psalm 8 echoes it, and the Coronation Psalm, 2, helps to complete the picture. The *az* of verse 5 ('*Then* shall he speak...') is thought, under this scheme of things, to be an allusion to the 'First Man', the 'Son of God', elected at the time of Creation; his 'adoption' as 'Son of God' becomes, thus, the 'ritual repetition' or 'actualization' of the primordial institution of King and Kingship. 'What happened then to the Patriarch of Kings and Men happens again to the actual "King" and "Man" in the Coronation Rite. Psalm 8 contains the same identification of "Man" and "King". The "Son of Man" in 8^{5ff} is King "nearly a god" (5), "crowned" (5), "ruler of the world" (6), and of the animals (7ff).'[53]

Since our Lord so clearly in Mark 14^{62} and its parallels referred to Dan 7^{13}, it does seem that the Danielic use of the title was much in His mind. The collective character of Daniel's conception (e.g. 7^{18}, where 'the one like unto the son of man' = 'the saints of the Most High') points, in turn, to our Lord's thought of Himself, as representative not only of man in general, but as the One through whom the new Israel comes to birth.[54]

[51] Aage Bentzen, *King and Messiah* (E. T.), 1955, p. 12.

[52] In *Opphavet til den senjödiske forestilling om Menneskesonnen N.T.T.*, 1944, referred to in A. Bentzen, *King and Messiah*, p. 39. Mowinckel, at the same time, declares that the affinity of these ideas is not to be found in the *Urmensch* doctrines and myths of the later Gnosticism.

[53] So Bentzen, ibid., pp. 41f. Note, in the Pauline theology, the antithesis between Christ and Adam, with Christ as the head of the new humanity and the second creation. In Jesus, the image of God, marred and spoiled, is seen in 'man' again. All this is a direct outcome from this interpretation of the meaning of 'Son of Man'.

[54] J. Klausner, *The Messianic Idea in Israel*, (E.T.), 1956, pp. 229f, says that the plain meaning of the 'son of man' (meaning 'human being') is the same as the 'saints of the Most High', and refers to oppressed Israel, 'portrayed as a *human being* coming from heaven with the clouds'. But in a comparatively short time, he goes on to say, it was thought that this 'son of man' was the Messiah. 'There is no *individual* Messiah in

The term is quite obviously one with wide echoes and many connotations, not as innocuous as has sometimes been represented. Indeed, as Ethelbert Stauffer declares, so far from this, ' "Son of Man" is just about the most pretentious piece of self-description that any man in the ancient East could possibly have used:' Stauffer ends his short chapter on this theme in his *New Testament Theology* with the sentence: 'In calling himself the Son of Man Jesus had already taken the decisive step in claiming cosmic history as his own.'[55]

It is not only as 'Son of Man' that Jesus is portrayed in the Synoptics, but as 'Son of God' or 'Son' (of the Father). There is the 'Johannine boulder', as it has sometimes been called, of Matthew 11^{27}; and the reference to the 'heir' in the Parable of the Wicked Husbandman (Mk 12^{1ff}). The Voice at the Baptism (Mk 1^{11}) and the voice of the Tempter (Mt $4^{3,6}$) both appeal to His Sonship. The saying in Mark 13^{32}, freely confessing the limitations of His knowledge, carries the impress of genuineness upon it, and witnesses again to our Lord's thought of Himself as 'Son' of the Father. Jesus is thus, as in John, the unique (ἀγαπητός, Mk 1^{11}, etc.: μονογενής in Jn) Son, through whom many souls are brought to glory. All this language had Messianic connotation.[56] In Matthew 16^{16} and 26^{63} (Peter's confession and the High Priest's question at the Trial) the term 'Christ' and 'Son of God' are set side by side.

These titles, then, were used by Jesus, or used by others of Him. In addition, too, He thought of Himself in terms of the Deutero-Isaianic picture of the 'Servant of the Lord'.[57] All these titles coalesced for New Testament writers in the general

Daniel', he states categorically. See T. W. Manson, *The Beginning of the Gospel*, 1950, p. 23, where he expands his earlier interpretation (*The Teaching of Jesus*, pp. 212, 227) in the following terms: 'The "Son of Man" can be taken to represent a community consisting of all those who are completely given over to the service of God. But the historical fact is that the ideals which Jesus embodied were fully realized only in Himself, so that, in truth, He, and He alone, is the "Son of Man". As Jesus used it, the term has no plural.' Note E. W. Heaton (*Torch Commentary* on 'The Book of Daniel', p. 184): 'It is understandable that there should have been a close connexion between (and therefore terminology common to) the People of God referred to here and the individual figure who came to be thought of as its principal and embodiment. This intimate relationship between Messiah and messianic community was readily expressed in Hebrew thought, because of the ease with which it moved from the representative individual to the group he represented.'

[55] Ibid., pp. 108, 111.

[56] Cf. 4 Ez 7^{23}, 13^{23}, 14^{19} for examples of this.

[57] For the contrary view, see, e.g., Morna Hooker, *Jesus and the Servant*, and C. K. Barrett's article in the *Festschrift* for T. W. Manson.

conception of the 'Messiah', the Christ, anointed and empowered by God.

Whilst this is so, G. S. Duncan sounds an important warning when he reminds us that Jesus set little store by titles, and disdained the kind of authority gained by their use (cf. Mt 7[21], 23[8ff]; Lk 6[46]). Messiahship, especially, was an idea which, once claimed, led to the gravest misunderstandings. 'Life as Jesus saw it', he comments most cogently, 'consisted essentially of obedience to the will of God. Hence for Himself the decisive question could never be "In what way shall I fulfill the role of Messiah?" It could only be: "What is the way of life which the Father has marked out for the Son"?'[58] Perhaps it would be better to say that these titles themselves are to be understood alone in terms of the life and work of Jesus.

It is this kind of insight into the motives of our Lord that delivers us from the rigidity with which some commentators have investigated the Messianism and eschatology of the Gospels.[59] Jesus lived as a witness to God. His contact with the Father was immediate and real. He lived for God and in God, and His 'Messiahship', like everything about Him, was a response to what He knew of God, not to a set of ideas which He found ready-made and uniformly accepted. We must not make the mistake of arguing from Messianic conceptions to Jesus. If we think of Him in Messianic terms, then we must allow these to be interpreted, first, by Him.

[58] *Jesus, Son of Man*; pp. 120ff and 133.

[59] Note, e.g., how Schweitzer in his *Mystery of the Kingdom of God* (E.T.), 1901, approaches the records with predetermined ideas concerning the Messianic programme. Texts such as Joel 2[28ff] and Mal 4[5] provide him with a time-table and a test. John did no miracle: therefore he could not be the Forerunner; that was the guise in which Jesus appeared before His contemporaries. Signs and wonders and the pouring out of the Spirit are to occur *before* the Messianic era. Elijah will be sent before the Great Day (see, e.g., pp. 115, 125, 152). It is a similar kind of rigidity in dealing with the facts that has led men back again to the position in which the 'miracles' of Jesus are thought of, first, as evidences of His 'claims'. Isa 35[5ff], 61[1], 29[18f] and many references which can be adduced from Rabbinic literature (see, e.g., C. K. Barrett, *The Holy Spirit in the Gospel Tradition*, pp. 57f, 70f) show that the Messiah was expected to do 'miracles' and deal with evil spirits. The speeches in early Acts show how the fulfilment of this expectation in Jesus was appealed to as evidence of His significance (Peter in Acts 2[22]—'a man approved of God unto you by mighty works and wonders and signs [δυνάμεσι καὶ τέρασι καὶ σημείοις], which God did by him in your midst'; cf. 10[38]). That the miracles were signs is most certain. They are witnesses to the inbreaking of the Kingdom in salvation. They show Jesus as the Lord of Life, the One fulfilling the role of God's vicegerent, Himself the agent of power. But the springs of these happenings is not to be found in the Lord's desire for authenticating signs (see, e.g., Mt 16[1ff]), but in motives of compassion, matched with available power.

III. THE HOLY SPIRIT

Old Testament prophecy spoke of the divine endowment to be given to the coming King. 'The Spirit of the Lord shall rest upon him' (Isa 11^{2}), to provide him with equipment for his task. Similarly, the Servant of God was to be anointed with the Spirit,[60] in order to open blind eyes, heal the deaf, proclaim release to the captives, raise the dead, and to announce 'the year of God's favour' (Isa 61^{1ff}—which our Lord declared, significantly, was fulfilled in Him: Lk 4^{18f}). This is in harmony with the Old Testament conception of the *ruach* of God given to artificer, leader, statesman, or king in accordance with God's commissioning.

More than that the whole Messianic era, the days of 'God's right hand', of His Kingdom, were to be days of the 'outpouring of God's Spirit' (cf. Joel 2^{28f}, the prophecy Peter knows to be fulfilled at Pentecost). 'The bestowal of the Spirit', as Bultmann states, 'is an eschatological gift' (cf. Acts 2^{16ff}; 1 Pet 1^{3ff}). The baptized, having become partakers of the Holy Spirit, have already 'tasted . . . the powers of the age to come' (Heb 6^{4f}).[61] All this was, of course, to be discovered by the disciples after the Lord's Death and Resurrection, when the Spirit revealed the gospel in these events, and gave the disciples power to witness to it. At the first, the Spirit was concentrated upon the person of the Messiah.

The circumstances of Jesus' birth, like everything connected with the unfolding of the Messianic era and the coming of the Kingdom, have all to do with the Spirit's creative activity. Matthew 1^{18} tells us that Mary was found with child 'of the Holy Ghost', and Joseph is told by an angel (Mt 1^{20}), 'that which is conceived in her is of the Holy Ghost'. The story of the birth is set, in Luke's account, amid circumstances witnessing to an outburst of the Spirit's activity in prophecy and inspiration (cf.

[60] Cf. also Isa 28^{6}, 42^{1ff} (quoted in Mt 12^{18ff}); 1 En 49^{3}, 62^{2}; Ps Sol 17^{37}, 18^{7}; Test Lev 18^{7}, Test Jud 24^{2}, and the Zadokite fragment in *Apocrypha and Pseudepigrapha of the Old Testament* (ed., R. H. Charles), II.10: 'And through His Messiah He shall make them know His Holy Spirit.' A haggadah on Gen 1^{2} says that the Spirit of God will be manifested in the spirit of the Messiah, and will spread His wings, and bestow His grace upon Israel (Gen Rabbah 2, quoted G. W. H. Lampe, *The Seal of the Spirit*, p. 31).

[61] *Theology of the New Testament* (E.T.), I.155. John the Baptist's promise (Mk 1^{8}) concerns the widespread experience of the Spirit's power in the coming days of the Messiah (cf. Acts 2^{23}).

$1^{15, 41, 67}$, $2^{25ff, 36ff}$). The angel says to Mary (Lk 1^{35}) 'The Holy Ghost shall come upon thee, and the power of the Most High shall overshadow thee'.[62] In the Hebrew parallelism of this verse *πνεῦμα ἅγιον* (anarthous) is here obviously synonymous with *δύναμις ὑψίστου*.[63]

At the Baptism, when Jesus associated himself fully with all that the Baptist's ministry of preparation implied,[64] Mark records: 'He saw the heavens rent asunder and the Spirit as a dove descending upon him' (cf. Mt 3^{16}). Luke 3^{22} adds, *σωματικῷ εἴδει ὡς περιστερὰν*, and Codex Bezae gives the reading *εἰς αὐτόν* for the *ἐπ' αὐτόν* common to all the Synoptists.[65]

It is not necessary to suggest that Matthew and Luke soften Mark's 'driveth him forth' (*ἐκβάλλει*, Mk 1^{12}) when they refer to the way in which the Spirit led Him into the wilderness. It may well be that here we are dealing with two divergent accounts of the Temptation.[66] The fact of the reference to the Holy Spirit in both streams of narrative would thus become doubly impressive. The temptations, as recounted in Matthew and Luke, involve the question of the right use of the power of which He, just designated Messiah, is now vividly aware. In Luke's account it is as One 'full of the Holy Spirit' that Jesus is 'led by the Spirit'.[67] in the

[62] G. W. H. Lampe notes that *ἐπισκιάζειν* is used in the Old Testament (e.g. LXX, Ex 40^{35}) to describe the tabernacling of the cloud among God's people, and (Ps 91^{4}, 139^{8}, LXX) of the protection and shielding of men by the divine presence. It is also the word used later (Mt 9^{7} and parallels, of the overshadowing of Jesus and the disciples by the cloud at the Transfiguration. See 'The Holy Spirit in the Writings of St. Luke' (*Studies in the Gospels*, ed. Nineham, Oxford, 1955), p. 167.

[63] From His birth, says Grundmann (*Der Begriff der Kraft*, p. 61), Jesus is endowed with power and is the bearer of power. δ. *ὑψίστου* is 'the wonderful effective creative power of God. For Luke, δ. is charged with the notion of a power-substance. The endowment with a power-substance—concerning the manner Luke says nothing—evokes the pregnancy of Mary'.

[64] And showed by it that He was 'moving in the same circle of prophetic and eschatological concepts as the Baptist' (C. K. Barrett, *The Holy Spirit and the Gospel Tradition*, p. 35).

[65] G. W. H. Lampe suggests (ibid., p. 168) that the 'bodily' reference would be meant to contrast with a transient experience of the Spirit's invasion, such as came to prophet or seer; and *εἰς αὐτόν* to indicate that the Holy Spirit did not 'come upon him' in some external manner, but entered right into Him.

[66] So Streeter's *The Four Gospels*, p. 187. Matthew may, however, have taken from Mark the reference to the ministry of the angels, and Luke, perhaps, the *πειραζόμενος ὑπὸ τοῦ* δ. of 4^{2} (C. K. Barrett, op. cit., p. 47). See, however, above, p. 79.

[67] 'It is Luke alone who emphasizes the completeness of our Lord's Spirit-possession in connexion with this event, and so brings the struggle with the devil within the scope of the Spirit's operation . . . the activity of the Spirit is often associated by St Luke with the conflict against the adversary (cf. Lk 10^{22} in its context in this Gospel)' (G. W. H. Lampe, ibid., p. 170).

wilderness to suffer these temptations of the devil. He is thus put to the test (πειράζειν), experiencing in mind the very temptations to which the circumstances of His future ministry will subject Him. All these are based on His consciousness of special relationship to God, and on the use of spiritual power in conformity either with human expectation and desires or with the divine will.

The other third-person references in the Synoptics to the Lord's empowerment by the Spirit are few. There is Luke 4^{14}, in which, significantly, 'power' and 'Spirit' are joined, 'And Jesus returned in the power of the Spirit unto Galilee'. There is also the passage from Isaiah 61^{1} which Jesus quoted in 4^{18} in the synagogue at Nazareth; and the reference in Luke 10^{21} to His rejoicing 'in the Holy Spirit' when the disciples returned from their successful mission. The fact that this is a passing reference makes an important point. This thinking and acting 'in the Holy Spirit' is assumed by these writers as the Lord's consistent approach to all that happens. It is made evident by the way each Synoptist tells his story that Jesus, as Messiah, is anointed and equipped in this very way.[68] References in Acts indicate that this is a presupposition concerning the Lord (Acts 10^{38}; cf. 4^{26f}).

The difficulty concerning the paucity of references to the Spirit in the Synoptic Gospels becomes more pressing when applied to the teaching of Jesus. The Early Church was conscious that it existed in the era of the Spirit. Its references to the Spirit's guidance, power, and inspiration were constant and explicit. Why does not Jesus use language of this kind? 'Why, for example', Vincent Taylor asks, 'does Jesus not exhort His disciples to receive the Spirit, to be filled with the Spirit, not to quench the Spirit, to manifest the fruits of the Spirit, to be "temples" of the Spirit, to be strengthened, sanctified, sealed, united by the Spirit?[69] The Fourth Gospel fills in the lacuna here (not only with the Spirit-passages in Chapters 14–16, but also in the references at 3^{5ff}, 6^{51ff}, 7^{37ff}). Behind these Johannine references we are wise to detect actual sayings of Jesus, for thus we are provided with a bridge between the Synoptic Ministry and the experience and teaching of

[68] G. B. Swete in *The Holy Spirit in the New Testament* p. 56 comments that Luke intends his readers to understand from Luke 4^{14} that this reference to the spirit covers the whole of this Ministry.

[69] As he says (*The Doctrine of the Holy Spirit*, Headingley Lectures, 1937, pp. 57f), this is 'the religious vocabulary of early Christianity'.

the Apostolic Church.[70] Vincent Taylor indeed suggests that, so far as the Synoptists are concerned, 'sayings about the Spirit are few in the recorded words of Jesus just because the doctrine was dominant'. The argument on which he bases this unexpected dictum is founded on Form Criticism. 'Pronouncement-stories' did not concern things which were taken for granted. They concerned matters especially raised in controversy or experience.[71] The doctrine was certainly dominant in the community in which the Gospels took shape, but, going back to the days of the Ministry themselves the fact is that the basic reference in the teaching of Jesus, as the Synoptists make clear to us, is not to the Spirit, but to the Kingdom.

The power of the Spirit during the days of the ministry is concentrated upon the figure of the Messiah Himself. 'God anointed him with the Holy Ghost and with power: who went about doing good, and healing all that were oppressed of the devil' (Acts 10^{38}). By His Death and Resurrection, and His Exaltation, He then 'sends forth the promise of my Father' upon the disciples (Lk 24^{49}). They are told to 'tarry in the city' 'until ye be clothed with power from on high'.[72] 'While Jesus is in the flesh, there can be no other incarnation.'[73] 'The general gift of the Spirit belongs to the time of the vindication and manifestation of the Messiah and of the Messianic Kingdom.'[74] As Luke tells the story in the second volume of his work, it is obvious that he sees the age of the Spirit inaugurated now by the events outlined in Vol. I. Acts 1^{5} (cf. 11^{16})

[70] W. F. Lofthouse, in an article, 'The Holy Spirit in Acts and in the Fourth Gospel' (*Expository Times*, 1940–1, III.334ff), argues that the way in which the activity of the Holy Spirit is portrayed in Acts 1–15 presupposes exactly the emphasis of the five Holy Spirit passages in Jn 14–16; cf. the same author's *The Father and The Son* (1934), p. 176: 'The convictions of the Church as the writer describes them would be unintelligible unless Jesus had actually said precisely what He is represented in the Fourth Gospel as saying.'

[71] Ibid., pp. 54^{ff}. But there is much teaching in the Gospels based on matters which could not be considered as likely to be raised only in controversy or to clarify points of belief and conduct. They are told because of the way that they reveal the Lord and His Gospel, and for no other reason. And in any case, as C. K. Barrett points out (op. cit., p. 142), there *was* controversy on the subject of the Spirit. Acts 18^{24}–19^{7} indicates this.

[72] Cf. Isa 32^{15} *ruach mimarom*, 'the spirit from on high; LXX, πνεῦμα ἀφ' ὑψηλοῦ The Targum comments that the Spirit is from His Shekinah in the heights of heaven. *Mimarom* is also a circumlocution for the divine name. Strack-Billerbeck, *ad loc.*

[73] J. A. Findlay, *The Gospel according to St Luke* (1937), p. 28: 'saints and prophets might be *visited* by the Spirit before He came, only after He has gone can they be "filled" with the Spirit'.

[74] C. K. Barrett, ibid., p. 159, who refers also to Büchsel, *Geist Gottes*, Chapter IX. This is in line with Jn 7^{39}, 'this spake he of the Spirit, which they that believed on him were to receive; for the Spirit was not yet (given); because Jesus was not yet glorified'.

refers to days when the Baptist's prophecy of Spirit-baptism is being fulfilled. The book reveals how the Spirit, which had anointed the Messiah, now empowers His disciples, enabling them to be witnesses to Him and to the gospel which is in Him and the events through which He passed.[75]

This, surely, is the fact illuminating the paucity of references to the Spirit in the Synoptists, and shedding light on their nature. We can understand at the same time, that words of Jesus must have been given, preparing the disciples for the stage of personal empowerment and inspiration into which they were to enter after the events of the Passion. These lie behind the references to the Spirit in John's Gospel.

The parallel passages in Mark 3^{23ff}, Matthew 12, and Luke 11 prove to be of great significance when seeking to understand the secret of our Lord's own endowment. Matthew's reference to casting out devils 'by the Spirit of God' (12^{28}) becomes in Luke pictorially, and therefore in all likelihood, originally, 'by the finger of God'. No doubt Luke prefers this form of the saying because it echoes Exodus 8^{19}, LXX, and strengthens the allusions in his writings to the prophet like unto Moses, e.g. Luke 13^{33}; Acts 7^{51f}; Luke 11^{50}; cf. Deuteronomy 18^{15},[76]. References in Acts, however ($4^{28, 30}$, 11^{21}, 13^{11}), indicate that expressions concerning the hand (or finger) of the Lord virtually mean the same thing as the Spirit (cf. Ezek 3^{14}). The context—that of the attacks made on Jesus in connexion with the Beelzebub slander—provides this significant personal statement regarding the Spirit from the lips of Jesus.

Not being able to gainsay Jesus' evident power in healing and exorcizing, His opponents fell back on the only possible explanation—if God was not in this, then it must be Satan—and, in arguing thus, they found the complete way to discredit Him. In the Marcan story (3^{23ff}),[77] Jesus' reaction to the suggestion that He had made a bargain with Beelzebub is strong—even violent:

[75] See G. W. H. Lampe, op. cit., pp. 188f. Thus the promise of the Spirit recorded in Lk 24^{49} corresponds in some degree to the Annunciation. Like Mary, the Apostles are to be endued with 'power from on high'. At Pentecost they actually receive the power of the Spirit, in which Jesus had preached, healed, and exorcized.

[76] G. W. H. Lampe, ibid., p. 172.

[77] Bultmann (*Geschichte*, pp. 10–12, etc.) thinks that the Marcan version is a 'Pronouncement-story', preserved because it dealt with this very charge. It found also a place in Q in a version that would seem closer to the original, because of its connection with an actual case of exorcism.

'All their sins shall be forgiven unto the sons of men, and their blasphemies wherewith soever they shall blaspheme: but whosoever shall blaspheme against the Holy Spirit hath never ever forgiveness, but is guilty of an eternal sin.' This reaction, as Mark indicates (verse 30) was 'because they said, He hath an unclean spirit'.

It should be noted that Matthew records the story immediately after quoting Isaiah 42 [1ff] (Mt 12[13ff]). By this very conjunction, the Evangelist is witnessing to the belief that Jesus is 'my servant whom I have chosen; My beloved in whom my soul is well pleased: I will put my Spirit in him', and that His ministry (as referred to in verse 15) is accomplished as Son of God, and Servant of God, in the power of the Spirit.[78]

One interpretation of the title Beelzebub is that it means 'Lord of the house'.[79] In his exercise of lordship over vast areas of human life, and in particular in the matter of demonic invasion of human personalities, Satan is 'not such a fool'[80] as to allow an alliance with him to work against his own household! Clearly another power is at work in these exorcisms.

Many commentators have suggested that the 'stronger' (ἰσχυρότερος) of Luke 11[22] is the Lord Himself.[81] 'It may be', says Vincent Taylor, 'that, in the light of His temptation, Jesus believed Himself to be the binder of Satan.'[82] But it may also be that He attributed the binding to God.[83]

The influence of Deutero-Isaiah is of paramount importance in the interpretation of Jesus' mission in the Gospels. Grundmann therefore sees this logion in Luke 11 as an appeal on the part of Jesus to the passage from Isaiah 49[25], which it echoes. He is telling the lawyers, in a language they would understand, that He *is* the appointed Servant of God: at the same time this logion lays bare the background to all Christ's actions, which stem from the fact that He has 'power' as the 'Stronger' over the 'Strong', bringing God's Lordship in the place of Satan's. In the theology of the

[78] The Matthean story seems a conflation of Mark and Q and, apart from this introductory allusion, does not need separate study.

[79] *Ba'al Zebul* in Mischnaic Hebrew. The aptness of the references in verses 17 and 21 immediately becomes apparent. Geldenhuys, *Comm.*, p. 332, prefers 'Lord of the High Place', found thus in the Ras Shamra tablets. Ironically, in 2 K 1[2ff] this is denigrated to *Ba'al zebub*, 'Lord of flies'.

[80] T. W. Manson, *Sayings*, p. 85.

[81] E.g. Plummer, Geldenhuys, etc.

[82] *The Life and Ministry of Jesus*, p. 86.

[83] So Creed, Rawlinson, Ernest Percy, and Otto.

Church, the Death and Resurrection of Jesus is regarded as His triumph over the might of Satan and his demons. In our logion, which must come from the Lord Himself, the decisive battle, however, is already presumed: it took place in the Temptation. Jesus's whole activity corresponds to the robbing of the spoils.

Luke 11²² would seem best interpreted, however, as our Lord's description of the power in which He, as a human being, consciously did His work and exercised His Ministry. The Fourth Gospel is full of references of this kind, tracing the source of His inspiration, His work, and His words not to Himself, but to the Father (e.g. Jn $5^{19f, 30}$, 8^{28}, 14^{10}). We feel that the whole tenor of Luke 11^{21f} is in line with the references in verse 20 to the Kingdom and the finger (Spirit) of God.

Otto is typical of many exegetes who see the ἰσχυρότερος of this passage[84] as God the Father stripping Satan of his armour, and proceeding, through the working of Jesus as exorcist, to take from him his spoil. Jesus was sent by God, and is working by God's power. From the standpoint of the Christian community later, says Otto, it was a matter of dogma that Christ Himself had gained the real victory over Satan, and it is this later dogmatic assumption that lends obscurity to the narratives in Matthew and Mark.[85] Thus Satan's overthrow has been realized in Heaven.[86] Now, as the Kingdom comes in Jesus and with Him, in His ministry and mighty works, it is being worked out 'in earth as it is in heaven'.[87]

When we say of the Lord that He was a 'charismatic'[88] or 'pneumatic'[89] person we are not denigrating Him. Rather we are shedding lustre upon these terms! 'It is impossible to avoid the conclusion', says H. Windisch, 'that Jesus Himself traced the

[84] He gives priority to Luke's account of the Beelzebub controversy. In accordance with his theory (outlined in pp. 82ff of *The Kingdom of God and the Son of Man*), he thinks Luke is following an older form of *Stammschrift* than Matthew and Luke.

[85] Ibid., p. 101 and footnote, p. 102. It is this tendency, says Otto, that causes the omission in Mark of 'then is the kingdom of God come upon you'. 'From the standpoint of later Christology, this saying was scarcely tolerable. For it clearly presupposed that Christ did not himself bring the Kingdom of God, but that His own appearance was actually only a result of the fact that the Kingdom had already come, that the powers of the Kingdom were working in Him and through Him, but in such a way that He Himself was part and parcel of this inbreaking entity of the Kingdom, which was superior even to Him.'

[86] An idea which lends peculiar point to 'I beheld Satan fallen as lightning from heaven' in Luke 10^{18}.

[87] Ibid., p. 105. [88] So Otto, C. K. Barrett, etc.

[89] H. Windisch, art., 'Jesus und der Geist nach Synoptischer Überlieferung', in *Studies in Early Christianity*, ed. S. J. Case, New York, 1923, pp. 229ff.

powers, abilities and authorities in Him back to the Spirit working in Him.' This writer suggests that, even in the days of the oral tradition, the tendency was to reduce this emphasis, and that in the original form of these stories, 'the element, the impulse of the spirit, and its inspiration appeared more frequently and more powerfully'.[90] The lack of such references in the Gospels compared with the abundance in post-Resurrection narratives and documents is to be understood, says Windisch, by taking account of two processes working in opposite directions: one anxious to displace the 'pneumatic' element in all to do with Jesus and the other concerned with the full development and encouragement of this same element in the Christian community. Is not the solution, however, to be found along the lines suggested above, coupled with the undisputed fact of our Lord's humility and of the 'hidden' nature of so much connected with the Messiahship? As we have seen, the records show that our Lord realized His endowment with the Spirit, and those who write about Him equally understand it; but He makes no outward and continual reference to it, for the following very good reasons: 'To have claimed a pre-eminent measure of the Spirit would have been to have made an open confession of Messiahship', since the Messiah was expected to be so endowed. More than that, the secret involved in His Messiahship—that it would result in suffering and death—also precluded such references. Jesus had yet to make it clear that God's Servant, bringing the Kingdom, and achieving salvation, under the full authority and power of the Spirit, would do this in circumstances of humiliation, defeat, and death.[91]

John's Gospel discloses a view of the Spirit corresponding with the interpretation we have been following. The testimony given to the Baptist in 1[33] witnesses, at the outset of the story, to the Lord's endowment by the Spirit, and to the way He will pass this gift on to others: 'Upon whomsoever thou shalt see the Spirit descending, and abiding upon him, the same is he that baptizeth with the Holy Spirit.' The Spirit 'descends' and 'abides' upon Him. He bestows the Spirit; but this bestowal does not take place until He is 'glorified' (7[39]). All the references in the Upper Room

[90] Ibid., pp. 231ff.

[91] C. K. Barrett, ibid., pp. 158f, refers to the Temptation as the place where Jesus won His victory in terms of humility and the voluntary abnegation of certain uses of power. It is from this time, as he significantly observes, that references to the Spirit almost disappear from the record.

are associated with future tenses.[92] After the Resurrection (20^{22}), 'He breathed on them, and saith unto them, Receive ye the Holy Ghost'. Now they can act as Apostles, remitting and retaining sins. The Spirit that had been fully upon Him is now upon them, too.

Having examined some of the conceptions providing the eschatological background to the Gospels, and observing something of their history when the Apostolic era opens, we must return to the days of the Ministry in order to look at two further keywords, *ἐξουσία* and *δύναμις* ('authority' and 'power'). These words, and what they illustrate, are of utmost importance in the Gospel records.

[92] And 3^{5}, 6^{63} refer to the future elements of Church life (C. K. Barrett, op. cit., p. 74).

CHAPTER ELEVEN

THE OUTWORKINGS OF POWER: (1) ACTS OF 'AUTHORITY'

WE have followed some of the clues provided in Mark's dramatic opening regarding the One 'possessed' by the Spirit, filled with power, who is both brought by, and brings, the Kingdom. In Mark 1^{15} Jesus announced that the Kingdom is at hand and 'the time is fulfilled'. In the succeeding verses there are striking indications of the 'authority' with which He acted. This is to be seen in the calling, and answering, of the disciples (1^{16ff}), in the tone and character of the teaching in the Synagogue (1^{21f}),[1] and in the healings and exorcisms that follow (1^{23ff}). Chapter 2 introduces us to a story, not only involving healing, but demonstrating power to forgive sins. In this way, these opening verses of Mark's Gospel enable us to feel something of the impact of the teaching, actions, and presence of Jesus of Nazareth ($1^{22, 27}$, 2^{12}).[2]

The people who first shared in these happenings lived in days of widespread unrest and fear. The shadow of the Evil One and the power of his demons hung continuously and threateningly over their lives. Now this cloud was being dissipated in a new, vivifying light. In place of powerlessness and fear was a new teaching and a new acting, with authority.

Regarding the teaching, apart from the parables of Chapter 4 and the apocalyptic chapter, 13, Mark, though often referring to it and its ἐξουσία,[3] makes little reference to its substance. Matthew

[1] Windisch (art., 'Jesus und der Geist', *Studies in Early Christianity*, p. 225) says that the antithesis ὡς ἐξουσίαν ἔχων και οὐχ ὡς οἱ γραμματεῖς particularly emphasizes the prophetic-pneumatic character of this concept.

[2] 'Hidden in the human body of Jesus there was a divine power which, like the Spirit of Jn 3^{8}, cannot be seen; it can only be felt. Men of earthly mind . . . watch the 'power of Jesus in dumb astonishment, precisely because they belong to this world, and He—since the Spirit had entered into Him—belongs to the other; for the present there is no point of contact . . . they can only say, 'We never saw it like this!' J. A. Findlay, *The Way, The Truth, and the Life*, p. 94.

[3] Derived from the verb ἔξεστι, the basic idea of this word is that of the right, the liberty, to do something: hindrances are out of the way. While δύναμις concerns the ability or capacity to perform an action, ἐξουσία involves the possibility of its performance in freedom, without obstacle either from right or might.

remedies that omission. Indeed, in all matters he adds a special emphasis concerning the ἐξουσία of Jesus.[4] The Kingdom of God, subject of the teaching, provides the setting for this. Grundmann sees a direct relationship with Daniel 7[14]: 'His dominion (ἐξουσία) is an everlasting dominion, which shall not pass away, and his Kingdom that which shall not be destroyed.'[5]

The Sermon on the Mount contains dicta reinterpreting Old Testament Commandments and preceded by the formula 'but I say unto you' (5[22, 28, 34], etc.). The Sermon ends with a declaration that the words are those of the One who speaks for God with authority (7[29]).[6] So that the miracles of the chapters which immediately follow (8 and 9) afford evidence of this authority: as they prove, this extends into the realm of healing and exorcism. In Matthew's telling of the story of the paralytic, the forgiveness of sins is explicitly referred to Christ's ἐξουσία and is plainly the point most at issue.[7] 'All things have been delivered to me by my Father', He declares in 11[27]; and in this sums up His authority to reveal the Father and act for Him.[8] This He manifests also in His power over nature (8[26]) and over life and death (9[25]). Before the era of dogma and theological interpretation, as Windisch says, 'the man with authority' was a designation for Jesus: the phrase preserves the impression made by His very appearance.[9]

The incident of the Roman Centurion's servant (παῖς, Mt 8[5ff], δοῦλος, Lk 7[2ff]) is illuminative, and for this we quote Lk 7[8] 'for I also am a man set under authority,[10] having under myself soldiers: and I say to this one, Go, and he goeth; and to another, Come, and he cometh.' The Centurion discerns the relationship in

[4] Cf. W. Grundmann, *Der Begriff der Kraft*, p. 57: 'For him the Christ is the one who has ἐξουσία—a characteristic word for Matthew.'

[5] Cf. Mt 24[30], 26[64], where Jesus Himself refers to the Danielic picture. (See C. H. Dodd, *According to the Scriptures*, pp. 67ff, for the echoes of Dan 7 in this Gospel.)

[6] Strack-Billerbeck, *in loc.*: 'The one who has Authority in God': this is the sense of the phrase. 'Jesus does not teach from Himself, from His own opinions, but rather as a prophet, who speaks as the mouth of God.'

[7] Cf. T. H. Robinson (*M.N.T.C.*) *ad loc.* Mark tells the story (2[1–12]) as illustrative of the conflict between Jesus and the religious leaders. Matthew is not concerned with that at all. As Messiah, it is His divine right to forgive sins—that is His concern. It is important to bear in mind Jn 20[22f], at this point, also (p. 100, and, later, pp. 131f).

[8] Grundmann, *Der Begriff der Kraft*, p. 58, says E. Norden rightly judges here that (πᾶσα) ἐξουσία could stand here for πάντα.

[9] Windisch, op cit., p. 226.

[10] H. J. Schonfield, *Authentic New Testament*, p. 139, notes that these were the words used by the Roman legate Petronius to the Jews gathered at Tiberius in Galilee when trying to persuade them to accept the erection of Caligula's statue in the Temple. (Josephus, *Jewish Wars*, ii. 10. 4).

which Jesus works. As a soldier, he himself operates in a hierarchy of delegated authority. This is what Jesus does! *Under* God's authority, He therefore acts *with* authority. Because of His ἐξουσία, His command is obeyed in the spiritual realm.

The question of Matthew 21[23ff] (Mk 11[28]) throws further light on this: 'By what authority[11] doest thou these things? and who gave thee this authority?' What is in dispute is not His acts of miracle, but the forthright cleansing of the Temple; and the Lord's answer is not just a clever way out of a difficult impasse: it provides evidence of His consciousness of the seat of His authority—it comes from the same source as that which inspired the Baptist: it is rooted in God.[12]

The material in Matthew's Gospel is most carefully arranged. His account of Passion Week is meant to bring home the fact that at the centre of all that happened throughout that week it is the *authority* of Jesus that is at issue. The controversy rages in one long debate round the theme, 'What is real authority, and where does it reside?' The 'little apocalypse' and the three following parables of doom are all comment on this. They concern those failing to recognize the true authority and to know their 'day of visitation'.[13] When, at the close of the week they crucify Him, it is thus the One claiming unique authority that they put to death.

'All authority hath been given unto me in heaven and on earth' is the announcement of the risen Christ (28[19]). It is in virtue of this that He is able, as the Gospel ends, to empower His disciples for their mission. It is this authority, too, that provides the setting for what will be discussed later, the δύναμις demonstrated by Jesus, and the power and authority shared by believers in the context of the Church.

John's use of this conception is also important: more especially since the words for power, δύναμις, ἰσχύς, κράτος, ἐνεργεία, etc., which occur elsewhere in the New Testament, are exiled from his writings. 'Authority' (ἐξουσία), by contrast, is found some eight

[11] Ludwig Bieler, *Wiener-Studien*, LV., Vienna, 1937, p. 188, says that ἐξουσία here is no more than the conception of 'rights' transferred to the religious sphere. That may be exactly what this meant on the lips of the questioners: but as Jesus uses the word, and Passion week progresses, the question goes much deeper than this.

[12] He also, by His answer, 'proves that there are subjects on which they are not qualified to speak. They are no judges of authority, for they cannot pass an opinion on so obvious an instance as that of John' (T. H. Robinson, *M.N.T.C. ad loc.*).

[13] G. P. Gilmour: *The Memoirs called Gospels*, 1959, pp. 190ff.

times in the Fourth Gospel (1^{12}, 5^{27}, 10^{18} (2), 17^{2}, 19^{10} (2), 19^{11}).[14] There is an affinity between John's usage and that of Matthew. Jesus is the 'unique' Son of the Father.[15] As such He has full, unlimited authority.[16] At the outset of the 'High-priestly prayer', Jesus declares 'thou gavest him authority over all flesh, that whatsoever thou hast given him, to them he should give eternal life'. This power over men is in accordance with the Father's purposes, so that the Son may bring them to His own quality of living, i.e. to Sonship (cf. 1^{12}).[17]

5^{27} speaks of the power, or authority (*ἐξουσία*), which He, as Son of Man, has received to act as Judge.[18] Of the 'I have power' (*ἐξουσίαν ἔχω*) of 10^{18}, C. K. Barrett thinks this means little more than *possum*.[19] It would seem, however, that what is being emphasized is the freedom the Lord has in relationship with the Father.[20] He can thus declare concerning His own life, 'I have power to lay it down.' He is the 'absolute Lord of His life and death. Death can have not the slightest power over Him. He gives His life. He takes it again. In death and in rising again, He is the determining agent.'[21]

[14] 'He avoids the word *δύναμις*, not only when meaning a mighty work but also in the sense of "power". He abstains from the word "powerful", and from the synonymous words "strength" and "strong". He seems to desire to show that heavenly power is far above "might" and deserves a higher name. Accordingly he calls it by the term "authority" (*ἐξουσία*)' (E. A. Abbott, *Johannine Vocabularies* (*Diatasserica*), 1,669).

[15] *μονογενής* (Jn $1^{14, 18}$, $3^{16, 18}$; 1 Jn 4^{9}). See Moulton and Milligan, *Vocabulary of New Testament Greek in the light of Papyri*, for instances of this word meaning 'unique' (cf. also Liddell and Scott, new edition, and Bauer). *ἀγαπητός* Mt 3^{17}, etc., 'only-beloved', inclines to this meaning.

[16] Foerster in *T.W.z.N.T.* III.572: 'An important part is played by *ἐξουσία* in interpreting the work and personality of Jesus. It means the full authority to act granted Him by God.'

[17] Note the verb *γενέσθαι*. In 1^{12} instead of what the Gnostics and others understood as man's inherent 'right' to become a child of God, the very opposite is being declared: all is of God's free grace. It is also noteworthy that those who 'receive' Jesus become, in John's language *τέκνα*, while Jesus is invariably the *υἱός* (cf. 1 Jn 3^{1}). The words that follow in 1^{12f} emphasize also what are the conditions for the granting of *ἐξουσία*.

[18] 'John stands in here with the whole New Testament proclamation' (Grundmann). This text 'starts from the common Christian belief that Christ, as Son of Man, is judge of quick and dead' (C. H. Dodd, *The Interpretation of the Fourth Gospel*, p. 209).

[19] *The Gospel according to St. John.* He compares 7^{1} (W a b) and 19^{10}. It is true that in the later instance what Pilate possesses is *potestas* (see later p. 313).

[20] Foerster, *T.W.z.N.T.*, III.565. Note the usage in 1 Cor 9^{44}: *ἐξουσία* in the sense of 'freedom to act'.

[21] Grundmann, *Der Begriff der Kraft*, p. 81. The change of emphasis here and at 2^{19} must be noted. Elsewhere (Acts 2^{24}; Rom 1^{4}, etc.) the Resurrection is clearly portrayed as due to God's action. Hoskyns and Davey (*The Fourth Gospel* at 10^{18}) point out that the contradiction is more apparent than real: the whole Gospel is an essay on the closeness of will, purpose etc. between Father and Son (cf. 5^{30}). Note that 2^{23} and 21^{14} use the customary passive.

There is to be noted, too, in the expression of the Lord's ἐξουσία, as in the Synoptists, a double emphasis upon words and deeds.[22] Just as the listeners to Jesus's teaching in Mark 1^{21ff}, Luke 4^{31ff} were 'amazed', recognizing it as 'having authority', so the officers sent to arrest Him report in John 7^{46}, 'Never man so spake.' Similarly, healing power follows His word. The introductory stories in the second episode of the 'Book of Signs'[23] describe how two people, as good as dead, found life through His word: concerning the man at the Pool of Bethesda (5^{1ff}) C. H. Dodd comments: 'The will to live, together with the power to live, is given in the word of Christ.' The discourse following has as its dominant theme the statement in verse 21: 'the Son also quickeneth whom he will'. This 'quickening' happens through listening to the Word believingly (verse 24).[24]

Christ's words are spoken from the centre of His complete unity with the Father (12^{50}, $14^{10, 24}$).[25] In this Gospel, they are all words of self-revelation, pointing to the Father's purpose, calling men into personal relationship with the Father through Himself. In this way 'all the revelation that He brings is concentrated in the great "I am" statements'.[26] With His 'It is I', says Bultmann,[27] 'Jesus therefore presents Himself as the One for whom all the world is waiting, the One who satisfies all longing.'

The author of the Fourth Gospel has no qualms, as have the Synoptists, about viewing the miracles of Jesus as evidences of His ἐξουσία. The Lord appeals to them directly in that way Himself,

22 See above p. 101 (cf. Acts 1^{1}).

23 Following the scheme set out so persuasively in Dodd's *The Interpretation of the Fourth Gospel*.

24 Later the story of the raising of Lazarus fulfils all that Jesus claims in these verses. At His commanding word, dead Lazarus 'comes forth' (11^{43f}).

25 There is an identity, as Bultmann notes, between the word of Jesus and the Lord Himself. As He is 'life' and 'truth', so are His words (6^{63}, 17^{17}; cf. 5^{24}, 11^{25}, 14^{6}). As He must be 'received' (1^{12}, 5^{43}) so must His words (12^{48}, 17^{8}) and His 'testimony' ($3^{11, 32f}$). To reject His word, is to reject Him (12^{48f}). His words are to be our final judge, just as He is (cf. $5^{22, 27}$) (*Theology of the New Testament* (E.T.) II.63f).

26 Analogies to this style of speech can be found in the magical papyri and the Hermetic literature; cf. the inscription cited by Deissmann *Light from the Ancient East*, pp. 134ff, and Bernard, *International Critical Commentary*, pp. cxviiff: 'I am Isis, Queen of every land, instructed by Hermes. . . . I am the first who has brought the fruits of the earth to men.' The ἐγώ εἰμι statements in the papyri were all meant to be used as spells and charms, by which one aligned oneself with the δύναμις of the God in question. More important analogies are found in the words of God uttered by the prophets in the Old Testament (Isa 62^{6}; cf. 43^{25}, 51^{12}). There are equivalent statements of this emphatic nature in the Synoptists, e.g. Mt 11^{27ff}; Mk 14^{62}. We are also reminded—and probably, meant to be reminded—of the divine name of Ex 3^{14} (R. H. Strachan, *The Fourth Gospel*, pp. 19f); Bernard, *I.C.C.*, pp. cxviff.

27 Ibid., p. 65.

and expects His claims to be granted by virtue of them (5^{36}, 10^{25}, 14^{11}). Avoiding the expression *δυνάμεις*, John instead calls them *ἔργα*.[28] As in this Gospel Christ insists that His words are not His, but the Father's (12^{50}, 14^{24}), so He makes the same claim for His 'works'. 14^{10}, indeed, brings the two conceptions together: 'the words that I say unto you I speak not of myself: but the Father abiding in me doeth his works'. These 'works'—and, indeed, as John would have us see, His whole 'work' (cf. 4^{34}, 17^{4})—bear upon them the sign-manual of God, witnessing to His Love and Power, and to Christ's share in the Father's purposes and activity.

[28] Only once used of Christ's works in the Synoptics, e.g. Mt 11^{2}, and then not directly by Christ Himself. Even more characteristically John describes the miracles as 'signs': see later, pp. 111f.

CHAPTER TWELVE

THE OUTWORKINGS OF POWER: (2) *DUNAMIS* AND MIRACLE[1]

WE have seen that the Gospels provide a picture of Jesus exercising God-given powers. Through Him the Stronger (ἰσχυρότερος) is vanquishing Satan's Kingdom and asserting His own sovereignty. Jesus bearing God's commission, His 'authority', is also anointed by His Spirit, acting with 'power' (the Greek word so translated—δύναμις—represents innate power, strength to do). We look now at specific references to this endowment and its outworking.

Noting the regulative concepts of the individual evangelists, it becomes evident that while Matthew and John lay special stress on ἐξουσία, Luke's characteristic word is this one: δύναμις. Only once does Mark use this word in the sense of 'power of healing' (5^{30}) and Matthew never. Luke, however, has it at 5^{17}, 6^{19}, 8^{46} and Acts 3^{12}, 4^{7}, 6^{8}.

Luke sees Christ as the bearer of power, anointed and endued with Holy Spirit. Significantly, in Luke 4^{36}, after verse 32 has told us that 'his word was with authority', the two words 'authority' and 'power' are joined in the testimony given by the people: 'What is this word? for with authority and power he commandeth the unclean spirits, and they come out.' The Lord's 'authority' both in preaching and healing is referred to in this section of Luke, and in Chapter 5 we meet the reference to His 'authority' to forgive sins (5^{24}). It is noteworthy, however, that the emphasis in this instance is no longer upon that particular ἐξουσία, but rather, as in the re-written introduction to verse 17, upon 'the power of the Lord to heal'. The clearance of the man's sense of guilt[2] is thus seen as a necessary stage in the story of his cure.[3]

[1] Miracle has already been discussed on pp. 84, 91 n. 59, 102, 105f.

[2] There are modern cases of paralysis in which physical treatment has not been effective until an underlying guilt-sense has first been dealt with (see, e.g., L. D. Weatherhead, *Psychology, Religion and Healing*, p. 72).

[3] Sometimes it is argued that Mk 2^{6-11} reflects the standpoint of later days. The question, 'Who but God alone can forgive sins?' would be a familiar question in the early church. But although this story (e.g. as a 'Pronouncement-story') would provide a powerful answer to that question it preserves the authentic indications of a cure in two stages.

Some of Luke's references to healing δύναμις call for closer examination. They seem strangely 'physical'. There is, for instance, the reference already noted in 5[17f]: 'And it came to pass on one of those days, that he was teaching . . . and the power of the Lord was with him to heal.'[4] 'In other words', comments Otto, 'the charismatic power had its particular hours, when it was present for healing, and manifestly also those when it was not present. It is therefore stronger or weaker. It comes and goes.'[5]

The picture conveyed by Luke 5[18], several commentators have suggested, is similar to that of being filled with an electric potential. This analogy is, of course, one which is only possible in our day: but what is impressive is that Luke, reporting these phenomena, did so in terms analogical to us in this way. The fact that so many of Jesus's miracles involve the use of touch heightens this impression. The instinct of the woman with the haemorrhage led her, very successfully, to this kind of conclusion. Mark's comment (5[30]) leaves little doubt that he understood that this touch was felt by Jesus in such a way that He knew that δύναμις had gone from Him: 'perceiving in himself that the power from him had gone forth'. Branscomb[6] thinks this saying merely represents a popular conception of the way Jesus's healing works were accomplished, and Lagrange[7] interprets the phrase 'perceiving in himself' as a contrast with the kind of knowledge that the woman had ('she felt in her body'). His consciousness was an 'intellectual' one, as over against something made clear by the senses. Lagrange, therefore, does not think Mark's expression is meant to indicate a physical sensation. But whatever expedients are used to interpret this phrase, it would seem that the writer meant it to convey our Lord's awareness that the divine healing power which dwelt in Him had been 'tapped' by some needy person.[8]

In Luke what Mark gives as comment becomes a statement from Jesus (8[46]), thus deepening the impression considerably. Luke 6[19] is in the same vein: 'for power came forth from him, and

[4] αὐτόν in the original can be understood as having been changed to αὐτους (thus C, R, D, etc.). The force of the statement is that God's power is on Him (Jesus) for Him to heal with. So Plummer, Geldenhuys, Bruce.

[5] *The Kingdom of God and the Son of Man* (E.T.), p. 342.

[6] *M.N.T.C. ad loc.*

[7] *Evangile selon Saint Marc, ad loc.*

[8] 'How Jesus was conscious of the appropriation of His power we do not know; it is part of the secret of His spiritual consciousness' (V. Taylor, Comm. *ad loc.*).

healed all'. 'Behind these formulae', as Grundmann remarks, 'lies a conception of power-substance with which Jesus is thought to be filled, and which is reduced in the moment of a healing'.[9]

Friedrich Preisigke's book, *Vom göttlichen Fluidum nach ägyptischen Anschauung*, investigates the recurring idea of impersonal *mana*-force in the civilizations of the Near East. He traces the source of these ideas to ancient Egypt, where the Godhead was pantheistically identified with the Life-force.[10] Efforts to share in this power and manipulate it for personal purposes lie behind much of the magic and religion of the Near East. It must be remembered, however, that Judaism kept clear of this stream of ideas. The 'power of the Lord' is something different from *mana* and all its associated conceptions. Pantheistic ideas find no place in typical Old Testament views. Friedrich Preisigke, however, sees a connexion between the early Christian conception of the Power of God and conceptions of this kind. For him the story of the woman with the haemorrhage is regulative. He thinks of the δύναμις mentioned here as something automatic and quasi-physical, like a fluid or operating like an electric current. The bearer of 'power' needs this fund of power. It passes through him as its living agent.[11]

One thing seems certain: that in laying the particular stress he does on δύναμις in its aspect as healing power, Luke lays himself open to the charge of being influenced by Hellenistic notions.[12] The truth, however, is not so much this as that Luke is providing a testimony to what occurred in rather dubious terms. On other levels, our Lord, as a human being, needed seasons of refreshment and re-energizing. Crisis occasions and times of strain find Him, quite naturally, seeking fresh strength and inspiration in prayer.

[9] *Der Begriff der Kraft*, p. 62f: 'This power Jesus broadcasts on His disciples (Lk 9^1), who then as apostles use healing power, which in two places Luke can describe in the fashion that is completely primitive, a description which disperses the last doubts of the conception of a power-substance by Luke (Acts 5^{15}, 19^{11f}).'

[10] Grundmann, ibid., pp. 27ff. Preisigke is not necessarily right in this. Such ideas were very widespread, even in the earliest days. They were not exclusive to Egypt.

[11] Otto Schmitz, *Der Begriff δύναμις bei Paulus* (*Festgabe für Adolf Deissmann* Tubingen, 1927), pp. 158f. The bearer needs δύναμις, Schmitz quotes Preisigke as saying, as his 'fund of opportunity' (sitzgelegenheit).

[12] Bultmann (*Theology of the New Testament* (E.T.) I.157) writes of the Hellenistic conception of the θεῖος ἀνὴρ. He is of 'higher nature than ordinary mortals, filled with mysterious divine power, which makes him capable of miraculous insights and deeds. The term for the power in him is not . . . as a rule πνεῦμα, but δύναμις, power ("grace" also occurs): but in substance it means the same thing as the πνεῦμα of early Christianity (dynamistically understood).'

Mark 1^{35} is an indication of this kind, and Luke himself provides many further illustrations of the Lord's praying at great crises of His ministry (3^{21} at His Baptism; 6^{12} before choosing His disciples; 9^{18} at Caesarea Philippi; $10^{17, 21}$ on the return of the Seventy; 22^{39ff} in Gethsemane; and $23^{34, 41}$ on the Cross).[13]

There is a connexion observable between prayer and the reception of the Spirit, which becomes particularly noticeable when we move from the Gospel (comparatively sparing in its references to the Spirit)[14] to Acts.

In the 2nd volume of Luke's work, it is in prayer that the Church, like Jesus at His Baptism, awaits the descent of the Pentecostal Spirit (Acts 1^{14}), the 'prayers' are one of the chief features of the Church's life in the Spirit (2^{42}), the disciples are filled with the Spirit and enabled to speak the word boldly while they are engaged in prayer (4^{31}), prayer accompanies the ordination of ministers of the Church and the commissioning of its missionary preachers (6^{6}, 13^{3}, 14^{23}); prayer, accompanied by an imposition of hands, is the means whereby the Samaritans receive the Pentecostal Spirit (8^{15ff}) and prayer precedes the doing by the apostles of mighty works of healing and of raising the dead (9^{40}, 28^{8}). In all these instances there is a close connexion between prayer on the part of man and the communion from the side of God, of the power, inspiration, or guidance of the Holy Spirit.[15]

No one who has been engaged in any kind of ministry even remotely resembling that exercised by the Lord but will have known what it is to feel drained of energy and in need of recuperation. Intense sympathy, in itself, leaves one feeling empty. Luke's references, then, may point to something very real in the human experience of Jesus, best understood not by any quasi-physical analogies to 'electric potential', or 'refilling' with 'a fluid', but by referring to prayer and a renewed experience of communion and fellowship with the Father in spirit.

In Luke's second volume there are a number of references to the same word in the plural: the *δυνάμεις*, the 'mighty works' which so clearly witness to the power available to Jesus. In Acts 2^{22} Peter appeals to this evidence: 'Jesus of Nazareth, a man ap-

[13] Note also 5^{16} (the parallel to Mk 1^{35}), 11^{1} before teaching His disciples to pray, and 22^{31} for Simon, that his faith fail not. Luke's Gospel is rich, too, in acccounts of the Lord's teaching on prayer.

[14] Though note especially 3^{21f}, where Luke tells us that the Holy Spirit descended upon Jesus as He was praying.

[15] G. W. H. Lampe, art., 'The Holy Spirit in the Writings of St Luke', *Studies in the Gospels*, ed. Nineham, p. 169.

proved of God unto you by mighty works and wonders and signs, which God did by him in the midst of you, even as ye yourselves know.' In 10³⁸ Peter again speaks of Jesus as the One 'equipped by God to do miracles',[16] 'anointed with the Holy Spirit and power' (δύναμις), 'God being with him'. In these summaries, as W. Manson points out, there is no appeal to the ἐξουσία of his teaching, nor the impact of His person. They are 'true to the Hebrew-Jewish conception of history in which God makes himself known by mighty acts and by an outstretched arm'.[17]

There is a sense in which our Lord Himself seems to interpret His miracles as authenticating signs of His Mission. The writer of the Fourth Gospel makes much of this (Jn 5^{36}, 10^{38}, 14^{11}), but the idea is also in the Synoptics (Mt $11^{4ff, 21f}$). These are the signs of Isaiah 61 and 35; and anyone with ability to understand, Jesus seems to say, should understand them (Mt 16^{3f}). Had similar things occurred in their midst, Sodom and Gomorrah would have repented (Mt 11^{23ff}). Matthew 9^{33} (cf. Jn 9^{32}, 15^{24}) also refers to His sense of the superlative character of these mighty works.[18]

They were not, however, performed in order to stun people into acceptance of His claims. The Temptation can be understood as the story of resistance to a series of suggestions to do what was expected of the Messiah. Part of the Synoptic emphasis, as distinct from the Johannine, is that our Lord consistently refused to grant the Jews the kind of testimony asked of Him (Mt 16^{1ff}).[19]

We must look a little more closely at the attitude of the Fourth Gospel towards the ideas of miracle and δύναμις. We have referred already to John's avoidance of this noun, either in singular or plural form, and to his preference for the word 'work' (ἔργον) instead.[20] John's characteristic term for miracle is not this, however, but 'sign' (σημεῖον).[21] This is used in a double sense (1)

[16] Bauer, *Lexicon*, p. 377. [17] *Jesus, the Messiah*, p. 33.
[18] Otto Borchert, *The Original Jesus* (E.T.), pp. 402f.
[19] The reply to the Baptist (Mt 11^{4ff}) can bear another explanation than that of authentication. In his announcements of the 'Coming One' the Baptist had suggested a discipleship needing supreme qualifications. What was unfit would be destroyed. John needed to know that Jesus was exercising *the* ministry even if working it out in ways different from that which John had expected.
[20] See above, p. 106.
[21] The word is used in the Stoic vocabulary, and occurs in contemporary Hellenistic religion; but the roots of the conception are in the Old Testament. Its use in Ionic days for a 'mark', a 'sign or token by which something is known' (so Liddell and Scott), leads to its use in the LXX for *'oth*. It comes thus to have a special connotation in connexion with prophetic activity—a symbolical showing forth of God's meaning and purpose (see C. K. Barrett, *The Gospel according to St John*, p. 43).

concerning the sign in its visible aspect, as something noteworthy, an exceptional miraculous event, and (2) connecting with the Old Testament prophetic conception of a 'sign' as a revelation of God's will and intention.[22] In this second sense the invisible meaning is most in mind, and the sign can be thought of as a kind of acted-out parable.

In 6^{30} the word is used in the first sense: 'What then doest thou for a sign, that we may see, and believe thee?'[23] 6^{2} provides another instance in which 'sign' is clearly used as an equivalent for 'miracles', 'outward wonders'. But at 2^{11}, and thenceforward in connexion with the seven signs forming the framework of the central part of the Gospel, the word is employed in John's typical sense of a 'sign' whose inner meaning is known only to faith. As a result of this sign in Chapter 2, we are told (verse 11), 'his disciples believed on him'. Faith has the capacity to pierce through the outward event to its inner meaning, and to discern the glory of the Lord.

There is this further point of interest: though it is true that John avoids the noun *δύναμις*, he employs the corresponding verb in certain instances in a manner conforming to other New Testament writers' use of the noun.[24] In most cases (e.g. 1^{46}, 3^{3ff}, 5^{44}, 6^{44}, etc.) *δύνασθαι* has the meaning, as elsewhere in the New Testament, 'to be possible', or 'to be able'. It is coupled with other verbs almost with the force of an auxiliary, with the meaning 'can'. Grundmann notes, however, the peculiar force *δύνασθαι* has in some Johannine texts. In 3^{2}, for instance, *δύναται* is to be interpreted as equivalent to 'except God be with him'. What is being discussed is the Lord's power, defined as that which He shares with the Father through fellowship and partnership.[25]

The once-blind man in Chapter 9 declares[26] categorically, 'If this man were not from God, he could do (*ἠδύνατο*) nothing' (verse 33).[27] In his allusive manner, John may mean us to gather

[22] E.g. Isa 8^{18}.

[23] Of all the Johannine references, this question connects most directly with the typical use of *σημεῖον* in the Synoptics. In the latter it is not used of 'miracles', but of the confirming evidence, such as the *Bath Qol*, the voice from heaven, expected when Messiah comes.

[24] John seems to dislike nouns like knowledge, faith, wisdom, possibly because of their Gnostic associations, but he makes great play with the corresponding verbs.

[25] Grundmann, *T.W.z.N.T.*, II.304.

[26] An incident providing the Johannine parallel to the Beelzebub controversy.

[27] In 10^{21} the people give the answer to the 'Beelzebub' suggestion: 'Can a devil open the eyes of the blind?' This 'shatters the idea of reducing the power of Jesus to the power of demons' (Grundmann, *T.W.z.N.T.*, II.304).

something from the way in which this cure was effected (verses 6ff). At the time of Jesus, saliva was regarded as a healing agent; but even more importantly Jesus's method of making clay suggests a parallel to the way in which, according to the Genesis narrative, God made men out of the dust. Spittle, as J. A. Findlay reminds us, was regarded as liquid breath.[28] That John is thinking in these allusive terms is confirmed by the reference to the interpretation of 'Siloam'.[29]

In the story of the last great 'sign', before the culmination of His own Death and Resurrection,[30] some of the Jews say about Jesus, 'Could not this man (οὐκ ἐδύνατο οὗτος) which opened the eyes of him that was blind, have caused that this man also should not die?'

5^{19} ('The Son can do nothing (οὐ δύναται ποιεῖν) of himself, but what he seeth the Father doing') stresses the fact of His unity with the Father. The 'can do' is usually taken to refer to the character of the Lord's working, i.e. in complete unity with the Father, rather than to limitations on His power.[31] But if we follow Grundmann's clue regarding the way this verb is used in John, then this becomes a verse in which Christ's power is traced to its origin. Set against the background of the Sabbath controversy, the sign emphasizes who He is who wrought it.[32] God's continuing creative activity is shown in what the Son is doing. He claims that the power to perform this healing comes from God.[33] As Grundmann says: 'His δύνασθαι is fully rooted in God: "I can of myself do nothing" (5^{30}).'[34]

[28] 'The Son can do nothing, except when He sees the Father doing something' (5^{19}; Findlay quotes in his *The Fourth Gospel: Expository Commentary*, 1956, p. 89), 'and here is a case in point . . . the Son is imitating the Father's method of creation; He is not healing old eyes, but making new ones!' Irenaeus (*Adv. Haer.*, 5. 15. 2) and other early writers note the connexion between Jn 9^{6} and Gen 2^{7}.

[29] It meant 'sent', so John tells us—Jesus was the 'One that is sent' (13^{16}, 6^{29}, etc).

[30] In which 'the sign and its meaning coincide' (C. K. Barrett, *The Gospel according to St John*, p. 65).

[31] 'The sole condition on which the Son exercises divine functions is that He acts in complete unity with the Father; a unity which has the form of unqualified obedience to the Father's will. Given such unity, every act which the Son performs is an act of the Father' (C. H. Dodd, *The Interpretation of the Fourth Gospel*, p. 327; cf. LXX of Num 16^{28}, in which Moses asserts the nature of his works: 'I have not done them of myself').

[32] See C. K. Barrett, *The Gospel according to St John, ad loc.*

[33] R. H. Strachan, *The Fourth Gospel, Its Significance and Environment*, p. 169, cites Mt 11^{27}, 'all things have been delivered unto me', as a Synoptic parallel'. W. F. Howard shows that the ἴσον ποιεῖ ἑαυτὸν τῷ θεῷ of 5^{18} corresponds to a rabbinic tag which meant 'to make oneself independent of God' (so Odeberg, Schlatter, and others). His reply, therefore, stressed His dependence and complete unity of purpose with the Father.

[34] *T.W.z.N.T.*, II.304.

We can say then that Jesus did not traffic in signs or portents. The truth is that His miracles were signs for the simple reason that this is how the One who is the Son of God will act in a world like this; and because men can read in them God's meaning.

But even if we grant that this is the Son 'working' as the 'Father worketh' (Jn 5¹⁷) or state that this outbreak of miracle is what was expected in the days of Messiah, we still have to seek after some further explanation of these events in the kind of universe we know. How did the 'power of God' operate in these instances? Must we think of these events as something beyond the scope of all ordinary sequences of cause and effect—as if in some 'uncaused' fashion, miracles 'happened' wherever Jesus went?

The key to these occurrences is in the direction John indicates. They occur, in the first place, because of our Lord's unique nearness to God, and because of His sympathetic understanding of human need and of the corresponding availability of spiritual power. These miracles are 'tokens of the coming of God's Reign in Jesus. They are the Kingdom of God in action—God's sovereign grace and forgiveness operative in Christ.'[35] What enabled them to happen was His direct awareness of God and of spiritual power. There was nothing 'irrational' about them. They follow certain causes and fulfil certain laws. Amongst these contingent circumstances we notice the necessity for 'faith'.[36]

On every occasion when people could contribute faith, our Lord seems to have expected it, or needed it. In the case of lunatics, or the demon-possessed, this could not be forthcoming, and He acted on the strength of His own powers. In the other instances, the contribution of those who were present helped to make the situation a responsive one, in which God's power could flow (cf. Nazareth, where the right atmosphere was missing).[37]

It is important to notice, also, the indications that as a healer Jesus used the medical methods of His time—and some of ours—as far as they would go. Notice, for instance, the questioning

[35] A. M. Hunter, *The Work and Words of Jesus*, 1950, p. 55.

[36] 'The nature of the faith that is the link with power' forms the subject of the last chapter of this book.

[37] Note what we might call the 'Faith stories' of the Gospels, in which the story leads to a statement about 'faith' (e.g. Mt 9²⁰ᶠᶠ; Mk 10⁴⁶ᶠᶠ; Lk 17¹¹ᶠᶠ in which the words 'Thy faith hath made thee whole' occur). Luke's story of the woman who was a sinner, where the healing was of a spiritual order, uses the same phrase, adding the words 'go in peace.' (Lk 7⁵⁰). The story of Mk 9¹⁴⁻²⁷ rings with the keywords 'to believe' and 'to be able' (Büber): *Two Types of Faith* (E.T.), 1951, pp. 17ff. Jesus was concerned to draw attention to the importance of 'faith'.

indicated in the story of the epileptic boy (Mk 9^{14ff}). Contemporary references[38] recounting treatments for paralysis, epilepsy and dumbness, and mentioning the use of saliva in assuaging eye diseases seem to indicate that our Lord used some of the contemporary remedies and methods. There are undoubted parallels in pagan and rabbinic literature to His exorcisms. C. K Barrett. criticizes Alan Richardson for minimizing the significance of these in his book, *The Miracle Stories of the Gospels.* 'In fact,' writes Barrett, 'we are driven to the conclusion that there is hardly anything in the Gospel exorcisms which cannot be paralleled in more or less contemporary pagan or Jewish literature (or in both).'[39]

E. R. Micklem brings to notice much that is valuable relating to this. He adduces instances from the modern mission field affording striking parallels with Gospel accounts of the expulsion of 'demons'. After discussing some of the classic stories of divided personality investigated by modern psychologists, he avers: 'Fundamentally, no doubt, the ancient method is the same as the modern, viz. "suggestion". It makes very little difference for therapeutic purposes whether the patient believes that the demon has left him, so long as he is persuaded and has accepted the "suggestion" that he is free from slavery.'[40]

The significance of these parallels, and the value of comparing the methods of Jesus, so far as we are able, with other methods of healing, both ancient and modern, is that three facts emerge: (1) He did not disdain 'ordinary' methods, but employed what was of value in them; (2) there were elements in His cures transcending the ordinary altogether; and (3) these latter elements are in alignment with what is already known to be healing and helpful—they indicate the reinforcement He is able to bring at this point because of His contact with God in love and power. The incredible swiftness of His cures, and the fact that some of them operated 'at a distance' (Mk 7^{24ff}; Mt 8^{5ff}), removes them from more 'normal' methods, as do the cases transcending ordinary experience altogether, such as the raising of the dead (Mk 5$^{21ff, 35ff}$, 7^{11ff}).

There would be two tendencies at work in the days of the early

38 E.g. Celsus in *De Medicina*, iii, 27, iv. 4, and Galen in *Nat. Facul.*, iii. 7.

39 op. cit., pp. 57f. The significance of the exorcisms of Jesus derives from the context in which they are placed, i.e. of His teaching and the announcement of the Kingdom.

40 *Miracles and the New Psychology*, p. 131.

Church: one to assimilate Jesus to contemporary healers, and the other to assimilate His miracles to His saving power in spiritual experience. The miracles are found in a setting of personal relationship, with trust on the one side and healing power on the other. It is to be noticed how often people beg Jesus to heal them. Bartimaeus breaks through opposition to reach Him. The noticeable instance is that of the woman with the issue of blood, in which the miracle takes place at two levels: first, as a drawing of power from Jesus without His consent, and then as a dealing between Him and the woman. The second tendency comes to prevail over the other in the tradition, though even in the Fourth Gospel both are present. The final result of the process would be the use of Gospel miracles in the form of remarkable parabolic pictures of the healing of the soul.[41]

In each of these tendencies it is possible that tradition has heightened and developed elements that were there from the beginning. The story of the Gadarene swine, as also that of the cursing of the fig-tree, show that the tradition ascribed actions to Jesus which do not seem true to His nature.[42] In each case, He has been assimilated to the wonder-worker of the time. It may be, also, that the healings have been spiritualized. All that we know of Jesus, however, makes it credible that He exercised His powers within a personal relationship rather than quasi-magically.

[41] A. Richardson, quoting R. H. Lightfoot, finds the explanation of the conjunction of the stories in Mk 8^{22-30} in their theological symbolism: the gradualness of the healing in 8^{22-6} corresponding to the slowness and difficulty of the disciples coming to full awareness, and the Blind Man of Bethsaida affording a parallel to Peter and the opening of his eyes at Caesarea Philippi (*The Miracle Stories of the Gospels*, pp. 84ff). Similarly, the picture of Christ calming the sea and walking on the water affords a parallel in other types of experience (ibid., pp. 92f).

[42] They do not conform to Otto's test of self-consistency of personality (*The Kingdom of God and the Son of Man*, p. 333).

CHAPTER THIRTEEN

POWER IN CROSS AND RESURRECTION

IN Jesus, the Messianic hope had been fulfilled, though in ways very different from popular expectation. As the agent and embodiment of the Kingdom, endowed with the Holy Spirit, Jesus is to be seen during His ministry achieving God's purposes, scattering God's enemies and demonstrating His goodness, holiness, justice, and love.

Conscious of His share in the powers of 'the age to come', and of His part in the overthrow of Satan and of the rescue of man from his dominion, Jesus knew that the supreme crisis lay ahead. Not only must He be ready for the ultimate in sacrifice; the time would come when the utmost would be demanded. He came to see that His Death would be the critical point in the conflict. It would be a moment pregnant with altogether new possibilities for the breaking through of the powers of the Kingdom.

So He who acknowledged His mission to be 'servant of all' knew that His service would be fulfilled in 'giving his life a ransom for many' (Mk 10^{45}). By His Death, He would bring the possibility of release from sin and Satan's bondage to all.[1] The references in John to 'laying down his life' (e.g. 10^{11}, 15^{13}) and the story of Gethsemane make clear that this conception of the value and purpose of His Death was dominant in His mind. He spoke of Himself as of a 'grain of wheat': 'Except it fall into the earth and die, it abideth by itself alone; but if it die, it beareth much fruit' (John 12^{24}; note the verses following).

This, then, is the act by which the new era is to be ushered in, and the powers of the Spirit passed to those who 'believe on Him': this totally unexpected laying down of His life in apparent weakness, giving Himself into the hands of His enemies, human and superhuman. At no point is the difference between the concept of power in Old Testament and New so pronounced. Here, in what represents the greatest paradox and surprise of all time, is

[1] In Aramaic, and in Semitic languages generally, there is no expression covering the meaning 'all men': 'for many', therefore, here means 'for all'.

discovered the supreme demonstration of power. By means of the Cross, a way is found of defeating sin in human nature, and, as St Paul would have us understand, bringing the cosmic powers of evil to their overthrow. Resurrection and Ascension complete these great acts of God by which the Gospel is achieved; and after Pentecost this becomes the Good News to which the Apostles witness.

By means of Christ's Death and Resurrection, in Beyschlag's phrase, a principle of victory (a δύναμις σωτηρίας[2]) has been declared. However far men are out of tune and out of touch with God through sin, by this they can be brought back into the life of God (Rom 5–6). This is the 'Gospel' the early Christians discover to be 'the power of God unto salvation' (Rom 1^{16}). 'It is not enough to say that the Gospel treats of God's power', comments Anders Nygren; 'it is itself God's δύναμις. Wherever the Gospel is preached, the power of God is effective unto salvation.'[3] The New Covenant is made clear and possible by God's mighty act in Jesus: the 'Strong One' is routed, and the ἰσχυρότερος is at work destroying Satan's lordship. The proclamation of this message becomes the Church's all-conquering weapon.

In the opening verses of his First Letter to the Corinthians, Paul, who is here defending his methods and message, speaks of the Gospel as δύναμις (1^{18}).[4] More particularly, it is the 'word of the Cross' which Paul, in opposition to the world's dismissal of it as 'foolishness', designates in this way: 'we preach Christ crucified . . . but unto them that are called, both Jews and Greeks, Christ the power of God, and the wisdom of God' (1^{23f}). Though it is Paul who elucidates the strength of the Gospel at this point, it must be remembered that, from the first, men found power in this message of a crucified Lord (Acts 2^{23f}).

In 2 Corinthians 13^4 Paul refers to the paradox at the heart of this gospel: 'he was crucified through weakness';[5] but this suffering voluntarily undergone on our behalf in the way of God's

[2] Quoted, art., 'Power', Hasting's *Dictionary of the Bible*, IV.30n.

[3] *Romans*, p. 66. Sanday and Headlam, *ad loc.*, call attention here to Paul's use of the word δύναμις rather than ἐνέργεια in this famous sentence. The choice stresses God's personal activity in the Gospel: 'it has all God's Omnipotence behind it'.

[4] 'It is the spiritual power of the Gospel rather than its wisdom, that Paul wishes to emphasize. Foolish or not, it does its work' (H. L. Goudge, *Comm. ad loc.*).

[5] But weakness self-assumed, as the ἐκ of this verse makes clear (cf. Jn 10^{17f}, 'I have power to lay it down'). The corresponding ἐκ of the next phrase indicates the ultimate condition of the Power of God, too (J. H. Bernard, *Expositor's Greek Testament*, *ad loc.*).

will issues in uttermost triumph: 'yet he liveth through the power of God'.[6]

Paul speaks in many ways of the power of Christ's Death, and of its results in the life of the believer. By it the sinner is justified, through it he receives adoption into God's family, he is saved, reconciled, redeemed, brought into the life of the second Adam. It has soteriological power: 'Christ died for our sins' (1 Cor 15^{3})—a statement of the Christian *kerygma* which is echoed throughout the New Testament.[7] Our Lord took our sin upon Him, suffered in our stead, trod down the powers of darkness. In Colossians 2^{14f} Paul speaks of Christ by His death on the Cross dealing with the curse of the legal statutes under which all of us are found guilty, and at the same time triumphing over the angelic powers[8] into whose hands He had resigned Himself. His rising again is the signal of that triumph (Phil 2^{10f}).[9] We need to remember that in all these statements Paul was feeling his way, using metaphors and concepts which are not entirely consistent. One thing, however, is clear: he knows for himself the power resident in the Cross, and is finding it also an instrument of power in bringing men to God.

Its power does not reside in any set of ideas concerning it, nor is it reduced in power the further the historical happenings recede in time. Though, as an historical event, it is located at a point of time and space, it demonstrates a pardon and forgiveness that is everywhere and immediately available. Part of its effectiveness lies in the fact that it speaks the language of action: this is the *proof* of God's Love (e.g. Rom 5^{8}).

The moment of the Cross epitomizes man's evil in the rejection of God's Son, and at the same time demonstrates such love and forgiveness as results not in man's damnation, but his salvation. It thus can bring home to men the nature of sin (that men could do

[6] 'Paul sees in this a rule concerning divine power. The power of God hides itself in weakness and defeat and gains its victory therein', W. Grundmann, *Der Beg. der Kraft*, p. 87.

[7] And here, quite characteristically, appealing to the witness of the Scriptures ('according to the scriptures') as indicative of this soteriological principle. No doubt Isa 53 is the basic Scripture in mind.

[8] Who were held to have drawn up the Law (cf. Gal $3^{13, 19}$). Redemption from the Law (cf. Gal 4^{4f}) is given through Christ who overcomes the lordship of the elemental spirits (see Grundmann, ibid., pp. 73f, and the later chapter, 'Principalities and Powers').

[9] See E. Stauffer, *New Testament Theology* (E.T.) p. 287 n. 408, for an illuminating quotation from *Acts of Thomas*, 39. 'Christ', he comments (p. 130), 'is the "Victor" who has beaten down the ancient enemy in the battle of His Passion'.

this to Him!), and at the same time reveal the love of God, concerned to find a way to deal with sin and to bring man to a new frame of mind completely.

Something of the *mysterium tremendum et fascinans* is felt by men looking at Christ's Cross.[10] Before this event the spirit quails.

What we are witnessing is not only a revelation of man's sin and the answering, engulfing Love of God: in the Cross we are also witnessing God's judgement on sin. The Old Testament teaching concerning God's wrath, working remorselessly against whatever is contrary to Him, needs to be borne in mind here. We are, says Paul, 'saved from the wrath through him' (Rom 5^{9}). That fearful process, which is set in motion by God is dealt with by God Himself in Christ!

Texts like Romans 4^{25} and 2 Corinthians 5^{15} remind us that the message of Cross and Resurrection are indissolubly joined. Behind these events is God's one great purpose of salvation. In the Synoptic Gospels it is impressive to note Christ speaking of what lay ahead in a way which, before the events occurred, linked them together. The Christ must suffer, be killed, and after three days rise again (e.g. Mk 8^{31}, 9^{31}, 10^{34}).

The Resurrection is the central fact of Christian evidence and theology. Without it there would be no Church. The gospel came into existence in fullness when Christ was raised from the dead (cf. 1 Cor $15^{14,\ 17}$, etc.). In itself it affords the greatest illustration of the Power of God; it invests all that had preceded it with meaning. The Cross can now be understood as the method by which God revealed His power for the world's salvation (cf. 2 Cor 13^{4}).

The New Testament insistence is that it was God who raised Christ from the dead.[11] The typical statement is in the passive, as at 1 Corinthians 15^{4}, 'hath been raised' (cf. Rom 4^{25}, 8^{4}, etc.), or, as at Acts 3^{15}, etc., Christ is referred to as the One 'who God raised from the dead'.

Some believe that Jesus referred to God's Resurrection power in His answer to the Sadducees in Matthew 22^{29}:[12] 'Ye do err, not

[10] Men have felt something of this before when face to face with the power of God in Jesus: 'Depart from me; for I am a sinful man, O Lord' (Lk 5^{8}).

[11] With this Jn 10^{17} is apparent in contrast: the Johannine statement, however, needs to be offset against its teaching of the complete unity between Father and Son, and the insistence that the Son does all things in obedience to the Father.

[12] E.g. Grundmann, *T.W.z.N.T.*, II.305.

knowing the scriptures, nor the power of God'. It is not certain, however, that this text affords evidence in the way usually understood. C. K. Barrett puts forward an attractive suggestion[13] that the latter part of the sentence refers to the Amidah prayer, the first two Benedictions of which are known as *Aboth* and *Geburoth.* The former addresses God in the style 'God of Abraham, God of Isaac, God of Jacob' (a formula of importance in the context of Mt 22^{29}), and the latter addresses Him as *gibbor le'olam*, and then as *ba'al geburoth.* The 'mighty acts' referred to are His acts of omnipotence in nature, followed by this reference: 'Thou sustainest the living with loving-kindness, quickenest the dead with great mercy, and keepest thy faith to them that sleep in the dust.'[14] The suggestion is that Jesus in His reply would be referring to these benedictions, mentioning the name *geburoth*, which was changed later to the δύναμιν (sing.) of our Gospels by someone not aware of the allusion. What Christ was originally saying, would thus be, in effect, 'You know neither the Bible nor the Prayer Book!' The point, however, still remains, *Geburoth* (the Jewish Prayer Book) witnesses to the power of God to quicken the dead, just as does the reference to God's δύναμις, as usually understood.

The Resurrection of Jesus, mightiest of all the mighty acts of God, is closely linked in New Testament thinking with God's acts in Creation (1 Cor 15^{45}; 2 Cor 5^{17}; 1 Pet 1^{3}, etc.) and, more particularly, with the Exodus and the Red Sea deliverance (1 Cor 10^{1ff}; 1 Pet 1^{18f}, 2^{9}; Heb 13^{20}; cf. Lk 9^{30f}).[15] A. M. Ramsey's book on the Resurrection has a chapter 'According to the Scriptures', in which he quotes the speech in Acts 13^{16-41} as a witness to the unity to be discerned between God's acts in Israel, and His acts in Christ. The God of Israel is a God who 'raises up'. The phrase is of constant occurrence in the Old Testament:

He raised up prophets, judges, the poor, the nation, the fallen tabernacle of David (Amos 9^{11}), a righteous branch (Jer 23^{5}), a shepherd in the land (Zech 11^{16}). . . . The history of Israel is a series of crises wherein in hours of catastrophe God stretches out His arm in judgement and mercy. Finally a day comes when Jesus Christ, identifying

[13] *The Holy Spirit and the Gospel Tradition*, p. 74. He acknowledges his own indebtedness for this suggestion to the late H. M. J. Loewe.

[14] C. K. Barrett quotes Israel Abrahams (*Companion to the Authorized Daily Prayer Book* (IX), for the suggestion that this may have been inserted into the Amidah as a result of disputes between the Pharisees and Sadducees regarding the Resurrection (possibly in the reign of John Hyrcanus 135–104 B.C.).

[15] Doubtless, also, the Return from the Babylonian exile is also in mind.

Himself with Israel, bears the destiny of Israel with Him to the Cross and the grave; and God raises Him, and with Him Israel, from out of death.[16]

The speeches in the first part of Acts witness also to the early Christians' sense of unity with what they are discovering to be implicit in the Old Testament. God has vindicated His Servant, humiliated and crucified by men ($3^{13ff, 26}$, $4^{10f, 27}$, 10^{40}) and life and salvation and forgiveness are to be found through Him. Isaiah 53, and especially verses 4 and 10ff, is discernible behind many of these references. Daniel's 'Son of Man' figure (7^{21f}) suffering eclipse and defeat, followed by vindication and the power to vindicate others, is also clearly in view.[17]

In the phrases of Romans 4^{25} Paul may be quoting 'a snatch of *kerygma* from the pre-Pauline Christian tradition'.[18] If so, it is important as defining the place of the Resurrection in developing theology: 'who was delivered up for our trespasses' (Isa 53 $^{4f, 12}$ again!) referring to the Cross and its annulling of past sin, is balanced by 'and was raised for our justification'. Paul, when thinking of Christ's Death, passes immediately to the thought of His Resurrection and Ascension (Rom 8^{34}: 'It is Christ Jesus that died, yea rather, that was raised from the dead, who is at the right hand of God'). Without doubt, he connects the Resurrection itself with Christ's atoning work. 'It is God that justifieth' he has just announced in the previous verse. In Rom 10^{8f}, again, he seems to be reproducing an apostolic credal formula. It is introduced by the words ἔστιν τὸ ῥῆμα τῆς πίστεως ὃ κηρύσσομεν ('the formula which expresses faith'[19]) 'because if thou shalt confess with thy mouth Jesus (as) Lord, and shalt believe in thy heart that God raised him from the dead, thou shalt be saved'. Deuteronomy 30^{11-14}, just cited by Paul, provides him with 'with thy mouth' and 'in thy heart'; the rest of the statements cover the necessary basic conviction of the believing Christian: that 'Jesus is

[16] *The Resurrection of Christ*, p. 27.

[17] See art., 'From Defendant to Judge—and Deliverer', by C. F. D. Moule, *New Testament Studies*, III.45f: 'When Daniel's Human Figure comes with the clouds to the Divine presence, that means (says the interpretation in the same chapter) that the people of the saints of the Most High are given judgement. The defendant, vindicated at his trial, is discovered to be the judge.'

[18] So A. M. Hunter, *Paul and His Predecessors*, p. 35, who quotes Weiss (*Hist. of Prim. Christianity*, p. 104) as reckoning this verse 'among the doctrinal statements which St Paul derived from the early Church.'

[19] C. A. Scott, *Christianity according to St Paul*, p. 119.

Lord' and that 'God raised Him from the dead'.[20] By this, says Paul, you come to salvation.[21]

Romans 1[3f] show signs of this formulary character also,[22] and 2 Timothy 2[8] echoes the same kind of statement, in which Christ's earthly life (as the Messiah, 'of the seed of David') and His being raised by God ('risen from the dead') are referred to as the two focal points of Christian belief. H. Windisch, in an article on 'The Christology of the Pastoral Letters',[23] discusses this doctrine of the two existences under which we have known Christ. He declares that the addition of the two phrases, 'according to the flesh' and 'according to the spirit' in Romans 1[3ff] and the use of the verbs γενομένου and ὁρισθέντος decisively underline this doctrine. These verses should certainly be approached with this clue in mind.[24] We are thus helped to place the reference to 'with power' in this much-disputed text. Sanday and Headlam's suggestion that it should be coupled adverbially with ὁρισθέντος (the Resurrection then being referred to, as at 2 Cor 13[4], etc. as a signal manifestation of Divine Power) does not seem adequate.[25] Though He was 'declared' to be Son of God by 'the resurrection of the dead', yet Paul (Rom 8[3, 32]; 1 Cor 10[4]; 2 Cor 8[9], etc.) knows that this He has been all the time. In the first phase, however, 'according to the flesh', He has known weakness and humiliation. Now, with the Resurrection, a new era has been ushered in. In this phase, 'according to the spirit', He is known to be the Son of God

[20] A. M. Hunter, ibid., pp. 31ff, who quotes Bousset (*Kyrios Christos*, p. 102) for the statement, 'The formula "Believe in the God who raised Christ from the dead" may have been a piece of tradition when he got it'. The recurrence of this phrase, already noted, e.g. in Rom 4[25], 8[1]; 2 Cor 4[14]; Gal 1[1]; 1 Pet 1[21], helps to confirm this impression.

[21] 'Without the resurrection the work of Christ is not finished, and salvation-history does not reach its goal' (E. Stauffer, *New Testament Theology*, pp. 136f).

[22] Bultmann, indeed, in his *Theology of the New Testament*, I.49, suggests that Paul desires by his use of this handed-down formula to 'accredit himself to the unknown Roman Church as an apostle who advocates right doctrine'.

[23] *Zeitschrift für die neutestamentliche Wissenschaft*, 34 (1935), pp. 213ff.

[24] A. M. Hunter, *Paul and His Predecessors*, pp. 26f (he is following a suggestion from T. W. Manson) suggests an acceptance of Rom 1[3ff] as found in the Peshitta. The Syriac yields the following: 'concerning this Son: who was born according to the flesh of the seed of David's house; and made known as Son of God with power and holy spirit; who rose from the house of the dead, even Jesus Christ our Lord'. This triadic arrangement of the clauses avoids the adoptionist flavour of the text as we have it, or at least puts this back, past the Resurrection, to the Baptism. The balancing phrases κατὰ σάρκα and κατὰ πνεῦμα and the two participles do not, however, suggest an original triadic form. We would think that here the Peshitta is endeavouring to improve on Paul.

[25] *Romans* (*International Critical Commentary*), p. 9.

'with power'. Elliptically, of course, this phrase spreads over the whole of verse 4. The central point, however, is that Christ in tasting death for every man has defeated death. God's power, in Him, has won a complete victory over everything in Satan's dominion. This is the full sign of the arrival of the new age. To Christ, therefore, at His Resurrection (as in Phil 2^{9ff}) there has come 'a great accession of glory and power. He is from henceforth Jesus Christ, *our Lord*, bearing the name that is above every name.'[26]

All this is made clear in Romans 5^{21}, 'that, as sin reigned in death, even so might grace reign through righteousness unto eternal life through Jesus Christ our Lord'. Anders Nygren declares that Chapter 5 of Romans[27] distinguishes between two realms in opposition to each other: (1) the kingdom of death (cf. 'death reigned' of verses 14, 17, 21), the 'age of Adam', and (2) the kingdom of life (cf. 'reign in life' of verse 17), the 'age of Christ'.[28] 'In the old aeon, which began with Adam, death rules with unlimited power over all the children of Adam. In the new aeon, which burst upon man with the resurrection of Christ, life has come to dominion still more mightily.'[29]

Behind Hebrews 2^{14} (cf. 1 Cor 15^{26}) there lies this same conception of the two aeons, and of Christ's own tasting of death 'that through death he might bring to nought him that hath the power of death, that is, the devil; and might deliver them who through fear of death were all their lifetime subject to bondage'. Death is the supreme point of Satan's lordship. By Christ becoming Himself subject to death, the very crux of Satan's power became the point of his defeat.

Acts 2^{23f} affords an early witness to this circle of ideas.[30] Jesus 'being delivered up by the determinate counsel and foreknowledge of God, ye by the hand of lawless men [i.e. Gentiles] did crucify and slay: whom God raised up, having loosed the pangs of death; because it was not possible that he should be holden of it'.

[26] C. A. Scott, *Abingdon Bible Commentary*, p. 1138.

[27] I.e. from verse 12: 'The high-point of the Epistle, in the light of which the whole is best to be understood' (*Romans*, p. 20).

[28] Col 1^{13f}. It is through Christ's victory that we have been redeemed and take our place in the new era, delivered now out of Satan's sphere of power (ἐξουσία).

[29] Nygren, ibid., p. 23.

[30] Which, indeed, is also to be observed in Zachariah's Song in Luke's Gospel ($1^{68f, 79}$).

Peter is saying that it was impossible that death could assert its lordship over Christ. Also through Christ, the 'pangs of death'[31] are 'loosed'. Its might—by which the scriptures mean also, Satan's might[32]—is broken. 'He had his life from the power of God. As God's power had fitted him for his deeds of power, so also for the *new life*. That is now the apostolic testimony concerning his Resurrection.'[33]

Christ, as the leader of the new race, forerunner of the new era, in whom all is made possible, offers the resurrection life to all who will share in it. He is the 'second Adam' (Rom 5^{14}; 1 Cor $15^{45, 47}$) 'For since by man (came) death, by man (came) also the resurrection of the dead. For as in Adam all die, so also in Christ shall all be made alive'. (1 Cor 15^{24}). The 'new creation' of 2 Corinthians 5^{17} becomes possible 'in Christ'. The passage in Romans 6 in which St Paul speaks of the significance of baptism makes clear that, through the believer's identification with Christ's Death and Rising Again, it is possible to 'die to sin' and rise again, with Him, to newness of life (verses 3–14). 1 Corinthians 6^{14} echoes the same thought as Romans 6^{4}: 'God both raised the Lord, and will raise up us through his power.' God's power[34] is to be seen, supremely, at work in raising Christ from the dead (cf. Eph 1^{19ff}) and then in raising us up in Him (cf. Rom 4^{17-24}; Acts 26^{8}; 2 Cor 4^{14}, etc.).

Consideration of the nature of our part in the life of the new era introduces the whole question of the 'power' available to the Christian. It has to do with the tension of the eschatological situation revealed in the New Testament. The new era is here in Christ, ushered in with power at His Resurrection, and assured by the fact of His Ascension and of His reign 'at the right hand of God'. In the life that now is we already partake of it. Yet the Christian is still subject to the onslaught of evil, living in a world in which sin seems largely undefeated. Though invited to share in the 'resurrection life', the fact of which he is most sure is that bodily death awaits him at the end of his course here.[35] 1 Corinthians 15^{24ff} seems to envisage a programme by which Christ's

[31] ὠδῖνες θανατοῦ; cf. LXX, Ps 17^{5} (18^{4}), 114^{3} (116^{3}).

[32] 'Satan, the impulse to evil, and the angel of death are identical' (Rabbi Simeon ben Lakish), (*Baba Batra*, 16a: Moore, *Judaism*, I.492).

[33] W. Grundmann, *T.W.z.N.T.*, II.305.

[34] The word is δόξα, not δύναμις, in the parallel to 1 Cor 6^{14} in Rom 6^{4}; see Bultmann, *Theology of the New Testament*, I.156.

[35] Cf. Cullmann, *The Early Church*, p. 165.

lordship is progressively asserted.[36] 1 Peter 1^{3ff} speaks of the way God 'begat us again into a living hope by the resurrection of Jesus Christ from the dead'. This 'inheritance, incorruptible, and undefiled, and that fadeth not away' is 'reserved in heaven for you, who by the power of God are guarded through faith into a salvation ready to be revealed in the last time'. Christians are living 'in the power of God'.[37] The fullness of their destiny lies still in the future (cf. Rom 8^{24f}.; Col $1^{5, 23}$, 2 Tim 4^{8}). Christ Himself has vanquished Death and Satan, in His Resurrection, but only at the Parousia will His lordship conclusively and finally be manifested (2 Thess 1^{7ff}).[38]

In this intervening period of tension the earnest (ἀρραβών) of the Spirit has been granted to us, Paul declares in 2 Corinthians 5^{5} (cf. 2 Cor 1^{22}; Rom 8^{16}; Eph 1^{14}). 'But if the Spirit of him that raised up Jesus from the dead dwelleth in you he that raised up Christ Jesus from the dead shall quicken also your mortal bodies through his Spirit that dwelleth in you' (Rom 8^{11}). Thus we, who have the 'first fruits of the Spirit', wait in hope for 'the redemption of our body' (Rom 8^{23}). So the body 'sown in weakness', 'is raised in power'; and it is raised as a 'spiritual body', fitted for the full life awaiting it (1 Cor 15^{43f}).[39] In the meanwhile, the Spirit renews our inward man day by day (2 Cor 4^{16}; Eph 3^{16}) and, though we have to wait for the time when our carnal bodies shall be changed into spiritual bodies, yet, the Spirit as the force overcoming death is already at work repelling death, in the realm of the 'flesh'.[40]

It is therefore in the light of the Resurrection that Christianity understands all else concerning its faith. The early believers thought, felt and acted from the standpoint it provided. Their

[36] Cf. Schweitzer, *The Mysticism of St Paul*, p. 313: 'Paul pictures the glory of the Messianic Kingdom not as repose, but action. The whole period of the Messiah's reign is filled by a succession of victories over the God-opposing powers. In the moment when, by defeating the last of these enemies, death, he has brought all things into subjection to Himself, He will deliver up the rule to His Father, and thereby put an end to the Messianic Kingdom.'

[37] Cf. Ignatius, *Ep. to Eph.* 11.

[38] W. Grundmann, *Der Begriff der Kraft*, pp. 78ff.

[39] Cf. Phil 3^{21}. Our present mortal body will become like Christ's 'body of glory', through the active, divine energy to which all things (all earthly authority, enemies, power, death—everything!) are subject. This power of Christ, as J. J. Müller (*Epistles of Paul to the Philippians and to Philemon*, London, 1955, pp. 134f) says, is 'the guarantee that He is able to make our body of lowliness like unto His body of glory'.

[40] All disease, as Oscar Cullmann reminds us, is but a 'particular form of death'. This recedes before the Spirit (see *The Early Church*, pp. 165f).

lives were a constant communion, in new degree and after a different order, with Him whom once they had known in bodily form and in whose spiritual presence they now rejoiced (Mt 28[20]). He, now exalted and 'raised to God's right hand', furnishes the point from which they set out to explore and interpret everything. It must be remembered that their records of His Life and Ministry are written from this starting-point.

'The gospel preached by Jesus' came to be merged completely in the Gospel that *is* Jesus: this is what the Apostles proclaim. It is still the Gospel of God (Rom 1[1]; 2 Cor 4[4]). It is still the Gospel of the Kingdom (Acts, *passim*). But its content is Jesus. The striking phrase 'to gospel Jesus' appears (Acts 5[42], 8[35], 11[20]). They preach His Life, Death, Resurrection, and gift of the Spirit, for all this constitutes the drama of the mighty acts of God who came to deliver and to reign.[41]

The life of the new aeon, the 'Resurrection-life', is, in other words, a life in fellowship with Him whom God raised up in power.[42] Thus it is that the phrase ἐν χριστῷ becomes regulative for St Paul[43] Christ is the context of the Christian's life. Bultmann sees in the phrase 'in Christ' no mystical formula, but a reference to the quality and whole historical life of the believer as Christ-determined. 'To live in Christ', he says, means the same thing as 'to live as a Christian'.[44] The Pauline usage is, however, something different from this. We would follow Deissmann in his classical treatment of this phrase which he conceives as 'the peculiarly Pauline expression of the most intimate possible fellowship

[41] A. M. Ramsey, op. cit., p. 10. On pp. 15f the author writes of the way in which John in the Fourth Gospel merges into a unity the fact of the Jesus, 'according to the flesh' and the living Jesus whom they now know, 'according to the spirit'. The theme of *Life*, which runs through the Gospel, binds Ministry, Passion, Resurrection, the Gift and Coming of the Paraclete into one message of the Lord bringing Life in place of Death—the death of the body and the death of sin.

[42] Cf. Schweitzer, *The Mysticism of Paul*, p. 3: 'The fundamental thought of Pauline mysticism runs thus: I am in Christ, in Him I know myself as a being who is raised above this sensuous, sinful and transient world and already belongs to the transcendent; in Him I am assured of resurrection; in Him I am a child of God.'

[43] The phrase in this form occurs twenty-nine times in the Pauline Epistles (not counting 'in the Christ', Eph 1[10, 12, 20]). 'In Christ Jesus' is even more common, occurring thirty-two times. 'In the Lord' is found twenty-four times, 'in the Lord Jesus' thrice, and, 'in the name of the Lord Jesus' twice.

[44] *Theology of the New Testament*, I.311, 328f. In his *Primitive Christianity* Bultmann declares that it is a Gnostic cosmic conception, with an ecclesiastical application, and at the same time an eschatological formula, 'since with the establishment of the body of Christ the eschatological event has been inaugurated' (p. 197). Bultmann will not accept it as offering mystical interpretation.

of the Christian with the spiritual Christ'.[45] Speaking of this spiritual relationship in which the Christian dwells, Deissmann also says that 'the living Christ is the Pneuma' (e.g. 2 Cor 3^{17}; 1 Cor 15^{45}, 6^{7}). He notes the parallel use of the mystical formula 'in Christ' and 'in the (Holy) Spirit'. His comment is that 'it always refers to the same experience, whether Paul says that Christ lives in Him (Gal 2^{20}) or that the Spirit dwells in us (Rom 8^{9}), and whether he speaks of Christ making intercession for us with the Father (Rom 8^{34f}) or of the Spirit who helps in prayer (Rom 8^{26ff})'. W. H. P. Hatch expresses it in this way: the 'pneumatic' Christ is the atmosphere or element in which the believer lives: 'It can also be said that Christ, or the Spirit, or even God dwells in the Christian'[46] (e.g. Christ: Rom 8^{10}; the Spirit: Rom $8^{9, 11}$ adjacent verses to the former! 1 Cor 3^{16}, 6^{19}; God: 1 Cor 14^{25}; 2 Cor 6^{16}). Nor must the eschatological and social character of this experience be omitted from the picture: to be ἐν χριστῷ is to share in His new community—to become part of the new Israel of God.[47] 'To be "in Christ" ', declares John Knox, in his *Chapters in a Life of Paul*, 'is to be a member of the ultimate eschatological order, the divine community of love, proleptically present and partially realized in the Church, whose spirit is the very Spirit of God and the very presence of the risen Christ.'[48]

In developing his picture of the Melchizedek priesthood of Jesus, the writer to the Hebrews speaks of the 'power of an endless life'. This is the power now in Christ, conquering all transitoriness and destruction.[49] It is not surprising, then, that in the statement

[45] *Paul*, p. 140. He vividly portrays (p. 178) the 'old man', the pre-Damascus Paul, languishing in the dark prison enclosed by the many walls of the seven spheres of evil, 'in' the flesh, 'in' sins, 'in' Adam, 'in' his overhanging fate of death, 'in' the world, 'in' sufferings. The 'new man' (cf. 2 Cor 5^{17}) lives and works 'in' Christ within the sphere of light and holiness, into which all those dark terrors cannot reach.

[46] W. H. P. Hatch, *The Pauline Idea of Faith* (Harvard, 1917), pp. 39, 41.

[47] Recent interpretation has stressed this aspect of the 'being in Christ'. W. D. Davies, for example, says that this social interpretation of the phrase is clearly shown in such a passage as 1 Cor 12^{12} (*Paul and Rabbinic Judaism*, p. 86). He quotes C. H. Dodd (*Romans*, pp. 86f), R. N. Flew (*Jesus and His Church*, pp. 212f), and C. A. Scott (*Christianity according to St Paul*, pp. 151f) in support of the view that the phrase represents a social concept first of all. See also Oepke *T.W.z.N.T.*, II.538, and E. Best, *One Body in Christ*, pp. 19–30. C. Ryder Smith (*The Bible Doctrine of Grace* (London, 1956) will have none of this: 'There is no scriptural warrant', he says, 'for claiming that "in Christ" means "in the body of Christ" or "in the Church of Christ" ' (p. 210).

[48] op. cit., p. 158.

[49] Grundmann, *T.W.z.N.T.*, II.306. The contrast is with 'the law of a carnal commandment' (and, as Bultmann points out, the antithesis is not formed by means of the concept πνευματικὸς, but of δύναμις—so often synonymous: *Theology of the New Testament*, I.156).

of 1 Corinthians 1^{24}, writing of the Gospel achieved and liberated in Him, Paul sees focused in Christ the 'power' and the 'wisdom of God'. In Him God has acted in the fullness of His power and wisdom. Sin, death, and evil are overthrown. Just as surely as it could be said of the Kingdom that, in Christ, it is *αὐτοβασιλεία*, so Christ, as the subject and the content of the gospel, is Himself 'the power of God' (1 Cor 1^{24}).

CHAPTER FOURTEEN

APOSTOLIC POWER

THE Lord's Death and Resurrection represent the great watershed of the New Testament. By all that happened then, the disciples were made supremely conscious of God's Love and Power, and, on the inner side of life, the forces of sin and death were overwhelmed and defeated. The impetus of the movement by which this 'Gospel', 'the power of God unto salvation', spread throughout the world was at first concentrated in the little group who had gathered around Jesus. They were, in the primary and obvious sense, 'witnesses' of these things. They became witnesses in a still deeper way, knowing the power of these events in their own experience, and becoming conscious that the Spirit that had been incarnate in Jesus was now 'shed abroad' in them. This stage in the story is of immense importance. It concerns the way that Jesus, the embodiment of the Kingdom of God, and the bearer of power, equipped His disciples by the gift of the Spirit as effective preachers and witnesses to the message that was in Him and His gospel.[1]

In his Gospel, Luke, like the other Evangelists, gives many indications of the disciples' role during the days of the Ministry. As if in anticipation of what is to come, he sometimes calls these men 'Apostles'[2] (e.g. Lk 17^{5}, 22^{14}, 24^{10}) while referring to them in

[1] 'The message given by Jesus Christ was itself the message about Jesus Christ. The definitive content of the preaching of the primitive Church was not a gospel of the love of God and the love of one's neighbour (thus Harnack), and not simply a gospel of the holy God who condescended to sinners (thus Holl), but the gospel of the Christ-event' (E. Stauffer, *New Testament Theology*, p. 158).

[2] A. M. Farrer (*Apostolic Ministry*, p. 124) tells us that 'if we look to the New Testament itself, we see presently that ἀπόστολος is a function-word rather than a traditional title: it suggests to ἀποστέλλεσθαι, the being commissioned or sent, and it is on the verb rather than the noun that we should concentrate.' J. B. Lightfoot (*Galatians*, pp. 92ff) discusses the term, and notes its antecedents in Hebrew. In later Judaism itself, the term was used to cover the authorized representatives from Jerusalem to the Jews of the Dispersion. Dom Gregory Dix gives illustrations of this (*Apostolic Ministry*, p. 229) and concludes: 'It was, therefore, a well-known Jewish institution of which our Lord made use in the foundation of the Church.' An Apostle, says Rengstorf (art., ἀποστέλλω *T.W.z.N.T.*, I.422), is one who is 'validly commissioned with the representation of the person and case of another party'. Note the Rabbinic adage, cited no less than nine times in the Talmud, 'A man's *shaliach* is, as it were, the man himself' (or 'like himself'),

adjacent passages as 'the disciples', 'the Twelve' or 'the Eleven' (e.g. 17^{22}, 18^{31}, 22^{47}, 24^{9}). His other references conform to what is Mark's and Matthew's almost invariable usage. During the Ministry they are rightly described as 'disciples', learning from the Lord. Only when sent on mission are they legitimately designated 'Apostles'.[3] They are then the Lord's *shelichim*,[4] receiving from Him power and authority to do the two things distinctive of His ministry: to preach and heal.[5] After the Resurrection, having become His *shelichim* indeed, empowered by the same Spirit that came upon Him at His Baptism, they carry forward His work, as 'witnesses' and 'Apostles', 'in His Name'.

From such indications as Mark 9^{18} we notice that the power to work the works of their Master was not always with them in the days of their discipleship. They were part of the 'faithless generation' with which He had to bear (9^{19}). The events of the Passion and of Pentecost had to happen before these men were able to venture boldly and successfully on their own into the fields open to faith.

The risen Jesus of Matthew 28^{18ff},[6] to whom 'all authority hath been given . . . in heaven and on earth', commands them: 'Go ye therefore, and make disciples of all the nations'. The 'therefore' (*οὖν*) of verse 19 must not be overlooked. It stresses that it is the risen Christ, with dominion over all things, who commissions them, with every right so to do. It also links the fact of His universal authority with the universal nature of the mission now to be theirs.

In the Fourth Gospel, which repeatedly emphasizes the 'sending' of the Son by the Father, Jesus, after the Resurrection, sends out His disciples. Recipients of the Spirit,[7] they now possess the

Ap. Min., p. 229. Dix, in *Jew and Greek: a Study in the Primitive Church*, believes that the idea of the *shaliach*, the 'man sent', ultimately derives, as do so many Biblical terms and conceptions, from Persia. 'Only the "man sent" from the court of the Great King at Susa could override the authority of the local Persian satrap' (ibid., p. 8).

[3] Note again the full force of Mk 3^{14}. They are first 'to be with Him' in order that they might be sent out.

[4] N. Geldenhuys, *Supreme Authority*, 1953, p. 56.

[5] The parallel mission of the 70 in Lk 10 is instructive also in that the successful missioners report, 'Lord, even the devils are subject unto us in thy name.' All is accomplished 'in His Name'.

[6] See G. R. Beasley-Murray, *Baptism in the New Testament*, 1962, pp. 77–92, for arguments upholding the authenticity of this passage.

[7] Breathed into them as God breathed the breath of life into Adam (R. H. Lightfoot, *St. John's Gospel: a Commentary*, p. 333). The hour has now come when the Spirit can be given to the disciples (cf. 7^{39}).

'authority' to forgive sins (Jn 20^{21ff}). All that happens hereafter is a fulfilment of the Lord's promises in John 14–16. They possess the power to witness: their understanding of all that He was, said, and did is deepened and extended. The 'Spirit of Christian Paraclesis'[8] is upon them.

The opening verses of Acts, similarly, indicate that a new chapter is now beginning. 'The former treatise' concerned 'all that Jesus began both to do and to teach,[9] until the day in which he was received up, after he had given commandment through the Holy Spirit unto the apostles' (their title from the very first in Acts) 'whom he had chosen . . . speaking the things concerning the kingdom of God'. These verses suggest further, and final, preparation of the Apostles during the period between the Resurrection and Ascension, and a commissioning similar to the insufflation in John 20^{22}, 'through the Holy Spirit'.[10] This latter phrase, used in verse 2, seems like the announcement of a new dispensation. This is certainly what it is. A new era is about to dawn. As these men listen to their Risen Lord, they know they are in contact with 'the powers of the world to come'. We can imagine that the Lord had vividly in mind the parallel between His own baptism, when the Spirit descended upon Him with power, and the baptism of the Spirit now about to impinge upon His infant community.[11]

By the actual happening at Pentecost, the coming of the Spirit is afforded a definite historical setting.[12] In the recollection of the primitive Church, it was this that marked the beginning of the

[8] C. K. Barrett, in an article on 'The Holy Spirit in the Fourth Gospel' (*J.T.S.*, April 1950), notes the connexion between Paraclete and παρακαλέω and παράκλησις. He does not favour the customary interpretation of this description of the Spirit as either advocate or intercessor (a Pauline rather than a Johannine conception). He thinks instead of 'the Spirit of Christian Paraclesis', who takes 'the things of Christ' and declares them to the Church. (What this means, says Barrett, may be noted from Jn 2^{22}, 12^{16}. It is a kind of *midrash* on Jesus' life, interpreted in terms of the Old Testament.) The equivalent expression, 'Spirit of Truth', confirms this interpretation. Barrett instances 2 Cor 4^{2} for an illustration of how ,both in Jewish and early Christian literature, 'truth' is used as a synonym for missionary proclamation.

[9] The same two notes again: the teaching (preaching) and the doing (healing, etc.).

[10] H. B. Swete (*The Holy Spirit in the New Testament*, p. 68) points out that the position of διὰ πνεύματος ἁγίου between τοῖς ἀποστόλοις and οὓς ἐξελέξατο has led some interpreters to connect the words with ἐξελεξατο rather than with ἐντειλάμενος. 'But, as Blass says, this is all but impossible.'

[11] Acts 1^{5}; Lk 24^{48}; H. B. Swete, ibid., p. 65.

[12] 'The doctrine of the Spirit thus becomes more than a theological influence from the character of God or of Christ, and does not remain a mere hope derived from the utterances of Scripture or of Jesus' (A. Schlatter, art., 'Holy Spirit', *Dictionary of the Apostolic Church*, I.574a).

new era.[13] H. B. Swete speaks of the Pentecostal outpouring as—

the advent of the Spirit, as the Incarnation was the advent of the Son. Not as though either the Son or the Spirit had been absent from the world before the Advent. Each coming was the new manifestation, and the beginning of a new mission. '*God sent forth His Son*', and when the mission of the Son had been fulfilled, '*He sent forth the Spirit of His Son*' to take up the work under new conditions.[14]

The physical accompaniments mentioned in the Pentecostal story need not concern us overmuch. They represent an attempt to describe the indescribable.[15] What *is* impressive is the immediate change in this group of men from powerlessness and fear to effectiveness and courage. Whatever we are able to understand by the phenomena of speaking 'with other tongues',[16] it is plain that, on this occasion, there was ready communication as from one mind to another.[17]

Peter, in quoting from Joel's prophecy (Joel 2^{28ff}) speaks for all in the apostolic group. They realize that the fullness of the Messianic times has come. This is the dawn of the promised era.[18] It is to be noted that the Spirit is to be poured out 'upon all flesh'. It is available universally now, in Christ's name. In verse 22 Peter speaks of Jesus of Nazareth as 'a man approved of God unto you

[13] There is no doubt, says W. L. Knox (*Acts of the Apostles*, p. 81), that the story of Acts 2 has been coloured by the belief that the coming of the Holy Ghost represented a new era in the history of the world. He goes on to suggest that the original story of Pentecost was a proclamation of the new Torah to the proselytes of the world (see p. 84).

[14] Gal $4^{4, 6}$. See H. B. Swete, ibid., p. 79.

[15] Cf. Lk's ὥσπερ and ὡσεὶ in Acts 2^{2f}.

[16] The problem is complicated by the phenomena of glossolalia of which we learn in 1 Cor 14^{2ff}, etc. There is nothing to suggest in Acts 2 that the listeners heard a flow of unintelligible sounds. The reverse is true. They understood perfectly 'as if in their own language'.

[17] Para-psychology may, perhaps, yield analogies here, e.g., of 'telepathic communication' in moments of great mental illumination or emotional stress. On another level, it is plain that there is implicit in the story, as it is told, a parallel to the event commemorated at Pentecost—the giving of the Law at Sinai. See art., 'Pentecost', *Dictionary of the Apostolic Church*, p. 1,626, and A. Schlatter, *Church in the New Testament Period* (E.T., London, 1955), p. 20. Jerome (*Ad Fabiolom*, §7) has a vivid passage showing the close analogy between the Jewish and Christian Pentecost. The event, too, is to be understood as a complete reversal of what happened at Babel (see F. F. Bruce, *The Book of the Acts*, p. 64).

[18] ἐν ταῖς ἐσχάταις ἡμέραις is not actually in the Old Testament of Joel 2^{28} either in MT or LXX. LXX has μετὰ ταῦτα, The phrase may be a conflation from Isa 2^{2} or Mic 4^{1}, expressing what is understood, in the apostolic era, to be the sense of μετὰ ταῦτα. There are other variations to be noted in the text of this passage (see, e.g., footnote 47, p. 68, F. F. Bruce, *The Book of Acts*). The 'last days', in any case, expand in Luke's conception to the era of the Church. See H. Conzelmann, *The Theology of St Luke*, p. 95.

by mighty works (*δυνάμεις*) and wonders and signs which God did by him in the midst of you'.[19] Because of these signs, showing that in Him the Messianic Age had come, He is thus known to be 'authorized' (*ἀποδεδειγμένον*) by God. The Apostle refers to Christ's Crucifixion—happening with God's foreknowledge and consent—and to His Resurrection. All this is attested by Old Testament citations, in accordance with what comes to be the typical statement of the *kerygma*. In verse 32 rings the note of witness: 'This Jesus did God raise up, whereof we are witnesses.' The next verse refers to His exaltation,[20] finding here the final explanation of this prophetic outpouring of the Spirit: 'Being therefore by the right hand of God exalted, and having received of the Father the promise of the Holy Spirit he hath poured forth this, which ye see and hear'. According to their view, the possession of the Spirit by the community of Christians is direct evidence of the Lord's Messiahship and special relation to God,[21] and the spirit of prophecy the Apostles now know is proof to themselves of their share in the Messianic endowment. Joel's words are fulfilled in their own experience.

The process began immediately by which, as Jesus had promised, the Spirit would lead them increasingly into the understanding and power of the message entrusted to them. On the day of Pentecost, in explanation of what had happened to them, they were forced to refer to Christ's Death and Resurrection. As Peter spoke, he discovered he was preaching a Gospel! His reference to the people's share in Christ's Death, and the announcement of God's vindication of His Servant, reached them in such a way as to 'convict them of sin and righteousness and judgement'. 'What shall we do?' they cried. Peter told them that repentance and baptism in Christ's name could lead them into the

[19] These words of verse 22, says Guignebert (*Jesus*, p. 295), constitute 'the exact definition of a prophet'. The prophet, 'like-unto-Moses' is here; cf. Lk 11^{30}; Heb 6^{5}. Added to Luke's typical word, *δύναμις*, here used in the plural and by its very nature pointing to the divine character of the power manifested in it, we have the phrase, *τέρατα καὶ σημεῖα*, which occurs no less than nine times in the first part of Acts ($2^{19, 22, 43}$, 4^{30}, 5^{12}, 6^{2}, 7^{36}, 14^{3}, 15^{2}). This latter is a common Old Testament phrase describing miracles, and is found in this form in the LXX.

[20] The faith of the primitive Church turned far more on the Resurrection-exaltation of Jesus than it did upon His Passion. These men lived amid the aura cast by the Resurrection. It was an event shattering in its implications, and these men had lived through the period when it had actually broken upon them. It was the centre of apostolic preaching, e.g. here 2^{22ff}, and 5^{29ff} and (Paul) 17^{31}, 23^{6ff}, 26^{1ff}.

[21] In these early days this provided the cardinal proof of the Lord's Messiahship. See here, in Acts $2^{33, 36}$ and 5^{31f} (G. W. H. Lampe, *The Seal of the Spirit*, p. 49).

same experience of invasion by the Spirit. They, too, could share in the power of the new era.

So the Apostles preach Christ (Acts $8^{5,\ 35}$) and by their 'many wonders and signs' (2^{43})[22] afford indisputable evidence, like their Lord, not only of their compassion and faith, but also of their authority and power in the spiritual sphere.[23]

One of the items to notice is that this invasion by the Spirit did not involve supersession of the Apostles' natural faculties. They acted like men 'empowered', but not 'possessed'.[24] The phenomena affecting the apostolic community, both on the day of Pentecost and thereafter, belong to the realm of the supernormal rather than the abnormal. 'The closing verses of the second chapter of the Acts', as H. B. Swete comments, 'with their picture of the simple, joyful, strenuous life of the newly baptized in the days that followed Pentecost, reveal even more than the miracles of Pentecost itself the nature of the Power which had come to dwell with the Church.'[25]

Apostolic teaching and preaching did not depend upon frenzy or ecstasy. The opposite is true. 'Filled with the Holy Ghost', Peter can state his case in such a way that the rulers marvel (Acts 4^{13}). Later in Chapter 4 we are told how, after the Apostles had regained 'their own company', following a time of prayer, something of a second Pentecost came upon all, 'and they spake the word of God with boldness' (verse 31). This 'boldness' is an impressive note in apostolic preaching (cf. 4^{13}). The witness to the facts concerning Jesus is given in a spirit of complete confidence. There is no theorizing or speculating. Jesus is proclaimed 'with unique assurance' as Christ and Lord, the Son of God.[26]

Chapter 3 of Acts records the first miracle done by the Apostles.

[22] Just as in Luke's phrase in Acts 1^1, Jesus' ministry could be summed up in the words, 'all that Jesus began *to do* and *to teach*', so the Apostles, too, 'had still to make the Kingdom of God known by words and by deeds' (Hort, *The Christian Ecclesia*, p. 40).

[23] By means of these signs, which belong 'to the essence of things, the messenger himself, has and supplies the proof that he really is Jesus' deputy and represents him' (Rengstorf, *T.W.z.N.T.*, I.430).

[24] A. Schlatter (*The Church in the New Testament Period*, p. 16) points out that even the Jews in Palestine were subject to the influence of Hellenistic religious ideas. There was always a danger of 'seeking the manifestation of the Spirit in states of religious ecstasy, of seeking the activity of God in the suppression of consciousness and the fettering of the will under the stress of overpowering emotions. . . . The disciples learnt that their personal consciousness, so far from being suspended by the operation of the Spirit, was actually sanctified and perfected.'

[25] Ibid., p. 80.

[26] Norval Geldenhuys, *Supreme Authority*, p. 81.

It happened, as is evident, without premeditation. Face to face with a man in need, Peter acts as he knows his Lord would have acted in similar circumstances. All that occurs is to be understood in terms of the Lord—happening because of Him, in awareness of His spiritual presence, and in the assurance of the availability of the same power He knew in the days of His ministry. 3^{6} is to be noted: 'In the name of Jesus Christ of Nazareth, walk.' The explanation of what happened, as the overloaded text of 3^{16} makes clear, is 'by faith in his name'—faith that touches the deeps and the powers that His Name represents,[27] faith that is exercized in His way and because of Him, used in His Spirit. It is in direct touch with the living power of God. It is the kind of faith He looked for and encouraged. His work is clearly being continued in His men.[28]

4^{24} includes an interesting reference, in the Western text, to the 'energy of God'. The released Apostles report to 'their own company': *οἱ δε ἀκούσαντες (καὶ ἐπιγνόντες τὴν τοῦ θεοῦ ἐνέργειαν D) ὁμοθυμαδὸν ἦραν φωνὴν*. . . . And in the (second?) Pentecostal summary in verse 33 it is stated: 'And with great power gave the apostles their witness of the resurrection of the Lord Jesus'. By the 'power of God manifested in mighty works' (F. F. Bruce), the Apostles went on giving this testimony.

The list of the actual 'signs and wonders' described in Acts is impressive. The story of Ananias and Sapphira represents, in the telling at all events, a switching of the power to heal into its opposite channel.[29] Verses 15 and 16 of Chapter 5, recounting the manner of the 'signs and wonders' mentioned previously in verse 12, do so in language reminiscent of Mark 6^{56}. The popular excitement arouses similar extravagances as are recorded later in 19^{12}.[30] Philip in Samaria exorcises unclean spirits and heals the

[27] With Chapter 3 the story begins of a conflict with the authorities over the use of the Name of Jesus. See Note xi on 'The Name, Baptism, and the Laying on of Hands', *Beginnings*.

[28] The healing work of the early Church is a continuation of the same ministry, carried on in the name of Jesus and in the power of his presence. Particularly significant are the words of Peter to Aeneas: 'Jesus Christ heals you' (Acts 9^{34}), G. B. Caird, *The Apostolic Age*, 1955, p. 65.

[29] 'Such a power to destroy is the necessary analogue to the power to heal and make alive', comments the note on this incident in *Beginnings*, IV.

[30] Knowling (*Expositor's Greek Testament*, II.147) quotes Baumgartner's comment here. It is not actually stated that miraculous power went forth from Peter's shadow, etc. But if no such power were implied, why introduce this reference at all into a narrative that purports to note the extraordinary powers of the Apostles? Grundmann sees in these two places (5^{15} and 19^{11f}) a description of healing powers, which is in 'completely

paralyzed and lame. At Lydda, Peter heals paralyzed Aeneas (9^{33ff}),[31] and at Joppa brings back Dorcas from the dead. 13^{6ff} tells how Elymas the sorcerer withstood Paul, 'seeking to turn the deputy from his faith'. Paul 'filled with the Holy Ghost' spoke in faith, and, in accordance with his word, Elymas was stricken with blindness.[32]

The first record that we have of *healing* through the word of Paul is at Lystra, where a lame man is healed (14^{8ff}).[33] Paul and Barnabas speak for all others through whom 'signs and wonders' are done in Acts: 'Not *in* us, but *through* us, is the power operating', is what in effect they say to the men of Lystra. 'We also are men of like passions with you' (14^{15}). So the record continues, as at Philippi Paul cures a clairvoyant girl (16^{16ff}), the name of Jesus proving powerful in exorcism. Though now, in the second part of Acts, 'wonders and signs' is no longer the formula,[34] the list of marvels continues. We have already referred to 19^{11f} and the 'special' (or 'unusual', 'extraordinary' miracles (*δυνάμεις τε οὐ τάς τυχούσας*) which God wrought by the hand of Paul. Here we are told of the efficacy of his 'handkerchiefs and aprons' as healing agents! Eutychus, taken up as dead after his fall from a third-story window, is brought back to life by Paul (20^{7ff}). In Malta Paul takes no hurt, though a viper 'fastened on his hand'.[35] Paul

primitive fashion'. He says that these two passages disperse the last doubts which anyone might have as to whether Luke thought of δύναμις along the lines of a 'power-substance'.

[31] See note 28, above.

[32] Lake has a valuable note on verse 12 (*Beginnings*, IV.147) regarding the 'astonishment' of Sergius Paulus at the miracle. He writes: 'In view of modern tendencies to regard Christianity as a wholly ethical movement, it is well to emphasize how much stress Luke puts on the miraculous power of the Apostles.' He continues: 'nor is this Lucan; it is early Christian'.

[33] It is curiously parallel in phrase and manner to the story of Peter's healing of the Lame Man at the Beautiful Gate (3^{2ff}). One of the subsidiary aims of the writer is to set the apostleship of Peter and Paul side by side, and to find, and emphasize, every parallel that he can. 'Luke wants to show that the course of the Christian mission was not in the last resort by one Apostle, such as Paul, or by men at all, but by a supra-human power. . . . In both the Apostles we are intended to recognize the type of the Christian missionary' (M. Dibelius, *Studies in the Acts of the Apostles*, p. 132). In this second story, it is worthy of note that Paul's action is contingent upon the man's faith: 'seeing that he had faith to be made whole'. This factor (cf. 3^{16}) links this miracle with the typical Synoptic healing (e.g. Lk 5^{20}, 7^{50}, etc.).

[34] The phrase occurs no less than nine times in the first part of Acts, and is not found at all in the second part. This fact in itself points to the Aramaic background of Chapters 1–15.

[35] 28^{4}. It is worth noting the fact that there are no poisonous snakes now on the island. Bruce (op. cit., p. 470) comments that 'there may, however, have been vipers there in Paul's time. (So, in Ireland, there were snakes before St Patrick, but none, we are told, "since his day".)'

also here heals the father of Publius, his method, again, being that of the imposition of hands, accompanied by prayer; and others in the island come to him and are healed (28^{8f}).

In all this, Acts witnesses to the emergence of power in ways comparable to those recounted in the Gospels concerning Jesus.[36] The power is not of men, but of God, who 'raised up Christ from the dead'. Its vehicle in Acts is not so much the Synoptic Kingdom of God as the 'Holy Spirit'. Through this gift believers are experiencing an invasion from the spiritual realm, an outpouring of δύναμις.

'Whoever is responsible for the basic details of those first chapters of Acts', writes Norman Snaith, 'knew exactly what the Old Testament meant by the *ruach adonai*.'[37] As in so much in these early chapters, we are dealing with an accent that is thoroughly Hebraic.[38] The expressions 'poured out', on the one hand, and 'filled' on the other, are words which seem to fit very naturally into the descriptions of the coming of the Spirit, suggesting an invasive force within the personality.[39] Joel, in the prophecy Peter sees so richly fulfilled at Pentecost (2^{17ff}; cf. Joel 2^{28ff}), uses the term 'poured out'. But, at the same time, we are moving away from the Old Testament conception of the Spirit of God to the personal Holy Spirit of developed Christian theology. The highest attributes of personality are His. He is the directing and compelling influence behind the missionary campaign. Not only does He appoint and empower individuals to special offices, giving instructions to them (8^{29}, 10^{19}, etc.), sending them forth (10^{5}; cf. 13^{2}), but He informs and blesses the whole community.[40] 'It seemed good

[36] Jesus had said (in Lk only 6^{40}) 'Every disciple when he is fully equipped (κατηρτισμένος) shall be as his master' and in the Acts we see the Spirit which had come upon Jesus and marked Him out as the world's Redeemer come also upon His followers, making them what He chose them to be, His 'apostles' (Lk 6^{13}; cf. Acts 2^{43}, 4^{33}) (J. A. Findlay, *The Way, the Truth and the Life*, p. 32).

[37] *The Doctrine of the Holy Spirit* (*Headingley Lectures*, London, 1937), p. 25.

[38] Concerning these chapters, A. M. Hunter writes: 'Here is nothing which might not be paralleled from the Old Testament.' One example will serve. The story of the rapture of Philip the Evangelist (8^{39}) strikingly recalls similar language in the Old Testament (1 K 18^{12}; 2 K 2^{16}) (*Paul and His Predecessors*, p. 113).

[39] And this way of thinking, and writing, of the Spirit, fits Luke's predilection to the idea of δύναμις as something of a *mana*-like 'power-substance'.

[40] Cf. closing verses of Acts 2 already referred to; and note, e.g., Acts 13^{52} where, in Luke's selective fashion, we are told of what happened to the converts made at Pisidian Antioch, the first church formed in Asia Minor: 'And the disciples were filled' (were continually filled) 'with joy and with the Holy Ghost'. 'The same feature of primitive Christian life repeated itself in every city where the Church was planted', says H. B. Swete (op. cit., p. 105).

to the Holy Spirit and to us' is a declaration typical of the early Church (15^{28}). Men can, on the other hand, 'resist' the Spirit (6^{10}) and put Him to the test, and 'lie' to Him ($5^{5,\,9}$). All these references are in personal categories.

The supreme endowment given to the Apostles is thus, the invasion of the Holy Spirit. But it is important, too, to notice to whom apostolic power is given. 'Nowhere in the history of the Apostolic Churches', writes H. B. Swete, 'is there a more suggestive picture of the character which is inspired by the Spirit of Christ', than in Stephen, 'a character' which, as he says, is 'at once strong and tender, forceful and spiritual'.[41] He is described in 6^{5} as 'a man full of faith and of the Holy Spirit' and in verse 8 'full of grace and power'. The Holy Spirit and Power are equated in these descriptions, the *δύναμις* of verse 8 is clearly power to work miracles: He 'wrought great wonders and signs among the people', (cf. 8^{13}, etc.) and, as clearly, in verse 10, it is the power of preaching.[42] This apostolic man, technically not one of the Apostles, furnishes a typical example of the endowment with power and the Spirit by which the Lord's characteristic work of healing and preaching was continued by His men.

In Paul's exposition, the same conceptions are followed which we have already noted. In Romans 15^{18f} he refers to the things 'which Christ wrought through me, for the obedience of the Gentiles, by word and deed' (the familiar apposition) 'in the power of signs and wonders, in the power of the Holy Ghost . . . ' In the Spirit, in the power of Christ, and in this personal relationship with Him, Paul carries forward his Gospel, and follows his Lord, as one of His Apostles,[43] in healing and preaching.[44] 'In regard to himself', writes Albert Schweitzer, 'Paul knows that the Spirit acts through him. If his preaching is effectual, that is because it is done in the power of the Spirit; if signs and wonders proceed from him, they are wrought by the Spirit.'[45] The same conjunction between Spirit and Power found in Luke is observable in Paul. We have noted the 'in the power of the Holy Ghost' of

[41] Ibid., p. 89.

[42] 'And they were not able to withstand the wisdom and the Spirit by which he spake.' The whole phrase, as R. J. Knowling says (*Expositor's Greek Testament*, II.176) is as an exact fulfilment of Lk. 21^{15}; cf. 1 Cor 1^{17}, 2^{6}.

[43] Paul proudly claims this title, on a par with any of the Twelve (e.g. Gal 1^{1ff}). Jesus called him, equipped him, to be 'apostle to the Gentiles' (Acts 22^{6ff}, 26^{16f}). He was given the Holy Spirit to equip him for his work (Acts 9^{17}).

[44] W. Grundmann, *T.W.z.N.T.*, II. 312.

[45] *The Mysticism of St Paul*, p. 169.

Romans 15[19]; 1 Corinthians 2[4] speaks of 'the Spirit and of power'; 1 Thessalonians 1[5] says of his work in Thessalonica that it was not 'in word only, but also in power, and in the Holy Ghost'; 2 Timothy 1[7] refers to 'a spirit of power'.[46]

The signs of an Apostle are δυνάμεις. 2 Corinthians 12[12]: 'Truly the signs of an apostle were wrought among you in all patience, by signs and wonders and mighty works' (cf. Gal 3[5]: 'He therefore that supplieth to you the Spirit, and worketh miracles among you'.[47]

Similarly, the words of an Apostle, since he is the messenger of the Gospel, appointed to his task by the Spirit, are 'with power'. We have referred above to 1 Thessalonians 1[5], in which St Paul states that the working of the Spirit at Thessalonica did not proceed by word alone, but as the Word united with 'power', with 'Holy Spirit', and 'much assurance'. 1 Corinthians 4[19f] reverses this, contrasting the word of the 'puffed up' in Corinth with 'power': 'And I will know not the word of them which are puffed up, but the power, for the Kingdom of God is not in word, but in power.'[48]

This continuity of Apostolic word and deed with the Lord's own power in preaching and healing is as clear an element in Paul's thought and practice, as in Luke's treatment in Acts. Both see the Holy Spirit as the force behind the power to preach and work miracles. *Πνεῦμα*, as Walter Grundmann comments, expresses the condition in which the exalted Lord is present. Power and might belong to Him, who Himself was endowed by the Spirit while living an earthly life. 'In the Spirit, Christ is present with His Apostle as dispenser of power, and in this given personal relationship, through the Spirit and in Spirit, the Apostle is as his Lord. He is not representing himself, but rather his Lord.'[49]

[46] Otto Schmitz, art., 'Der Begriff δύναμις bei Paulus' *Festgabe für Adolf Deissmann*, p. 145. The synonymity between Spirit and Power, he points out, is also developed in 1 Cor 15[43]: 'it is raised in power' is parallel to 'it is raised a spiritual body'. (Bultmann, *Theology of the New Testament*, I.156, also points to the closeness of the ideas of δόξα and δύναμις in this same passage.)

[47] In Gal 3[5], 'this gift (which has now become a determinative norm for the truth of the gospel) is now more specifically described as the divine operation (ἐνεργῶν) of forces (δυνάμεις) be it exclusively as spiritual gifts, or also as miracles of healing, and the like' (H. N. Ridderbos, *The Epistle to the Galatians* (*ad loc.*)).

[48] This contrast between 'word' and 'power' here, as F. W. Grosheide indicates in his *The First Epistle to the Corinthians* (*ad loc.*), is comparable to that in 1 Cor 1[17, 24] between 'wisdom of words' and 'power' and 2[1, 4] between 'excellency of speech' and 'power'.

[49] *T.W.z.N.T.*, II.312.

Paul is thus a *shaliach* of Jesus.[50] 'Paul, a servant of Jesus Christ, called (to be) an apostle, separated unto the gospel of God' is how he characteristically describes himself at the head of the Roman Epistle. At the beginning of 1 Corinthians, he pin-points the centre of his preaching: it is Christ Jesus, and His Cross, the Power and Wisdom of God. This gospel he *knows* to be power because of its efficacy to deliver men and to bring them into the life of God. 1 Corinthians 2^{4f} becomes doubly impressive in the present connexion: 'And my speech and my preaching were not in persuasive words of wisdom, but in demonstration of the Spirit and of power: that your faith should not stand in the wisdom of men, but in the power of God.'[51]

Otto Schmitz has a paragraph in which he shows how Paul, in all his missionary work, is driven by a 'godly energy' (ἐνέργεια). 'It is certainly', he says, 'a strong stream of the Power of Christ, which he experiences effectively (ἐνεργουμένην ἐν ἐμοι ἐν δυνάμει, Col 1^{29}).[52] So in Ephesians 3^{7}, after speaking of the Gospel, Paul continues: 'whereof I was made a minister . . . according to the working (ἐνέργεια) of his power'. This is not something he thinks of as peculiar to himself. Galatians 2^{8} makes that clear. The point is that 'the Apostolate is the sphere of the working of God's power'.[53]

In what manner does this power come? Never to inflate the recipient. Its effect is the opposite of the foolish 'boasting' decried by Paul. It is linked with humility and obedience; and it is often most at work when the Apostle is least conscious of it.

It is as an ordinary Christian disciple, as well as God's Apostle, that Paul experiences the way His power works through 'weak-ness'. 'But we have this treasure in earthern vessels, that the exceeding greatness of the power may be of God, and not from

[50] N. Geldenhuys (op. cit., p. 62) remarks that Paul, on his way to Damascus, was *shaliach* to the Jewish rulers, and that 'through the power of the Living Saviour the persecuting Jewish *shaliach* is changed to the ἀπόστολος κατ' ἐξοχήν'.

[51] Not that Paul in his preaching displayed πνεῦμα and δύναμις, but rather that the Holy Spirit and the power of God ($1^{18, 24}$) manifested themselves in his preaching (cf. Lk 10^{19}; Acts 28^{3ff}; Heb 2^{4}, etc., for similar refs.) (F. W. Grosheide, *The First Epistle to the Corinthians*, p. 61).

[52] Ibid., p. 146. Note also Gal 2^{8}; 1 Tim 1^{12}; 2 Tim 4^{17}; Phil 4^{13}.

[53] W. Grundmann, *Der Begriff der Kraft*, p. 100. Regarding the Apostolate, A. Schlatter (*The Church in the New Testament Period*, p. 36) gathers texts from John and Peter (Jn 15^{27}, 20^{19}; 1 Pet 5^{1}, 1^{8}, etc.) which show that no special glory attaches to the status of Apostle. The Apostle 'does not stand *above* the Church, but is *in* it'; cf. Edward Schweizer, *Church Order in the New Testament* (E.T.), 1961.

ourselves' (2 Cor 4^{7}).[54] It is the very weakness and poverty of the agent, *shaliach* though he knows himself to be, that proves beyond doubt the source of the power demonstrated in him. Paul has seen this principle at work in Christ Himself: 'crucified through weakness, yet he liveth through the power of God' (2 Cor 13^{4}; cf. Rom 1^{4}). So Paul can write (1 Cor 1^{25}) 'the weakness of God is stronger than men'.[55] He is one who has heard God saying to him: '(my) power is made perfect in weakness.[56] Most gladly therefore will I rather glory in my weaknesses, that the power of Christ may rest upon me' (2 Cor 12^{9}). In his trials, accepted as discipline, Paul has known Christ's power resting upon him.[57] So, instead of being afraid or ashamed of his 'weaknesses', Paul can actually bring himself to boast in them!

Notice, too, that Paul, though confessing his weaknesses, knows at the very same time that he is continuously made strong in Christ and His strength.[58] In the fragment in 1 Timothy 1^{12} he gives thanks to Christ, who 'puts strength into me' (the verb is in the aorist here: ἐνδυναμώσαντι με), and in this he is thinking especially of the time when he was 'appointed to his service'. Having received the call to the apostleship, he has continually been given strength to fulfil it.[59] In what Deissmann calls 'the heroic confession'[60] of Philippians 4^{13} (here the present participle of the verb is used), Paul cries: 'I can do all things in him that strengtheneth me.' He is sustained at all times by the power of Christ.

[54] This, says Grundmann (op. cit., p. 105), is the 'classical formula' of this law concerning power and weakness. 'The weakness and difficulties of the Apostle, pictured in the antithesis of the following verses, had first been experienced by Jesus. It is these very things that are the vessels for the power of God effecting the work of redemption; with the aim that the life of Jesus might be visibly seen as the factual basis in which the all-conquering power of God is manifested.'

[55] Grundmann, *T.W.z.N.T.*, II.317.

[56] Bultmann (*Theology of the New Testament*, I.351) writes: 'Paul's dictum "for power comes in weakness to perfection" is spoken as a basic principle, and holds true for any "weakness".'

[57] Notice the way in which Paul thus speaks, much in the same way as elsewhere he might describe the coming of the Spirit. The truth concerning Paul's equating of the Spirit with the exalted Christ (cf. e.g. Rom 8^{9f} and 2 Cor 3^{17}, etc.) is that 'experientially, they are one' (A. M. Hunter, *Interpreting Paul's Gospel*, p. 39).

[58] Cf. the Old Testament 'The Lord is my strength' of Ps 118^{14}, 140^{8}; Hab 3^{19}, Jer 16^{19}.

[59] E. F. Scott, *The Pastoral Epistles, M.N.T.C. ad loc.*

[60] *Paul*, p. 156.

CHAPTER FIFTEEN

POWER IN THE CHRISTIAN COMMUNITY

WE have looked at the power granted to individuals, rendering them Apostles and effective witnesses. This was known by men confessing that they were 'called' of God. The original disciples had known this calling and appointment by Jesus (Mk 3^{13f}; Jn 15^{16}), and Paul equally claimed that he knew it from God (Rom 1^{1}). Preaching and healing in the name of Jesus, the Apostles experienced guidance and empowerment in a deep, intimate relation with the Holy Spirit. The work that Jesus began to do and to teach prospered in their hands.

We have also noted that in making this endowment the Spirit overleaps barriers. Early in the story, the outworking of the Gentile mission fell from the hands of Peter and passed to Paul, who so far from being a disciple of Jesus had been 'a persecutor of the Church'. And apostolic power is seen most vividly in Stephen, called by the Church, not to apostolic office at all (he presumably did not possess what were then thought to be the necessary qualifications: cf. 1^{21}). His appointment was actually to a post relieving the apostles of a burden and releasing them for proper apostolic duties! Yet in him the Spirit's power was plainly shown. He was a man 'full of faith and of the Holy Spirit'.

What of the community in the midst of which, and for which, the Apostles laboured? Was it, in itself a sphere of power? Did it promise anything of this nature to those who were won for its membership?

In the beginning there was, of course, no preaching of a community. The men addressed already belonged to the covenant race of Israel. The good news was that these were the days of fulfilment, Messiah had come, God had visited His people, and—most incredible of all—the Holy Spirit was being poured out upon those having faith in the crucified peasant proclaimed as Messiah, and that, through linking oneself, in this way, with the events of

His Death and Rising Again (or, of His being raised-again) from the dead, *δύναμις* was to be experienced. No sense of discontinuity between 'Old Israel' and the 'New' was consciously felt in those early days.[1] These new experiences, however, as well as these claims, involved a distinctiveness soon evidenced in the way they referred to themselves or were designated by others.[2] Thus began the marking off of the 'New Israel' from the 'Old', It was, indeed, something implicit from the first. When Jesus came into Galilee and announced the Kingdom of God, everything to do with God's inbreaking in the person of His Son was bound to be divisive. Men would either enter into all that God had for His people, or refuse it.

In this way, therefore, the community began to gather round the Lord in the days of His Ministry. We have already noted His special choice of the Twelve, and His appointment 'that they might be with him, and that he might send them forth to preach, and to have authority to cast out devils' (Mk 3^{14f}). This was 'the living kernel of the coming Church',[3] which came to be founded upon the disciples' word and testimony.

There are two texts in Matthew's Gospel which speak, in anticipation, of the powers which the Church and its leaders were to exercise. The first is Matthew 16^{18ff}, where Christ's response to Peter at Caesarea Philippi is given in fuller form than either in Mark or Luke. Jesus has revealed His joy at Peter's faith and insight, which He declares arises not from any merely earthly promptings. He continues: 'And I also say unto thee, that thou art Peter, and upon this rock I will build my Church; and the gates of Hades shall not prevail against it. I will give unto thee the keys of the Kingdom of heaven: and whatsoever thou shalt bind on earth shall be bound in heaven and whatsoever thou shalt loose on earth shall be loosed in heaven.' Controversy has long

[1] F. G. S. Hopwood, *The Religious Experience of the Primitive Church*, Edinburgh 1936, *circa* p. 231, speaks of the difficulty of the 'New Israel' interpretation of the Church in early days, and says that this theory does not fully allow for the vital sense of oneness with Israel which the primitive Church possessed.

[2] E.g. *οἱ πιστεύσαντες*, or some other participle of *πιστεύω* (Acts 2^{44}, etc.—note the *οἱ πιστοί* of Acts 10^{45}—a notable use of the adjective in an active sense), *οἱ ἀδελφοί* (Acts 11^{1}, etc.), *μαθηταί* (Acts 6^{1f}, etc.), *οἱ σωζομένοι* (Acts 2^{47}), *ἅγιοι* (cf. Eph 2^{19}, above: Acts $9^{13, 32, 41}$, etc.), *ὤν τῆς ὁδοῦ* (Acts 9^{2}), and the names 'Nazarenes', 'Galileans' (Acts 24^{5}, 1^{11}, 2^{7}, etc.) which refer to their association with Jesus, finally culminating in the *χριστιανοί* of Acts 11^{26}. See Note xxx 'Names for Christians and Christianity in Acts', *Beginnings*, V.375ff, H. J. Cadbury.

[3] J. R. Nelson, *The Realm of Redemption*, p. 27.

raged over this text, e.g. as to its genuineness,[4] and concerning the powers here conferred, and the precise nature of what it was to which the Lord was responding and promising these powers, i.e. was it to Peter himself (and to his 'descendants'?) or was it to Peter's faith and insight (and to anyone else showing a like faith?) The fact that our Lord spoke in Aramaic helps to settle some of these matters. The purely Grecian distinction between πέτρος and πέτρα disappears, and 'Cephas' repeated on both occasions would seem, therefore, to refer clearly to Peter himself—though, of course, the meaning of the text immediately widens when we remember that the Peter referred to is the Peter of this moment of revelation and insight.[5] As R. N. Flew commented: 'In this passage Peter is to be as it were the forefather of the new Israel, as Abraham was the forefather of the old.'[6] Just as Abraham's faith began the story of Israel and made it possible for God to reveal Himself to his descendants, so Peter's understanding of who Jesus is sets in motion the possibility of the new Israel, the future Church.

Another clue from Aramaic is provided by the word into which we must translate the ἐκκλησία of the text. K. L. Schmidt suggests *kenishta* as the Aramaic equivalent[7] and carries the assent of many scholars with him in this suggestion.[8] As Schmidt explains, the word primarily meant a local Jewish community, but it could be used to cover the idea of a special group, i.e. the Messianic Remnant, which Jesus Himself represented and came to call out

[4] R. G. Nelson, ibid., p. 31, lists the names of some of the scholars who do not regard Mt 16^17ff^ as authentic (they are, of course, undisputed textually): T. W. Manson, R. Bultmann, P. Althaus, C. J. Cadoux, B. S. Easton, J. F. Foakes-Jackson, M. Goguel, K. Holl, G. Johnston, W. G. Kümmel; and on p. 34 a corresponding list of those who have defended their originality, e.g. A. T. Cadoux, O. Cullmann, R. N. Flew, C. Gore, P. G. S. Hopwood, A. Juncker, E. Lohmeyer, R. Otto, K. L. Schmidt, A. Schweitzer, H. D. Wendland, H. Windisch. Also in Dr Nelson's own pages, this text is admirably discussed.

[5] The Peter of a moment later can equally be referred to as 'Satan'. The 'Stone' passage of Isa 28[16] seems to be in view in this Matthaean reference. This predisposes us to view the matter most in the light of Peter's discovery of who Messiah is—for it is the latter who is to be the 'stone of stumbling'.

[6] Ibid., p. 129. Cf. also the midrash on Deut 21, which described God about to create the world, foreseeing faithful Abraham and saying, 'Now I have found a rock on which to build and establish the world' (Cox, *Torch Comm. ad loc.*). This homiletic midrash, *Yelammedenu*, is quoted in Moore, *Judaism*, I.538.

[7] *T.W.z.N.T.*, III.522ff. See also Burton, *Galatians*, pp. 417ff, Hort, *The Christian Ecclesia*, pp. 3ff, Hopwood, *The Religious Experiences of the Primitive Church* (Edinburgh, 1936), pp. 227ff.

[8] The Sinatic Syriac version uses this word to translate ἐκκλησία not at 16[18] (not preserved in this version), but at 18[17]. Flew ibid., p. 124. See also Schmidt, etc.

from the people of the Old Covenant, establishing it as the eschatological community of the Kingdom of God.[9]

The phrases concerning 'binding' and 'loosing' recur in the second of these two passages, Matthew 18^{18}. Here these powers are at the disposal not of Peter merely, but of the whole group. The terms themselves are usually explained by reference to Rabbinic usage, by which they meant 'forbidding' and 'permitting' in matters to do with religious observances etc.[10] Some commentators see the power conferred upon Peter, thus, as of 'laying down the law for his fellow-disciples, like a true Rabbi'.[11] Others[12] see it applied to admitting and excluding from the Christian community.[13] But, while these are Rabbinic terms, it is not necessary that this specialized use governs their meaning in this, obviously, figurative passage. The way the phrase is employed in the second passage, in a chapter outlining behaviour within the Christian group and the power of prayer when 'two of you shall agree on earth as touching anything that they shall ask', sheds light, surely, on its use in both contexts. It concerns the effective joining of heaven and earth, through the insight and faith granted to those who are where Peter was at the moment of his illumination and to those to whom Jesus is so real that He is with them as their unseen Lord and Leader (Mt 18^{20}). In the Lord's Prayer we are bidden to pray, 'thy kingdom come, thy will be done, on earth as it is in heaven': the keys of the Kingdom are those locking earth and heaven together in this way. To those possessing the keys, Jesus promises the power to command eternal forces. Their bindings and loosings—when done in this way and operated on this scale—are not ephemeral. They are linked with power.[14]

[9] For this see R. H. Fuller, art, 'Church' (*Theological Word Book of Bible*, p. 47). Hort years ago, made the suggestion (ibid., p. 10) that to substitute 'Israel' for ἐκκλησία in this sentence would give the approximate impression of its meaning to the listening disciples.

[10] R. N. Flew, ibid., p. 134, T. W. Manson, *Sayings*, p. 205, Strack-Billerbeck, I.738ff, etc.

[11] A. J. Mason in Hasting's *Dictionary of the Bible*, IX.30.

[12] e.g. Strack-Billerbeck, *ad loc.*

[13] If this is what it deals with, comments R. N. Flew, then the reference would seem to be to the apostolic preaching (which invariably divided people in their response to it); cf. Lk 10^{16}, 'He that heareth you, heareth me', etc. The 'loosing' would then = 'hearing' and 'binding' = 'rejecting' in the second text.

[14] It is thus to two or three of *you*—with the Lord in the midst (the strongest link between heaven and earth)—that the Father's creative power answers from the heavenly realm. This represents no stronger doctrine regarding prayer, and the powers open to it, than we meet with elsewhere, e.g. Mt 21^{22}; Mk 11^{24}; Jn 15^{16}; Jas 5^{14}ff. This is true 'prophetic prayer': see pp. 33f, 57 and pp. 190f, later.

The words in John 20[21ff] regarding the power to forgive (or retain) sins are similar. The divine community, acting under the power and inspiration of the Holy Spirit, can act effectively on earth in such a way that its actions are not transient, nor haphazard. They have eternal backing and eternal consequences.

The significance of the description of the Church as the 'Body of Christ' is best understood in this way.[15] This is the community empowered by the Spirit to witness for Him, and to proclaim the Gospel of the 'Christ-event'. It should experience the reality of the 'Lord in the midst', and, feeling His continual inspiration, continue His double work of preaching and healing. Using the power it possesses under the Spirit to bind and loose, to join heaven and earth in effective action, it must not be afraid, in the moment of the Spirit's direction and in Christ's name, to use the power He gave it and which He Himself exercised—to pronounce the forgiveness of sins in radical and absolute fashion.

There is a further point about the description of the Church as Christ's 'Body'. This title emphasizes the connexion between its existence and Christ's Resurrection. Its *raison d'être* is here. 'After three days' the Lord raised up the Temple of His own body, and at the very same time He raised up the body of His Church, to act as His continuing agent on earth (cf. Jn 2[18ff] and Mk 14[58]).

The earliest of the passages describing the Church as the Body of Christ (1 Cor 12)[16] is one detailing the various *charismata* given by the Spirit to individuals. These gifts, however, are not to foster individualism. They are all for the common good (πρὸς τὸ συμφέρον, verse 7). The use of the verb ἐνεργεῖν is noticeable throughout this passage (e.g. verse 6 and verse 11). It stresses the effective working out of God's power through the gifts poured out upon members of the Church: 'the word of wisdom', 'the word of knowledge', 'faith', 'gifts of healing', 'workings of miracles', 'prophecy', 'discernings of

[15] 'As Paul works out his theology of the Body, it has both a vertical and a horizontal reference. On the one hand, the Body looks up to Christ as its Head and Saviour (Col 1[8]; Eph 1[22]), from whom it draws its vitality (Col 2[19]; Eph 4[16]). On the other, those who are in Christ's Body are members one of the other, with gifts which vary, but are all needed for the good of the whole (Rom 12[4ff]; 1 Cor 12[12ff]).... The Church is the continuator of the Messianic Ministry of Jesus, called, like him, by service and suffering, to spread the Reign of God to the end of the earth, till all men are reconciled to him through Christ.' (A. M. Hunter, *Interpreting Paul's Gospel*, p. 44.)

[16] Note also 1 Cor 10[16f]. It may be that this metaphor had its origin in sacramental associations.

spirits', 'kinds of tongues', 'the interpretation of tongues'.[17]

Ephesians 4^{11ff} while providing a much more sober list of ministrations[18] ('And he gave some to be apostles; and some, prophets; and some, pastors and teachers') makes the same point —that all these agencies are for the 'building up of the body of Christ' (verse 12).

Galatians 3^{5} refers to 'He therefore that supplieth to you the Spirit, and worketh miracles (*ἐνεργῶν δυνάμεις*) among you (*ἐν ὑμῖν*: "to you"?)'. As in the Corinthian's passage, Paul is here assuming the possession of these extraordinary powers as 'an acknowledged fact' (J. B. Lightfoot). More particularly, the gift of the Spirit, 'has now become a determinative norm for the truth of the gospel', and it is evidenced by the divine working of *δυνάμεις*.[19] As if, perhaps, to offset the more impressive and showy manifestations of power, which might be in danger of catching the attention of the early Christians, Paul, later in the same letter (5^{22}) gives his list of ethical 'fruits of the Spirit'. These 'fruits' are something shared amongst all members of the community.[20]

Though not referring to *δυνάμεις* and exceptional gifts of the Spirit (except, perhaps, in the 'greater works than these shall he do' passage of Jn 14^{12}), the Fourth Gospel's picture of the Christian community and its endowment follows that already outlined. The word *ἐκκλησια* is not mentioned in the Gospel, yet throughout the Johannine writings the life of the Christian is all the time considered against the background of the eschatological community. The latter is the constant presupposition. The powers to be known by the Christian and in which He shares are discovered in the fellowship and apply to it.[21] The gift of the Spirit after the Resurrection is recounted in such a way in the Gospel

[17] By this recital we are brought right into the atmosphere of the early Church. The *ἐνεργήματα δυνάμεων*, carefully distinguished here from *χαρίσματα ἰαμάτων*, would seem to be the 'wonderful divine powers' of the Synoptic story (cf. Mt 11^{20}, $13^{54, 58}$, where the plural *δυνάμεις* is similarly used of Jesus's deeds of power), the lordship over demons, as distinguished from the healing of diseases (W. Grundmann, *Der Begriff der Kraft*, p. 114). At the end of the chapter, *δυνάμεις* are distinguished from *χαρίσματα ἰαμάτων* (verses 28f).

[18] Though this should be compared, not with 1 Cor 12^{8ff}, but with verses 28ff of that chapter, where not *gifts*, but types of men exercising them are listed. We notice, then, these omissions in Eph 4: *δυύαμεις* (workers of miracles?), *χαρίσματα ἰαμάτων, ἀντιλήψεις, κυβερνήσεις, γένη γλωσσῶν* (1 Cor 12^{28}).

[19] H. Ridderbos, *Comm. ad loc.*

[20] See G. S. Duncan, *Galatians M.N.T.C.*, p. 173.

[21] It needs always to be remembered that, for any New Testament writer, the Church is always a presupposition. He is, invariably, either writing *for* the group, or *to* the group.

(20^{22f}) as to emphasize the corporate nature of the gift, suggesting too, that the Spirit is to be the abiding authority behind the fellowship. The post-Resurrection charge to Peter (Chapter 21) is all of a piece with the strong 'pastoral' character of this Gospel.

The fact that the Spirit continues and fulfils the work of Christ[22] means a vocation of witnessing and preaching for the community. Through its witness the world is to be reproved of sin, righteousness and judgement (Jn 16^{8ff}).[23] The Spirit will thus convict the world of sin's essential nature; it is ἀπιστία, the refusal to 'believe on Him'. The prayer of Chapter 17 pictures the disciples as an 'unworldly or eschatological group', in the world, but not of it, given to Jesus by the Father (verse 2), living in unity with the Father and the Son, and by their witnessing bringing others into the circle of those who 'believe on me' (verses 20ff). The same indirect reference to the 'church' is made in the First Epistle when describing those whose fellowship is with the Father and with His Son, Jesus Christ (1 Jn 1^{3}). In 1 John 2^{7-17} the contrast is drawn between the eschatological community and the world: over against what is doomed and perishing is the society of the redeemed possessing the gift of forgiveness, knowledge of God, and victory over evil.[24]

The allegories of the Vine and the Good Shepherd fill out the picture of believers partaking in a community whose power, meaning, and purpose are all found in Christ. 'Believing' does not involve nor result in a solitary relationship with Him: one is a member of the flock, or a branch in the Vine, and in this relationship one is to 'bear fruit'—fruit which, again, finds its life in a similar 'abiding in the Vine'. One is a member of a group governed by the brotherly love commended by Christ (Jn 15^{12}; 1 Jn 3^{14}).[25]

[22] E.g. Jn $14^{18, 26}$, 16^{13}; I Jn 2^{27}, 5^{6f}. [23] See above, pp. 132 and 134.

[24] C. H. Dodd, *Joh. Epp.*, *M.N.T.C.*, p. 33. Note the way in which John can write in 1 Jn 3^{9} of the extent of this victory over evil. The one begotten by God has a δύναμις overcoming sin (John uses here the device of his specially adapted δύνασθαι). The new life expresses itself in love to the brethren and defeats sin (Grundmann, *Der Begriff der Kraft*, p. 113n.).

[25] Note that the sacraments observed by the believing community receive their power from the Spirit. Without the Spirit, the acts merely partake of the realm of 'flesh' in which they take place, and profit nothing (6^{63}). Reference must be made to the way in which Christians throughout the centuries, in diverse ways and with differing understanding, have received *strength* through partaking in the sacrament of Holy Communion. In Mass, Eucharist, and Breaking of Bread, they have 'discerned the body of the Lord', 'feeding on Him by faith' and feeling something of their share in the fellowship of His people. Dom Gregory Dix has a lyrical passage about this on p. 744 of his book *The Shape of the Liturgy*.

The Church is thus the agency continuing Christ's ministry, proclaiming His Gospel, carrying the fact and the power of His Victory to men, and bringing them into the life of salvation. It is also the fold into which others are brought, and is thus both the means and the object of strengthening and empowerment. The Church possesses the power to endure against all changes: as the Lord said to Peter in Matthew 16^{19}, 'The gates of Hades shall not prevail against it.' After noting the profusion of images for the Christian community in the New Testament,[26] Ethelbert Stauffer points out that practically every image has its antithesis, e.g. Christ's Church and the Synagogue of Satan (Rev 2^{9}, 3^{9}); the people of God and the men of this world (2 Cor 6^{14ff}); Christ's flock and the devouring beast (1 Pet 5^{8}); God's 'building' and the throne and city of Satan (Rev 2^{13}, 14^{8}); the Bride of Christ and the dreadful figure of the 'whore of Babylon' (Rev 2^{20}, 9^{21}, 17^{5}, etc.; cf. also Gal 4^{25}). In this way, he declares, the story of the Lord's struggle is continued in the life of the Church,[27] which is therefore not inappropriately, though daringly, designated as the 'Body of Christ'. Throughout his *New Testament Theology*, Stauffer continues to refer to these forces 'antagonistic' to God and his Christ, noting the age-long antagonism between the *civitas dei* and the *civitas diaboli* which Augustine made the central theme of his chief work. Christ's people need to know that the ἰσχυρότερος has charge of them. In the strength of His Victory over the Strong Man, they can go forward.

The letter to the Ephesians, giving the most developed picture of the Church as the Body of Christ, and of Christ as its Head (e.g. 1^{22}), contains a striking passage in Chapter 6 in which the Christian is bidden to 'be strong in the Lord, and in the strength of his might'. Though, with all other members of the Church, he is 'in the Lord', he is not thereby exempted from attack nor from the struggle of faith against the surrounding impalpable forces of evil. Delivered by the Lord from the power of satanic might, he is not guaranteed that he will be untouched by it.[28] Here, too, the need for the Christian's own faith and volition is emphasized. The

[26] It is, e.g., *ecclesia*, 'people of God', 'flock of Christ', 'God's planting', 'God's building', *ecclesia femina* (by which Stauffer means the Bride of Christ conceptions, etc.) and *corpus Christi*, *New Testament Theology*, pp. 156f.

[27] 'The Church is the body of Christ. In the story of her suffering and her glorification the destiny of Jesus Christ in His Passion, Death, and Resurrection comes to its conclusion' (E. Benz, *Ecclesia Spiritualis* (1934), pp. 26f., quoted by Stauffer, p. 156).

[28] W. Grundmann, *Der Begriff der Kraft*, p. 108; cf. Jn 17^{15}.

imperative 'be strong' (ἐνδυναμοῦσθε) invites him to enter into the heritage of power[29] that is already his in the Lord, but the initiative to do so is his own!

The power of God offered to the Christian is, therefore, not only a force working through him, but a strength safeguarding and holding him past all vicissitudes. 'No one is able to snatch them out of the Father's hand,' Jesus says concerning His sheep in John 10^{29}. Though negatively expressed, the words witness to the powerlessness of all other powers to break the fellowship forged with God in Jesus. He is the Good Shepherd, laying down His life for the sheep: both they and He are safe in the Father's hands.[30]

As the eschatological community, the Church exists in the scheme of time between Christ's Resurrection and the Parousia. Thus it is already tasting the powers of the 'age to come' (Heb 6^{5}), delivered from satanic might, but nevertheless still living here on earth, 'threatened and surrounded, waiting for the ultimate rescue and the overthrow of the enemy'.[31] This explains a recurring double emphasis: the paradox of existing in the state of deliverance, and yet continually being put to the test and needing constant reinforcement. So, in Colossians 1^{9ff}, Paul, praying for his fellow Christians, speaks of the Father 'who delivered us out of the power of darkness, and translated us into the kingdom of the Son of his love' (verse 13), but in the same prayer he petitions that they might be 'strengthened with all power, according to the might of his glory, unto all patience and longsuffering with joy' (verse 11). 1 Peter 1^{5}, referring to those 'who by the power of God are guarded through faith unto a salvation ready to be revealed in the last time',[32] is thinking of this overarching 'power' by which the Church is held until the final day of salvation. The need for Christian volition is indicated here, too, in the 'through faith' of this verse, and the phrase, 'receiving the end of your faith (even), the salvation of (your) souls' in verse 9.[33]

The Church is certainly not immune from attacks from without.

[29] Note the connexion of the verbal form with δύναμις.

[30] These words later find their vindication in the Lord's Resurrection (Grundmann, ibid., p. 120).

[31] W. Grundmann, ibid., p. 109; see pp. 125f, above.

[32] E. G. Selwyn (*The First Epistle of St Peter*, p. 125) finds a parallel to the expression used here in Ignatius's *Ep. to Ephesians*, verse 11, and declares that Peter's meaning is that Christians are to be thought of as living 'in' God's power.

[33] 'Our faith lays hold upon God's power and this power strengthens faith and so we are preserved' (Leighton, Comm. *ad loc.*).

But what of failure and betrayal from within? 2 Corinthians 13 concerns trouble which had caused scandal and disaffection within the Church. In verse 10 Paul refers to his apostolic authority, given him by the Lord, as he says, 'for building up, and not for casting down'. If need be he will have to use his disciplinary powers to the full, however, and in this way, also, prove he is Christ's representative (verses 3f).[34] The Apostle knows that his mandate is to extend the life-giving influence of the Word of God, but he knows—and they should know, too—that this power possesses a double edge.[35] The authority to discipline the community is a necessary corrolary of the commission to build it up and keep it healthy.[36]

The Church, the Spirit-possessed society,[37] is the realm of *δύναμις* and *ἐνέργεια*,[38] mediating and witnessing to the power of God as salvation (cf. Rom 1^{16}). It is also the sphere promoting growth in character and the 'fruits' of the Spirit. The consummation of all human history in Christ, and the coming to perfection of all things in heaven and earth in Him is the 'open secret' (*μυστήριον*)[39] of God, hid from all ages (Eph 1^{9f}). This 'secret' is now being revealed, *τοῖς ἁγίοις αὐτοῦ*, i.e. to the Church. It is 'Christ in you, the hope of glory' (Col 1^{26ff}): His indwelling in

[34] Note verses 3f. The very weaknesses the Corinthians have discovered in Paul provide a channel through which God's boundless power strengthens him to discipline the Church. Paul loses no opportunity to point to Christ's willing assumption of 'weakness', which made the Passion possible (J. H. Bernard, *Expositor's Greek Testament, ad loc.*), pp. 141f, above, we have discussed the principle which Paul sees concerning human weakness and God's power.

[35] 'The power to destroy' is 'the necessary analogue to the power to heal and to make alive' (comment on the Ananias incident in *Beginnings*, IV, quoted above at p. 136 n, 29).

[36] The strong use of apostolic authority is shown at 1 Tim 1^{20} and 1 Cor 5^{3}. To put offenders 'out of the Church' was to put them back into the sphere of Satan. It involved dread possibilities, but these strong measures could lead in the end to a real repentance and the ceasing to trifle with the incalculable forces of God (cf. also 1 Cor 11^{29ff} for Paul's teaching regarding 'unworthy' partaking of the Lord's Supper, and its possible results).

[37] 'The distinctive characteristic of early Christianity was the conviction that the community of believers possessed as a matter of present reality the indwelling of the Holy Spirit which had been hoped for by the prophets as the primary blessing of the future age of God's new covenant with men' (G. W. H. Lampe, *The Seal of the Spirit*, p. 48). He adduces Acts 5^{39}, 9^{31}, 15^{28}, 20^{28} as some among many indications that in the narrative of Acts the Church is envisaged as a Spirit-possessed society; cf. Acts 19^{1ff}: the disciples of John know nothing of the Holy Spirit, but the disciples of Jesus do! (see R. Otto, *The Kingdom of God and the Son of Man*, p. 80).

[38] Note how in Col 1^{28}, Phil 2^{13}, and 1 Thess 2^{13} *ἐνεργεῖν* and *ἐνέργεια* are the words more typically used; cf. p. 141, above.

[39] In the references to the *μυστήριον* (cf. also Eph 3^{9ff}) there is also a strong overtone regarding the fact that this has come to the *Gentiles*. Col 1^{25} makes it clear, however, that it is *ὁ λόγος τοῦ θεοῦ* that is the *μυστήριον*.

His people, His being among them as He has promised.[40] This is the goal set before every member of the Christian community (Col 1^{28}). Christ, in His inwardly renewing and transforming power, is to be proclaimed 'till we all attain unto the unity of the faith, and of the knowledge of the Son of God, unto a fullgrown man, unto the measure of the fulness of Christ' (Eph 4^{13}). This is the kind of maturity for which Paul looks within the Christian Church!

Two passages, in Ephesians 4^{15ff} and Colossians 2^{19}, together provide a picture of the way in which, through the Holy Spirit, God's energy and power works out in the Church. By the ancients the body was thought, not only to be held together, but also to be supplied with nourishment through the 'joints'[41]: every member, therefore, contributes toward the life of the whole, being part of the unity of which Christ is the 'head',[42] pouring life and energy into every part, and making for its growth 'in love'.

The life principle behind the Church is thus the power of God, energizing it in every detail, and informing and empowering the whole. Her destiny is to fulfil all that God promised to ancient Israel, and to continue 'all that Jesus began to do and to teach'. She is the vehicle of God's truth, the bearer of the Gospel, the agent of God's salvation in Christ, as well as the home and shelter of His people, where in the *κοινωνία* Christ's gifts are to be discovered and used.

[40] Of Christ's inward strengthening with power, Paul's prayer in Eph 3^{14ff} speaks in superlative terms. The doxology of verse 20 not only mentions the 'power that worketh in us' of the previous verses, but speaks of the ability of the One who wields this power 'to do exceeding abundantly' ('to do beyond all things') far beyond anything of which we have any kind of conception, either in our asking or thinking.

[41] E. F. Scott, *Epistles to Colossians, Philemon and Ephesians* (*M.N.T.C.*), p. 56, 114.

[42] In Col 2^{10} Christ is declared 'the head of all principality and power'. This idea is still in mind in verse 19. For the Church 'the powers of nature are finished with . . . it is free under Christ', $2^{14f, 20}$ (Eduard Schweizer, *Church Order in the New Testament*, 8a).

CHAPTER SIXTEEN

MAGIC AND SORCERY

WE have been observing the direct results of the Lord's ministry in the life of the men closest to Him, and in the community that gathered round Him. We need now to overtake some of the considerations devolving from earlier days and pre-New Testament conceptions. In previous sections of this book we have noted the contrast between the Biblical concept of power and that obtaining in the realm of magic; we have noted, too, the ideas concerning the mediation of God's powers through angels and *δυνάμεις*; we have discussed the authority of rulers, as conceived in the Old Testament and inter-testamental literature. We must now follow these themes as they emerge in the New Testament. We begin with 'magic'.

The Book of Acts provides a number of dramatic pictures illustrating the clash that occurred in connexion with the concept of 'power' as Christianity moved out from Palestine to invade the contemporary world. The contrast is between men guided and used by the Holy Spirit and knowing His power, and those who, by magical means, were searching for and exploiting any form of power available to them on the fringe of the psychic and super-normal.[1]

Behind much religious, as well as magical, practice in the ancient world lay this pursuit of 'power'. Much of the ritual of the Mystery religions in New Testament days, for example, was aimed at establishing a regeneration making possible some sharing of the divine nature[2] and therefore of the divine power.[3] The baptismal

[1] 'Very few in that age', states Sir Wm. Ramsay, 'were utterly superior to the belief in magical power' (*The Bearing of Recent Discovery on the Trustworthiness of the New Testament*, pp. 106f).

[2] Cf. 2 Pet 1[4], where the phrase appears in the New Testament itself. Deissmann (*Bible Studies*, p. 361f) sets out the Inscription by which the inhabitants of Stratonicea honour Zeus Panhemerios and Hekate, indicating the remarkable verbal parallels and assonances between this Inscription and 2 Pet 1[3ff]. In this passage we are right in the realm of 'the official liturgical language of Asia Minor'.

[3] A. D. Nock (art., 'Studies in the Graeco-Roman Beliefs of the Empire', *J.H.S.*, XLV (1925), pp. 84[ff]) points out that contemporary belief was much more directed to divine power than to divine personalities. He quotes Aristides in a striking passage saying of Serapis (*Orat.*, viii, i, p. 88): 'Who he is and what nature he has, Egyptian priests and prophets may be left to say. We shall praise him sufficiently for the moment if we tell of the many and great benefits to man of which he is revealed to be the author.'

lustrations of the Mysteries were designed to this end, the enacted drama of the resurrection of Osiris suggesting to the initiate his own rebirth,[4] the *epopteia* of the Eleusinian mysteries,[5] and the rite of the *taurobolium*, having a similar meaning.[6] Many magical procedures sought the same attainment hoping that by the means used man might be ennobled and raised to an altogether new level of living.[7] Magic is best thought of, however, not as a handmaid of religion, even of pagan religion,[8] but rather as 'reversed religion'.[9] The magician was considered to possess the skill and knowledge by which to compel demons to aid him in his purpose.

In the narrative of Acts there are stories of encounters with sorcerers: 8^{5ff}, 13^{6ff}, 19^{13ff}, as well as the incident of the girl with the pythoness spirit of divination in 16^{16ff}.[10]

The story in Acts 8 is most instructive. Philip, the deacon, exercising an apostolic ministry in a Samaritan city, proclaims Christ to the people (verse 5), and shows the signs of an apostle (verses 6f). Simon[11] is greatly impressed with what he sees. This

[4] The Orphic carried to the grave on his golden scroll the boast: first, 'I am the child of earth and of the starry heaven'; then later, 'I too am become God' (Gilbert Murray, *Five Stages of Greek Religion*, p. 181).

[5] In which it seems the symbolism of the ear of wheat miraculously growing out of season forms part (Walter F. Otto in 'The Mysteries', *Eranos Yearbooks*, New York, 1953, p. 25. Note reference to the rebirth symbolism in Orphism, ibid., pp. 82f).

[6] See S. Angus, *The Mystery Religions and Christianity* (London, 1925) for a full discussion of the likenesses and unlikenesses between Christianity and these faiths. The divorce between them is made very clear in Apuleius's *Metamorphoses* (which provides in its last chapter the one straightforward account in contemporary literature of what it was like to enter one of the Mystery religions). Robert Graves, in his translation in the Penguin Classics (*The Golden Ass*), points out that Apuleuis makes the worst of his characters, the baker's wife, 'reject all true religion in favour of the fantastic and blasphemous cult of an Only God.' (Introduction, p. 20.) He clearly scorns contemporary Christianity, and recognizes, however much he misunderstands it, that it belongs to a different thought-world.

[7] See, e.g., A. D. Nock, art., 'Studies in the Graeco-Roman Beliefs of the Empire', *Journal of Hellenic Studies*, XLV (1925), p. 87, who refers to *Paris Papyri*, ed Wessely, 1,665, p. 518.

[8] In Egypt, the right performance of ritual went so far as to make of it something almost magical. The sacred words were thought to compel the superior powers to obey the officiating priest (see F. Cumont, *Oriental Religions*, p. 93).

[9] F. Cumont, ibid., p. 191.

[10] *ἔχουσαν πνεῦμα πύθωνα*. Apollo, the giver of oracles, was regarded as embodied in a snake at Delphi (otherwise known as Pytho). *πύθωνες* were utterers of involuntary oracles Plutarch calls them *ἐγγαστραμύθους*, 'ventriloquists' (*de def. orac.*, ix, 414, E), regarded as inspired by Apollo (F. F. Bruce, *The Acts of the Apostles*, p. 315). Brought to full mental and emotional health, this girl was of no further use to her masters (Acts 16^{19}).

[11] Post-Apostolic literature makes a legendary figure out of this man. He is depicted as Simon Magus, the arch-heretic, founder of Gnosticism, antagonist of Peter later at Antioch and Rome (see Irenaeus, *Adv. Haer.*, i, 23, Justin, *Apol.*, i, 26). The latter adjudges a statue dedication, probably originally to a Sabine deity, to be meant for our Simon; see also the *Clementine Homilies and Recognitions* (in which Paul is made to

man has a tremendous reputation amongst his fellow-Samaritans, who were notoriously interested in magic (verses 9f). Known as 'That power of God which is called Great', it is not so much that he is claiming to be God himself,[12] as that he is thought to be one in whom something of the power of the supreme God has been localized and evidenced. But whatever be the exact significance of Simon's title, there can be no question as to his high standing in the eyes of the people and of his skill in the realms of magic and sorcery. So impressed, however, is Simon with the δύναμις working through Philip that he was amazed (ἐξίστατο—the same word used in verse 9 concerning the people's attitude to Simon) and 'believed'. This was evidently a very elementary form of belief, comparable to that of the Jews impressed by the words and works of Jesus in John 8^{30f},[13] whose faith was merely a surface matter, not continuing when put to the test. This belief, however, does witness to the fact that *this* man—who had dabbled in these matters for so long—knew himself to be in the presence of a power superior to anything he had known.[14]

'Baptized' and 'believing', Simon was amongst the group of converts visited by the Apostles Peter and John from Jerusalem. As yet, the narrative tells us, the Holy Spirit was not yet 'fallen upon' any of them (verse 16). The sequence of events regarding the invasion of the Spirit varies so often in the stories in Acts that one thing only seems to be underlined: that His coming does not conform to any set programme! In 10^{44ff} the Gentiles are baptized because their 'speaking with tongues' indicated that they had already been visited by the Spirit; the Ephesian group of 19^{5f}, knowing only 'John's baptism', received the Spirit, by contrast, after baptism in the Name of Jesus and the laying on of hands. Now, though belief and baptism had preceded, it is after prayer

figure as Simon!), and the *Acts of Peter*. Origen (*contra Celsum*, v. 62) tells us of 'Simonians' who say that 'Simon is the power of God', and who are therefore not really Christian heretics at all (see arts. in Hasting's *Dictionary of the Bible*, *Dictionary of the Apostolic Church*, etc., on Simon Magus, and by R. P. Casey in *Beginnings*).

[12] As Dalman, *Words of Jesus*, p. 200, 'God Almighty' (the Rabbinic periphrasis *ha-geburah*). Just as Luke adds τοῦ θεοῦ in Lk 22^{69} so he adds καλουμένη μεγάλη in this explanatory fashion.

[13] Regarding this kind of 'believing' the Evangelist provides his own comment in Jn 2^{23f}.

[14] Ramsay comments on this and on these other stories in Acts (*Bearings*, p. 19): 'It is a universal feature in these encounters with magicians, that the latter with their sensitively organized physique always recognize the divine power inherent in the Apostles and messengers of God; they feel themselves in the presence of a power greater than their own.'

and the imposition of hands, that the gift of the Spirit was received by the Samaritans. This is referred to in such a way (verse 18) as to leave no doubt that inward feeling and external manifestation (possibly the glossolalia of 10^{46} and 19^{6}) provided undeniable evidence that the eschatological gift had come.

'Now when Simon saw that through the laying on of the apostles' hands the Holy Ghost was given, he offered them money, saying, Give me also this power, that on whomsoever I lay my hands, he may receive the Holy Ghost'. (verses 18f). It was easy for Simon to make the mistake he did,[15] for this is the realm on the borders of which he had worked for years. He now sees it opening in the presence of these men, and grasps at the possibilities of greater power that seemed to be beckoning . Knowing no better, in exchange for the ἐξουσία which he now knows they possess, he offers money. Unfortunately, he is far from knowing how, truly, these are men 'under authority'. He uses the word, as Ramsay comments, in the way that he understands it, as a magician.[16] He wants to be able at will to pass on 'power' (which is all that he understands, at this stage, of the Holy Spirit) to others. Would the apostles share their secret knowledge with him, and pass on their magical 'trick'?[17]

Adolf Schlatter administers something of a salutary shock when, in his book on *The Church in the New Testament Period*, he reminds us that the Jerusalem rabbis would view Christian claims as very much on a par with those made concerning Simon, 'the power of God which is called Great'. The Samaritans who thus revered him 'ascribed to him a mediatorial rôle between themselves and God, incarnating as it were the highest potency emanating from God. Those who adhered to him and accepted his teaching and the rites he prescribed were under the protection of this 'great power', and were assured of salvation.'[18] Conventional religion at this time, whether Hellenistic or Samaritan, left a void in human hopes and

[15] A mistake which has introduced the term 'simony' into regular usage.

[16] *Bearings*, p. 124.

[17] It is, surely, to Simon's credit that we are told, before the story ends, that he asked Peter, 'Pray for me to the Lord, that none of the things which ye have spoken come upon me' (verse 24). Perhaps he is beginning to understand something of the motives that operate in these realms, and to realize that God's powers are to be used only for God's purposes. A very radical repentance is, however, needed by a man with such an outlook and background as Simon (verse 22). We prefer the last picture of this man given here to the Simon Magus of later tradition. The Western text adds ὃς πολλὰ κλαίων διελίμπανεν to verse 24.

[18] op. cit., pp. 90f.

experience. Anyone possessing *gnosis* or giving evidence of 'power' could swiftly gather a group of devotees. The rapid growth of Gnostic movements of one kind and another at this period is evidence of this. To those who saw no deeper, Christianity must have seemed a system of this kind, built round the personality and the claims of Jesus of Nazareth. Those who developed Gnostic forms of Christianity patently so regarded it.

The story of Elymas in Acts 13^{6ff} concerns a renegade Jew, typical of a class who 'perverted the right ways of the Lord' (verse 11) and gave themselves to astrology, magic, and sorcery, misusing the understanding they possessed of God's ways and doubtless making great play with claims to knowledge of the divine name of Yahweh.[19] Some of them acquired such a reputation that they were given positions in the courts of princelings and proconsular officials. This man was such a one: ('which was with the proconsul', verse 7). He was a 'sorcerer' (verse 8) When Paul (who in this incident first receives his Roman cognomen) speaks to Elymas, he is described as 'filled with the Holy Ghost'. At that moment he would be acutely conscious of his link with God's power. He did not spare Elymas, who was doing his utmost to withstand the faith and prevent the Roman proconsul from developing too close an interest in it. Elymas is addressed as 'son of the devil',[20] 'thou enemy of all righteousness'. Divine powers are being used unlawfully by him. The 'children of the devil', of whom Paul says this man is one, are those who have broken with God's love and obedience, and seek to employ the powers coming from him for other purposes than His. Paul's word in verse 11, uttered in the consciousness of power, becomes operative, and Elymas is blinded 'for a season', as Paul said he would be.[21] The Roman proconsul, tremendously impressed (verse 12), 'believed'.[22]

Acts 19^{11ff} also helps to establish the kind of background presented to New Testament Christianity in such a city as

[19] Schlatter (op. cit., p. 120) regards this incident concerning Elymas as a typical example related by Luke of Paul's struggles with Jewish Gnosticism.

[20] Some commentators see in this an intentional antithesis to the name, 'Son of *Jesus*'. Here, however, the meaning is plain. He is acting the part of Satan, the adversary.

[21] 'The apostle, remembering his own example, knew that from the darkness of the eyes the mind's darkness might be restored to light.' F. F. Bruce so quotes Bede in *Acts*, p. 258, and also refers, similarly, to Chrysostom *Hom.*, xxviii.

[22] This, surely, is the preliminary type of 'believing'; cf. Simon Magus in 8^{13}. Luke does not add 'and was baptized'. The proconsul was impressed with the reality of the divine power working through Paul (R. B. Rackham, *Acts*, p. 202).

Ephesus. In the lines given to Antipholus in *The Comedy of Errors* (Act I, Scene ii, lines 97–102), Shakespeare portrays the scene.

> They say this town is full of cozenage;
> As, nimble jugglers that deceive the eye,
> Dark-working sorcerers that change the mind,
> Soul-killing witches that deform the body,
> Disguised cheaters, prating mountebanks,
> And many such-like liberties of sin.

The place was proverbial as the resort of quacks, magicians, and sorcerers of every kind.[23] Again, be it noted, the special group to whom attention is drawn is described in verse 13 as 'certain of the strolling Jews, exorcists'. As if Ephesian standards had influenced the chronicler, a list of Paul's own remarkable cures and miracles is recorded in this chapter. Perhaps Luke, or his source, was anxious to prove Paul's superiority in this realm, or perhaps, all unconsciously, he is revealing the Ephesian response to the coming of the *δύναμις* of the Holy Spirit among them: for it is here we learn of remarkable healing power of articles of clothing etc. that he had once used or worn![24] News of some of the accompaniments to Paul's mission would certainly reach the ears of the curious in the city. W. L. Knox thinks that Paul himself might have been in contact with some of these practitioners.[25] For them, at any rate, the formula concerning the name of Jesus becomes a great find.[26] Some of the bolder spirits begin experimenting with it. Always ready to seize on anything holding the promise of power, they find that this name is very powerful indeed! It works for the seven sons

[23] Bruce M. Metzger, in an article, 'St Paul and the Magicians' (*Princeton Seminary Bulletin*, Vol. 38, No. 1, June 1944, pp. 1ff), quotes some interesting examples of magic formulae, etc. emanating from Ephesus. 'From one end of the Empire to the other', he says, 'everyone knew of the famed Ephesian letters'. These were certain rune-like figures engraved on the image of Diana. They were thought to form a most effective charm indeed. He also describes a contemporary Ephesian amulet (set out in Vol. III of *Papyri in the Princeton University Collections*, 1942, pp. 78ff) which was meant to be worn on the body in order to ward off fever.

[24] R. B. Rackham suggests that Paul's miracles (verse 11) indicated to the Ephesians the presence of a permanent power residing in him (as in the Lord, Lk 8^{46}) (*Comm.*, p. 353).

[25] *Paul and the Church of the Gentiles*, p. 148. These astrologers and exorcists 'were presumably drawn from the Synagogue, but had left it in favour of Christianity as a more potent system of magic, whose efficacy was vindicated by its results'.

[26] Cf. *Paris Magical Papyri*, 574.3018ff. ὁρκίζωσε κατὰ τοῦ θεοῦ τῶν 'Εβραίων 'Iησοῦ (cf. also Mk 9^{38ff}; Lk 10^{17}, and Justin, *Tryph.*, 85). Such use of the name of Jesus receives stern Rabbinic strictures (e.g. Tosefta, *Hullin*, II.22f; T. J., *Shabbath*, XIV, 4. 14d, etc.) F. F. Bruce, *Acts*, p. 358: see also *Beginnings*, IV.31.

of Sceva, but not in the way anticipated![27] The very description of Sceva in verse 14 as 'a chief priest' reveals the kind of person it is with whom we are dealing. He is described in *The Beginnings of Christianity* as a 'rascally Levantine who knew that the High Priest of the Jews alone knew the name of God'.[28]

The news of the discomfiture of the would-be exorcists would spread like wildfire through the streets of Ephesus; and the sense of power connected with Paul's teaching and with the name of the Lord Jesus affected a vast number of people. The result was the public burning of magical books worth, according to the text, some 50,000 drachmae. This fact in itself indicates the widespread nature of the cult in 'curious arts', but also, more significantly, it provides the most tangible of all admissions on the part of the books' owners that in Christianity something far more potent was being demonstrated; something nearer the truth of things; and before whose light the 'curious arts' began to appear as works of darkness.

Luke concludes this section of his narrative with one of his typical summaries,[29] his closing words depicting the effect of Paul's three years' ministry amidst this pagan background, with its false pursuits, and its gross misuse, of power and might: 'So mightily grew the word of the Lord and prevailed' (19^{20}).[30]

Before the power of the Living God working through His Apostles, the works of darkness were shown to be of little account—the shadow, or reversal of the power that is in Him.

[27] It would seem that in the realms of the 'unconscious mind', where the trouble of the man 'with the evil spirit' (verse 16) would be located, the names of Jesus and Paul are known! But as these men use these names, the question comes, 'But who are ye?': what right have you to use these names and associate with them? It is not a matter of a magical uttering of a name that counts in these realms, but fellowship with all that the name implies.

[28] Op. cit. IV.239. 'Luke did not have at his disposal the devices of quotation-marks or the use of "*sic*" to show that he was merely giving Sceva's own account of himself' is F. F. Bruce's comment.

[29] Cf. 6^{7}, 9^{31}, 12^{24}, 16^{5}, 28^{31}.

[30] Note κατὰ κράτος (only time in Acts; cf. Eph 6^{10}) and ἴσχυεν (used in verse 16 above, in the story of the would-be exorcists: the only two occasions this word is used in Acts).

CHAPTER SEVENTEEN

'PRINCIPALITIES AND POWERS'

IN Paul's writings there are a number of references to heavenly powers. The various categories in which they are described becomes apparent when the references are set out in the following fashion:[1]

1 Corinthians 15^{24}: 'all rule and all authority and power'
Romans 8^{38}: 'nor angels, nor principalities . . . nor powers'
Colossians 1^{16}: 'whether thrones or dominions or principalities or powers'
Colossians 2^{10}: 'who is the head of all principality and power'
Colossians 2^{15}: 'having put off from himself the principalities and powers'
Ephesians 1^{21}: 'far above all rule, and authority, and power, and dominion'
Ephesians 3^{10}: 'unto the principalities and the powers in the heavenly (places)'
Ephesians 6^{12}: 'against the principalities, against the powers, against the world-rulers of this darkness, against the spiritual (hosts) of wickedness in the heavenly (places)'

There is also a similar reference in 1 Peter 3^{22}: 'angels and authorities and powers being made subject unto him'.

The way for this set of ideas concerning 'principalities and powers' had been prepared in orthodox Judaism. Yahweh's heavenly court of Job 1 and 2, the *bene elohim* of Job 1^{6}, 2^{1}, the references to God's *mal'ak*, and then to angelic messengers (Zech 1–8; Ezek 3^{12}, etc.)[2] were forerunners of a process whose momentum increased enormously in post-exilic and Hellenistic times.[3] Some of the language Paul used can be traced to the LXX.[4] In Daniel 7^{27} ἐξουσίαι (authorities) and ἀρχαί (rule) occur in the two alternative versions, and in Daniel $10^{13, 21}$, 12^{1} the guardian angel of each people, their prince (*sar*), become ἄρχων. We

[1] Later, on pp. 166ff, we discuss Paul's references to στοιχεῖα.
[2] See pp. 16f, 48ff for a discussion of angelology and demonology in Old Testament and Apocalypse and Pseudepigrapha.
[3] See above, p. 46.
[4] G. B. Caird, *Principalities and Powers*, Oxford, 1956, pp. 11ff.

have noted, in previous sections,[5] something of the history of the term *YHWH tseba'oth*. Originally, as we believe, a cult name, through its progression to 'Lord of hosts', it came to be translated in the LXX as ὁ κύριος τῶν δυνάμεων (Lord of powers)[6] By means of this term and its translation, the way was open to think of a hierarchy of angelic forces and cosmic powers. Much of this language concerning 'principalities', 'dominion', 'rule', as well as the more common term 'angels', meets us in the books of the intertestamental period (e.g. Test Jud 25^{2}; 3 Bar 1^{8}; En 61^{10}; Test Abr 14). In Philo we have noted the specialized treatment of the conception of 'powers', preparing for these Pauline references.

Aspects of this usage to be observed at the outset are: (1) In some cases, the supernatural agencies referred to seem to be exercising powers that are good, and, in others, powers that are bad.[7] (2) Certain terms are of frequent occurrence, e.g. ἀρχαί, ἐξουσίαι, δυνάμεις. (3) The order in which the titles occur does not yield information about their relative hierarchical importance —the names occur in varying order.[8] (4) In all these references the one common factor is the place of absolute supremacy accorded to the Lord Jesus over each and every class of angelic beings.[9] (5) In some cases, e.g. Ephesians 1^{21} and Colossians 2^{15}, this supremacy is described as already accomplished, while in 1 Corinthians 15^{24} it is a phase of the final consummation. In 1 Peter 3^{22} (as at Phil 2^{10}) His supremacy has resulted from the Incarnation, the Cross, and the Ascension, while Colossians 1^{16ff} states that all in heaven and earth—all originally created by Him —becomes reconciled to God 'through the blood of His Cross'.[10]

These supernatural powers, Paul asserts in Romans 8^{38}, are unable to separate Christ's people from God's Love in Christ. One suggestion is that, since this rhetorical passage is built up on a series of contrasted forces ('neither death, nor life', etc.), 'angels', and 'principalities' may similarly be set in opposition, one term

[5] pp. 42f, 49, 62.

[6] Especially in Psalms and Jeremiah. Elsewhere the more frequent translation was ὁ παντοκράτωρ. Often the name was, however, transliterated (see above, p. 42).

[7] It is to be noted, as C. A. Scott points out in his *Christianity according to St Paul*, pp. 29f, that St Paul is more concerned about the intermediary powers of evil than other New Testament writers, but note 1 Jn 5^{19} and cf. Jn 12^{31} with 2 Cor 4^{4} for the Devil, and Stephen's reference in Acts 7^{42}, to 'serve the host of heaven'.

[8] Though it is to be noted that when the three recurrent categories are used, they are invariably in the same order, e.g. ἀρχαί, ἐξουσίαι, δυνάμεις.

[9] Edward Langton, *The Angel Teaching of the New Testament*, London, 1936, p. 122.

[10] E. G. Selwyn, *1 Peter*, p. 207.

standing for good angels and the other for evil forces, i.e. the 'principalities' who are working against Christ's rule in the heavenly sphere.[11] Any force separating us from Christ might be regarded inevitably as evil, but the logical step does not follow by which we are allowed to label these categories in that way, for the cause of separation might conceivably originate from the human side, e.g. in the 'worship' of angels, discussed in Colossians.[12]

These angelic orders themselves are not outside the realm of Christ's creation, nor of His redemption. Colossians 1^{16f} explicitly affirms that: 'for in him were all things created, in the heavens and upon earth, things visible and invisible, whether thrones or dominions or principalities or powers; all things have been created through him, and unto him; and he is before all things, and in him all things consist'.[13] Colossians 1^{20} speaks of the reconciliation effected through Christ's Death, which operates upon all the divided elements of the whole creation, 'whether things upon the earth, or things in the heavens'.[14]

There can be no question about the angelic beings in Ephesians 6^{12}. These are evil, requiring the Christian to 'wrestle' against them, clad in the 'whole armour of God'. The ἀρχαί, ἐξουσίαι, and δυνάμεις of 1 Corinthians 15^{24ff} as certainly seem to be powers at enmity with God (verse 25, 'all his enemies').[15]

The references to the treatment of these beings, so variously

[11] The 'nor powers' of Rom 8^{38} seems in the nature of an afterthought. It escapes the parallelism of these contrasted pairs of opposites. It may have originally been linked with ἀρχαί (as Sanday and Headlam, and Denney).

[12] Godet makes this point in his *Commentary*. What is good in itself may work out in evil, if our sense of indebtedness, or even, of adoration, stops short at the creature instead of rising to God.

[13] For 'thrones', peculiar in New Testament to Col 1^{16}; see Test Levi 3^7; 2 En 20^1. Lightfoot (*Comm. ad loc*) discusses all the terms used here and, using Test Levi 3 and other passages from apocalyptic literature affirms that 'thrones' were of the highest order in the celestial hierarchy, possibly signifying (1) occupants of thrones surrounding the throne of God or (2) supporters of the throne of God; cf. the Old Testament picture of the cherubim. His final conclusion (p. 154, *b*) is that 'it seems best to treat θρόνοι as belonging to the same category with κυριότητες, ἀρχαί, ἐξουσίαι, which are concrete words borrowed from different grades of human rank and power. As implying *royal* dignity, θρόνοι naturally stands at the head of the list.'

[14] Cf. Eph 1^{10}. Through sin (when, in a pre-mundane fall, under Satan, angels revolted against God, or, upon earth, man's sin upset the balance of the whole universe: Rom 8^{20f}) the original harmony of the universe was destroyed. Christ's redeeming work rights this, throughout the whole scheme of things; cf. Peake, Colossians (*Expositor's Greek Testament*, 1903), pp. 510f. Many Pauline passages harmonize with the view that the angelic world needed, and comes to share in, a reconciliation. 'The blood of His Cross' was effective to the furthest reaches of the heavenly realm.

[15] Selwyn, *1 Peter*, p. 207.

described, themselves vary. In Ephesians 3^{10} they are brought to new knowledge and fresh understanding; in Colossians 1^{20}, as we have seen, they are 'reconciled'; in Colossians 2^{16} they are triumphed over (ἀπεκδυσάμενος); in 1 Corinthians 15 they are destroyed.[16]

Lightfoot suggests that Paul did not treat these categories—and, presumably, the realities they were meant to represent—very seriously. He was, so it would seem, accommodating himself to the point of view of his readers and hearers. He thinks that the phrase added in Ephesians 1^{21} reveals this. After listing 'all rule and authority, and power, and dominion' he continues 'and every name that is named, not only in this world, but also in that which is to come'. Lightfoot thinks this is so little serious a way of referring to these entities that it appears 'that in this catalogue St Paul does not profess to describe objective realities, but contents himself with repeating subjective opinions. . . . His language here shows the same spirit of impatience with this elaborate angelology, as in 2^{18}.'[17] It is quite likely that in places where Paul is obviously echoing Gnostic speculation there are signs of impatience in his references, but it is impossible to escape the view (e.g. from Eph 6^{12ff}) that he himself shared in the general belief concerning angelic beings, that he thought in terms of various orders and ministries among them, and considered the redeeming work of Christ to be for them not only an object of interest, but of reconciliation and of change.

Paul, as he took the Christian Gospel to the people of Asia Minor and Greece,[18] had the task of pioneering it, not only in body and person, but also in mind and understanding. The circumstances attending him inevitably had a bearing on the way he shaped his message. Just as the Galatian controversy resulted in a more acute recognition of the relationship between grace and faith and the supersession of the law, so Paul's contacts

[16] Selwyn, op. cit. He contrasts 1 Pet 3^{19} with these Pauline statements, as reflecting Peter's caution in statement (p. 208). We doubt whether this preaching to spirits in prison is meant to refer to these same cosmic powers.

[17] *The Epistles to the Colossians and Philemon*, p. 152; cf. Beet on Col 1^{16}, 'in this verse . . . the existence of angelic powers is not absolutely assumed. Paul merely says that if there be such, be they what they may, they were created in the Son of God.'

[18] By virtue of his background as a Jew of Tarsus, his sense of call and ordination (Gal 1^{16}; 2 Cor 4^{6}, etc.) and the force of events (Acts 13^{36}, 14^{27}) Paul felt himself uniquely called to be the Apostle to the Gentiles. To him had been imparted the divine secret that to them, as well as to Jews, the promises are available (Eph 3^{2ff}; Col 1^{25ff}). To them all, the door of faith has been opened (Acts 14^{27}).

with Gnostics and pagan philosophers, and his controversies with them, would broaden his thinking concerning Christianity. W. L. Knox, in his book, *St Paul and the Church of the Gentiles*,[19] speaks of the remarkable way in which Hellenistic Judaism, secure because of its fundamental and unwavering allegiance to the Torah, played host to any form of thought that seemed suited to its purpose. He argues that Paul was willing to act similarly.[20] In this way, Knox contends, Paul adapted his message in terms of the Hellenistic cosmogony in which all the contemporary cults were expressing themselves.[21] Thus he transformed Christianity 'from a system of Jewish apocalyptic, with a purely local and temporal appeal, into a religion of salvation by faith in the historical Jesus as the first born of creation'.[22]

Within Judaism itself the effect of Persian ideas was increasingly being felt at this point.[23] The whole mediatorial system received exaggerated emphasis in days when God's transcendence was being stressed; when His Name was too sacred to be pronounced; and it was argued that even the Law—God's most wonderful gift to His people—must have come through the mediatorship of angels. The strict monotheism of the Jew prevented 'angels' or 'demons' from assuming any of the prerogatives belonging to God. Rabbinic Judaism was having, however, to be more than especially careful in New Testament days concerning ideas verging on the idolatrous 'worship of angels', just as Christianity had for years to come to fight most sternly not only against the outward forces of the Roman Empire, but against the possible debasement of Christian truth by Gnostic fancies.[24] The peril from Gnosticism was accentuated by the very fact that, like Christianity, it recognized the world of spiritual reality, and observed the dichotomy between this world (or this aeon) and the other world of spirit. Its mythology is of far less significance in itself than this central fact, and represents, merely, the attempt to interpret it. This sense of

[19] Pp. 25f.

[20] 'The wisdom of the world might indeed be foolishness, but he was ready to use it to glorify Jesus, just as Judaism was ready to use it to glorify the Torah' (Knox, ibid., p. 90).

[21] See, e.g., R. Bultmann, *Primitive Christianity in Its Contemporary Setting* (E.T.), 1956, pp. 146ff; F. Cumont, *The Oriental Religions in Roman Paganism*, Chicago, 1911 pp. 133f, 207f, etc.; and above at pp. 66f.

[22] Ibid., p. 181.

[23] See above, pp. 17, 48ff.

[24] Many of which, ultimately, owe their final inspiration to Persia and Babylonia.

dichotomy, as Rudolf Bultmann cogently comments, was new in the ancient world. Man had always felt, in a measure, at home on this earth. Now 'the world became foreign soil to the human self'.[25]

Naturally enough this coincident movement offered ideas and interpretations, on the one hand, that were both suggestive and helpful, and on the other, that were challenging and to be resisted at all costs. We think of Paul so much as Christianity's champion against Gnostic ideas (as in Colossians) that we overlook the fact that on the positive side he was doubtless influenced by some of its suggestions. If it be no more than that he used some of its vocabulary—in order to refute it!—there remains at least this measure of borrowing.

The Gnostic myth associates individual redemption with the need for redemption on a cosmic scale.[26] It is Gnostic language, says Bultmann, when Satan is called 'the god of this world' (2 Cor 4[4]), and 'the prince of the power of the air' (Eph 2[2]).[27] He sees the 'rulers' (ἀρχαί) of this world who 'crucified the Lord of glory' (1 Cor 2[8]) as the spirit-powers ruling this planet, 'figures of Gnostic mythology'. They are referred to in all the categories listed above, 'thrones' 'dominions', 'principalities', 'authorities', 'power', etc., and are included in the 'gods many and lords many' of 1 Corinthians 8[5].[28]

In Galatians 4[3, 9] and Colossians 2[8, 20], Paul uses a word not included in these lists. It is the designation στοιχεῖα. In all but the second of these texts the word occurs with the addition, τοῦ κοσμοῦ. Etymologically στοιχεῖα means a row, or rank, or line. Thus it came to be used for the elements of speech; the letters of the alphabet; and the elements of knowledge (cf. Heb 5[12]). Next it was applied to the elements of the universe, the physical material out of which the world is made (2 Pet 3[12]). The next stage in the history of its usage takes us into the realms of animism and

[25] *Theology of the New Testament*, I. 165.

[26] Ibid., p. 166. 'The individual self is only a spark or fragment of the light-treasure which is held prisoner by the demonic world-rulers in this world of darkness; and its redemption is only a detail of the redemption of all the sparks of light fettered here in prison but united with each other and with their origin by a 'kinship of nature' (συγγένεια). Individualistic eschatology—i.e. the doctrine of the emancipation of the individual self at death, and of its journey to heaven—stands within the context of a cosmic eschatology.' See also the same writer's *Primitive Christianity*, pp. 163ff, for an account of the Gnostic myth, and the relations of Gnosticism to Christianity.

[27] Cf. Jn 12[31], 14[30], 16[11] and 'the ruler of this Aeon', Ign Eph 19[1].

[28] *Theology of the New Testament*, I.173.

symbolism. Behind each element was its tutelary deity, and the word is used to denote these.[29] G. H. C. Macgregor tells us that in the Orphic hymns Hephaestus is described as στοιχεῖον ἀμεμφές, the 'perfect element', and the moon-goddess is described in the Paris magical papyri as στοιχεῖον ἄφθαρτον.[30] The identity of astral bodies with these elemental spirits is a familiar step in this sequence, and στοιχεῖα comes thus to be used of the heavenly bodies themselves. Macgregor also quotes from the Testament of Solomon a passage in which certain spirits approach Solomon with the words, 'We are some of the thirty-three στοιχεῖα of the κοσμοκράτορες τοῦ σκότους . . . and are stars in heaven . . . and we are invoked as goddesses. . . . We are some of the thirty-six στοιχεῖα, οἱ κοσμοκράτορες τοῦ σκότους τούτου.'[31]

In his commentaries on Galatians and Colossians, Lightfoot knows nothing of this suggestion. He favours the translation 'rudimentary instruction' or 'elementary teaching' (as Heb 5^{12}) for στοιχεῖα in both these letters. H. N. Ridderbos in a recent commentary on Galatians takes a similar view.[32] In Colossians 2^{8} he thinks the expression is used as a synonym for 'the tradition of men', and in Galatians as 'definite principles or axioms according to which men lived before Christ, without finding redemption in them'.[33] The meaning of the Galatian passage, however, conforms exactly to the Gnostic idea of the στοιχεῖα as star-forces or powers. In the service of the law, the Jews are 'minors', in bondage under

[29] We have already noted this development in Apocalyptic literature, e.g. Jub 2^{3ff}, angels of fire, wind, clouds, darkness, etc.; 2 En 4^{1f}, 5^{1f}, 6^{1f}, angels that rule the Stars, keep the treasure-houses of the snow, dew and flowers; cf. 1 En 60^{17f}, 66^{1f}; Bar 6^{15f}, 7^{3}, etc. This conception is obviously behind Rev 7^{1}, 14^{18}, 16^{5}.

[30] Art, 'Principalities and Powers: The Cosmic Background of Paul's Thought', *New Testament Studies*, I. 21.

[31] Ibid., p. 22. Macgregor notes the juxtaposition of στοιχεῖα and κοσμοκράτορες (cf. Eph 6^{12}). The phrase τοῦ σκότους (τούτου) is equally noteworthy in this connexion. Note Edwyn Bevan, *Hellenism and Christianity*, p. 77; 'The fear of these world rulers (κοσμοκράτορες), particularly the Sun, the Moon and the five planets lay heavy on the old world. The Mysterious Seven held humanity in the mechanism of iron necessity.'

[32] His reasons for this, however, seem most inadequate (*Comm.*, p. 153n). He says 'one cannot speak of an established linguistic practice, as the expression can be found nowhere else.' Instances are given above, and Everling (*Die Paulinische Angelologie und Dämonologie*, Göttingen, 1888, pp. 66ff), gives 'a wealth of citations from Jewish writings' (E. Langton, op. cit., p. 126).

[33] In support of Ridderbos' interpretation of στοιχεῖα in Gal 4^{9}, the verse following describes that in which this service of the rudiments consists—observation of all kinds of ceremonial regulations. The Revised Version has, of course, 'rudiments' as its consistent translation. Burton, *I.C.C.*, pp. 510ff favours 'elemental forms of religion superseded by Christ'. This is also favoured by W. L. Knox, *St Paul and the Church of the Gentiles*, pp. 108f.

guardians and stewards. These are the στοιχεῖα, the elemental spirits, angelic powers,[34] 'who kept them in dependence upon themselves, until God, through Christ, set them free from the curse of the Law'.[35]

Paul seems thus to be at the point where Jewish ideas concerning 'angels' and Hellenistic ideas concerning astral and cosmic powers intersect. There is no doubt that he recognizes the existence of beings after this order, and he can find warrant in Judaism for this belief.[36] Always, however, their power is thought of as subordinate and derived. They possess nothing approaching divinity. Their rightful condition is that of God's agents. Paul's view is also that whatever of wrongful power they have usurped, or whatever force they have misused, together with all that is out of harmony in their sphere is being—indeed, already has been—put right by Christ.

In the section on Christ's Death and Resurrection, we noted how Paul considered that the cosmic powers, standing behind all that happens in this world, had been the ultimate strategists behind Christ's Crucifixion (1 Cor 2^{6ff}), and in their very attempt to defeat Him had engineered their own defeat.[37] Colossians 2^{15} speaks of the way in which, by the Cross, Christ 'completely turned the tables', triumphing 'over the angelic powers who had drawn up the Law'[38] (cf. Gal $3^{13, 19}$). The ἀπεκδυσάμενος of verse 15 affords one of many points of controversy in these difficult verses. Lightfoot favours 'having stripped off from himself', which agrees with the Revised Version 'put off from himself'. J. A. T. Robinson, in *The Body*, makes the startling suggestion that the object (understood) of this 'stripping off' was His Body. He thus eluded the grasp of the principalities and powers. Macgregor[39] says that it is a consistent Pauline argument that Christ must first put himself under whatever it is from which He is to save men (e.g. under the law, under sin, etc.):

Now that part of man through which the evil spirit powers can lay hold of man and enslave him is his 'flesh'. Therefore Christ had taken upon

[34] Grundmann, *Der Begriff der Kraft*, p. 48; cf. 1 Cor 8^5, 10^{20}. Jew and Gentile are subject to cosmic spiritual powers (ibid., p. 49).
[35] A. Schweitzer, *The Mysticism of St Paul*, p. 70.
[36] See p. 161 above, and the pages in the Old Testament and Apocalypse sections which refer especially to angelology, etc. (pp. 16f, 48ff).
[37] See above, pp. 118f.
[38] See note 45, H. J. Schonfield, *Authentic New Testament, ad loc.*
[39] Art., 'Principalities and powers', *New Testament Studies*, I.23.

himself the physical constitution of man; God had sent Him 'in the likeness of sinful flesh'—'flesh' in which the 'principalities and powers' still could find a lodgement. In the act of dying he divested himself of that flesh, and with it 'stripped off the principalities and powers', thus breaking their dominion, and carrying with himself in his victory all those who through faith had come to be 'in him' and thus shared his experiences.

The Authorized Version has 'having spoiled the principalities and powers', which might have been rendered 'having plundered'. The Authorized Version form has the merit, however, of reminding us of the 'Strong Man' passage, and of the echoes of Isaiah 49^{25}, 53^{12} in the LXX that lie behind it. This suggestion is still further interesting because, grammatically, the subject of the whole sentence is not Christ, but God.[40]

There is a third possibility that the phrase means 'having flung them away from himself'; and yet a fourth that the ἀρχαί and ἐξουσίαι of the passage are 'good angels', and the triumph (θριαμβεύειν) over them is to be understood in the sense of their willing subservience gladly given to Him.[41] Lohmeyer[42] thinks of the phrase as reminiscent of court, picturing the public degradation of high officials, their mantles and insignia being stripped from them. Vincent Taylor[43] writes of Paul thinking 'of the work of Christ as a fight of God Himself with the hostile powers, a death grapple from which He emerged victorious, stripping His enemies of their apparel and leading them, like a Roman conqueror in triumph'.

The consummation of the process by which Christ triumphs over all angelic powers takes place at the Parousia (1 Cor 15^{20ff}). At the end of all things is the final destruction of Satan, and the last enemy, Death. Until that time, the 'rulers of this world' (1 Cor 2^{6ff}) are not yet destroyed, though their power to destroy has been taken from them in Christ. They are καταργούμενοι (1 Cor 2^{6}), 'being put out of action'.[44]

[40] E. F. Scott, *M.N.T.C.*, p. 46.

[41] First suggested by J. Peirce, *A Paraphrase and Notes on Colossians*, 1729, and followed by Alford, Ritschl, Beet, C. G. Findlay, and Peake; see *Dictionary of Apostolic Church*, II.274a.

[42] *Der Kolosserbrief*, pp. 118ff.

[43] *The Atonement and New Testament Teaching*, p. 63.

[44] Macgregor, op. cit., p. 23. 'Like the redemption of the Christian', comments G. B. Caird (*Principalities and Powers*, p. 28), 'the redemption of the powers is achieved by the Cross, worked out in the present, and consummated at the Parousia.'

With regard to the whole matter of Christ's subjection of the angelic powers, it is impressive to note the place Psalm 110 has in early Christian apology.[45] Throughout the New Testament the picture meets us of Jesus 'seated at the right hand of God', as do also other references going back to this Psalm. The 'enemies' referred to (obviously originally Israel's human foes) are in the New Testament interpretation as clearly the principalities and powers of the invisible realm. God has raised up Christ 'and made him to sit at his right hand in the heavenly (places), far above all rule, and authority, and power, and dominion' (Eph 1^{20}). Oscar Cullmann traces this typical assertion into early confessional formulae, as indicated in 1 Peter 3^{22} and Phil 2^{6} in the New Testament and in the Letter of Polycarp 2^{1}, and Ignatius' Trallians 9^{1} in early Apostolic literature. Christ's subjection of the angelic powers is not thus to be regarded as a 'peripheral assertion', but as an 'altogether central article of faith'.[46] An increasing hesitancy about the concept of angelic powers brought about its virtual disappearance at a later stage, but the survival of the picture of the heavenly session at the right hand of God witnesses to the original complete conception based on this thoroughgoing interpretation of Psalm 110[47] Paul, thus, is shown to share in a common Christian viewpoint.

Johannine and Synoptic references are of a piece with these conceptions. Jesus, as the living agent of the Kingdom of God, has come into this world, casting out the 'Strong One', overturning His house, and taking his spoils (Mk 3^{23ff} and parallels). Mark's Longer Ending (16^{19}) speaks of his triumph seated at the right hand of God' (cf. Acts 7^{55f}). By His Death, He has ransomed 'many'.[48]

In the Fourth Gospel there are no accounts of exorcism, no reference to the demons, nor any hint of the Pauline categories of 'principalities and powers'. All that the other writers suggest concerning a kingdom of evil, or spirits in revolt against God, is concentrated upon the figure of the devil.[49] This present world is

[45] Mk 13^{36}; Mt 26^{64}; Acts 2^{23f}, 5^{31}, 7^{55}; Rom 8^{34}; Heb 1^{3}; Rev 3^{21}, etc.

[46] See *The Earliest Christian Confessions* and *The State in the New Testament*, pp. 102f.

[47] *The State in the New Testament*, pp. 103f.

[48] Mk 10^{45} and the reference to this on p. 117.

[49] Throughout the New Testament Satan is 'the summary of spiritual forces, their first and master, as God is Lord of angels' (Grundmann, *Der Begriff der Kraft*, p. 49).

in Satan's grip: men stand under his lordship.[50] John states succinctly, 'To this end was the Son of God manifested, that he might destroy the works of the devil' (1 Jn 3^{8}).

Even more clearly than in the Synoptic Gospels, Christ is victor *throughout* His ministry. There is no suggestion (as in Phil 2^{9f}; Eph 1^{20ff}; 1 Pet 3^{21f}) that His supreme authority over the cosmic and demonic powers must wait for His Death and Resurrection. He is 'the Resurrection and the Life' (11^{25}) *now*, as the story of Lazarus proves (cf. 5^{26}).

John's message concerning the focal point of Christ's victory is, however, the same as that of all the New Testament writers. From the first chapter, the Gospel moves towards the Paschal drama: by means of this Christ bears away the sins of the world (1^{29})[51] In His 'lifting up'[52] He will draw all men unto Himself. With this act, judgement has come to the world, and the Prince of this world shall be cast out.[53] 'Now' is in the inbreaking of God's sovereignty in judgement and power. Thenceforward, the one to whom men will look will not be the Father of lies, but the Saviour of men. The devil will no longer be 'ruler'; nor will men any longer be under his sway.[54]

All authority and rule is now under Christ. This is the underlying fact of this era, even though not fully recognized by many of its participants! The Christian, living in the times of tension

[50] So remarkable is his power of infiltration into the realms of God's own authority that Jesus can say to the Jews in 8^{44}: 'Ye are of (your) father the devil'. In their determination to put Jesus to death—and finding their reasons and their authority in their religion—they are the tools of Satan. So far from claiming inheritance in the people of God, they are being used by God's enemy. From the beginning he has twisted the things of God. He is the 'father of lies'; a 'murderer from the beginning'. As Stauffer says (*New Testament Theology*, p. 66), his is 'the spirit of constant negation—of negation most serious for the cosmos and its history. Hence he answers every act of God with some counter activity, every historical advance with a contrary motion.'

[51] Note what H. E. W. Turner calls 'the principle of teleological interpretation' in John. By announcing the great saving fact underlying all Christ did and was, John 'puts his readers in possession of an important clue at the very beginning of the Gospel' (*Jesus, Master and Lord*, pp. 54f).

[52] The twofold meaning of this phrase should be kept in mind: (1) The actual lifting up upon the Cross, e.g. 12^{33}, and (2) the glorification and exaltation John always associates with Christ's Death, e.g. 14^{31ff}. (R. H. Lightfoot, *Comm.*, p. 252, points out that in the LXX of Isa 52^{13} ὑψόω and δοξάζω are used side by side.)

[53] 12^{31f}. For ἐκβληθήσεται ἔξω, cf. 6^{37}, 9^{34f}, 14^{30}, 16^{11}. Not 'cast out of the world', but 'cast out of office, out of authority' (C. K. Barrett, *Comm.*, pp. 355f). 'Nothing is said of his subsequent fate'.

[54] 'By His "uplifting" on the Cross, Jesus will be given world dominion: becoming *de facto* the *Saviour of the world*, as, in His human ministry, He was *de jure*. *I will draw all men unto myself*. These words are the Johannine counterpart of Mt 11^{28}' (R. H. Strachan, *The Fourth Gospel*, pp. 258f).

between the Resurrection and the End, is denizen of a world whose rulers, both terrestrial and celestial, do not yet all recognize Christ's authority. Because of this, perplexing questions are continually raised about the Christian's allegiance. Some of these questions affecting his relationship to the State and to earthly rulers will be discussed in the next chapter.

CHAPTER EIGHTEEN

CIVIL POWER: THE AUTHORITY OF THE STATE

BY the Hebrew, all rule was considered to be subordinate and subservient to God. In Old Testament days, as we have noted, earthly kings were considered to hold their authority under His command. Texts from Deuteronomy (e.g. 32^{8f} and 4^{19}) show that even the 'gods' of the heathen were regarded as holding their lordship at the will of Yahweh.[1] All angelic power ultimately derived its authority from Him. The close connexion made in thought between the earthly ruler, seen and known in this world, and the unseen angelic ruler who is the appointed guardian of each nation is emphasized in Isaiah 24^{21}, $34^{2, 4}$.[2] The relationship between them is that the earthly ruler embodies the counsel of the angelic *sar*, or 'watcher'. It would seem that this idea is continued in the thought of Paul. As for these 'princes' of each nation,[3] says G. B. Caird, 'Paul believed that society was controlled by angelic powers who, though corrupt and doomed to lose their power, retained as long as the present age lasted the stamp of their God-given authority'.[4]

Once this clue is provided, certain Pauline passages yield what would seem to be a possible double reference. In them, we may ask, is Paul speaking of earthly, or angelic, rulership? Or is there a subtle interweaving—so that while we are directed to think of one order of power, we are being reminded of the other? Who, for example, are the ἐξουσίαι of Rom 13^{1ff}? Some New Testament scholars take the view they are not earthly rulers at all, but the 'angelic powers' we have been considering in the previous section,[5] and, in particular, as suggested, that part of the angelic host who

[1] Quoted above at p. 17.

[2] See above, p. 37. All these texts are quoted in G. B. Caird's *Principalities and Powers*, pp. 5, 10.

[3] To give them the title (*sar*) accorded in Dan $10^{13, 20}$, 12^{1}, see above p. 48.

[4] Ibid., p. 22.

[5] E.g. Oscar Cullmann. See his *Christ and Time* (E.T.), 1951, pp. 194ff, and *The Early Church* (E.T.), 1956, pp. 134ff. He cites M. Dibelius, *Die Geisterwelt im Glauben des Paulus* (1909). Günther Dehn sets out the same view in *Engel und Obrigkeit* in *Theologische Aufsätze für Karl Barth 1936*, and the latter in *Rechtfertigung und Recht, 1938*, accepts it. See also K. L. Schmidt, *Das Gegenüber von Kirche und Staat in der Gemeinde des neuen Testaments* in *Theol. Blätter*, 1937, pp. 1ff.

'stand behind' the authorities ruling in this world. Paul's phrase thus carries a double reference—to the State, and to the 'invisible powers' of which it is 'the executive agent'.[6] It is difficult to accept this view in its most thoroughgoing form, though, at the least, one must grant that the kind of use Paul makes of this word elsewhere colours his choice of it here.[7]

In 1 Corinthians 2^8, where we take *οἱ ἄρχοντες τοῦ αἰῶνος τούτου* to mean 'the spiritual powers behind this world', the overtones work in reverse. The fact is that the earthly agents enacting the policy of the angelic rulers to bring Christ to death and humiliation were Pilate, Herod, and Caiaphas. So, as in Rom 13^1, we may consider the reference in the first instance is to the power of the State, and, secondly, to the *ἐξουσίαι* behind it, in 1 Corinthians 2^8 it is first, to the angelic powers, and then in its overtones to those who carried their policies into effect here upon earth.[8]

This relationship to earthly rulers and to the Spiritual *ἐξουσίαι* behind them forms part of the complex of Christian experience while living under Christ's Lordship in 'this present evil world'.

So far as he himself is called upon to exercise leadership, the Christian has clear guidance, and, of course, the perfect pattern. Jesus says in Mark 10^{42f}, 'Ye know that they which are accounted to rule over the Gentiles lord it over them; and their great ones exercise authority over them. But it is not so among you.' This is not the kind of rulership to be known amongst those who are Christ's.[9] For them there are very different standards: 'Whosoever would be first among you, shall be servant of all'.

As a subject in an earthly State, the Christian has to live his life

[6] So Cullmann, *Christ and Time*, p. 195, who quotes Irenaeus (*adv. Haer.* v. 24. 1) for the information that this is how Gnostics later interpreted Rom 13^1. (See also *The Early Church*, p. 137 and *The State in the New Testament*, London, 1957, pp. 93f.)

[7] Invariably elsewhere in Pauline usage *ἐξουσίαι* are 'angelic powers'; cf. Lk 12^{11} and Tit 3^1 for the plural used in the sense of earthly magistracy (see Foerster, *T.W.z.N.T.*, II.562).

[8] Cullmann says something very much like this at the foot of p. 135 of *The Early Church*. G. B. Caird (op. cit., pp. 16ff) finds reference to angelic rulers also in 1 Cor 15^{24}, 6^3, 11^{10f}. (In the latter text he says that women, according to Paul's dictum, must be veiled, out of deference to the angel guardians of the natural order of society—which ordains, of course, that women shall be subservient to men! The wearing of the veil is the mark of their honouring of this arrangement.)

[9] The Christian's citizenship is 'in heaven' (Phil 3^{20}). Earthly rulership is to be understood—whether one is suffering it, or exercising it—against the greater background (cf. Mt 17^{26}; see Nygren *Romans*, p. 427). Thomas Gilby's comment on Mk 10^{10-45} is illuminating: 'The political commonwealth may be healthy, and yet be no sort of final home for men made for the communications of heavenly society, its most efficient procedures will be clumsy compared with those delicate exchanges' (*Between Community and Society: a Philosophy and Theology of the State*, 1953, p. 317).

in this world. His Lord grants him no exemption from this (Jn 17[15]). His relationship to the ruling powers is set, therefore, as a Christian amid the tension of these times between the Resurrection and the End. The advice he receives is well set out in Romans 13[1-7], as also in 1 Peter 2[13-17]. The advice was, of course, pertinent in the first place to Jew and Gentile living then under the power of Rome. The Christian is to be subject to the Emperor and his governors 'for the Lord's sake' (1 Pet 2[13]; 'for conscience sake', Rom 13[5]). He is told—as one would imagine, somewhat surprisingly—'the (powers) that be are ordained of God' (Rom 13[1]).[10]

This teaching does not represent a counsel of expediency on the part of the Apostles, as if the Christian Church, already suspect of sedition, needed for safety's sake to be especially zealous in good citizenship. It is consistent with the orthodox Hebrew view of rulership and authority. Strack-Billerbeck, in adducing many contemporary instances, comments on Paul's statement 'for there is no power but of God' (Rom 13[1]): 'this is a proposition concerning which scarcely any divergency of view existed in the ancient Synagogue'.[11] In a passage addressed to kings and judges of the earth, Wisdom 6[3] emphasizes that 'dominion' and 'sovereignty' are from the Most High (cf. En 46[5]; Apoc Bar 82[9]). It is for this reason that secular government must be obeyed.[12]

God is the God of order, who created cosmos out of chaos. The preservation of order, therefore, is uniquely a matter for His concern and providence.[13] The ruler, occupying a functional position

[10] It is this that lends colour to the idea that these are the angelic rulers referred to here. Cullmann (*Christ and Time*, p. 204) asserts that this authority is theirs, since through the Cross of Christ the powers that govern the State have been brought within the kingdom of Christ (without knowing it). We agree with Caird's criticism of this point of view. The ἐξουσίαι, interpreted in this fashion, already possess authority in the economy of God. In any case, the ruler is there to maintain justice, and to act as a bulwark against chaos (see p. 36, above, E. Stauffer, *New Testament Theology*, pp. 81ff, and Caird, *Principalities and Powers*, pp. 24f). His authority, in other words, whether it be earthly or angelic ruler that is being thought of, has existed in God's 'natural order'. It is not dependent upon Christ's victory on the Cross.

[11] *Kommentar z.N.T.*, III.303.

[12] Cf. Josephus, *Jewish Wars*, ii, viii, 7. Sanday and Headlam (*Romans, I.C.C.*, p. 366) point out that the maxim regarding this divine appointment of kings and rulers is usually introduced in Hebrew literature in order to remind people that God is greater than all rulers, and that these should remember their responsibilities to him (e.g. as in Wis 6[1, 3], and En 46[5]).

[13] E. F. Scott (*Paul's Epistle to the Romans*, 1947, p. 69) reminds us of the motions of the stars, the movements of the tides, and says that the first law of God's universe is 'order'. 'The men who preserve order in a kingdom or a town or a business are to that extent doing God's work, and those who profess to serve God must support them.' Note, by the way, in this Rom 13 passage the number of words with the root τάξις—

as a centre of unity and of ordered government, can, in some measure, subserve the divine purposes.[14] Romans 13, with its reference in verse 4 to the wrath ('for he is a minister of God, an avenger for wrath to him that doeth evil'), sets the matter of subjection to the rulers squarely in this present aeon, which, with much out of harmony with God and His purposes, is the aeon of God's wrath. What the ruler does is to apply the law of retribution, denied in 12^{19} to the Christian.[15] Here again we face the dualism inherent in the Christian's situation. He is 'in Christ', under His Lordship, knowing the power of the Holy Spirit, to that extent living in the New Age; but he is also inextricably bound up in every way with the life of the world.[16] It is therefore the Christian, alone, who can see clearly what a ruler is meant to be, and in an enlightened manner, can yield him the kind of obedience to which his office really entitles him. As Paul expresses it, the ruler is 'a minister of God' (Rom $13^{4, 6}$) and his commission is to execute 'the wrath' on those who do wrong.[17]

In the Fourth Gospel there is one solitary, but very significant, reference to civil power; and in this (19^{10ff}) John shows himself completely at one with the view we can now describe as the biblical conception of civil authority. In verse 10 Pilate tries to stir our Lord to more useful efforts in His own self-defence: 'Knowest thou not that I have power (*ἐξουσία*) to release thee, and

ὑποτάσσεσθαι, τεταγμένος, διαταγή, etc. The whole stress is on the notion of 'order' (Cullmann, *Christ and Time*, p. 201). The condition of anarchy must be checked at all costs. 'That is the reason why, in the New Testament, the divine institution of the State is primarily based on criminal law'. (E. Brunner, *Justice and the Social Order*, p. 175).

[14] Cf. 2 Macc 4^6. Is this a possible guide to the interpretation of 2 Thess 2^{6f}? G. B. Caird interprets the reference to *ὁ κατέχων* here to Rome herself: 'Caligula has been removed, and all that he stood for is for the moment held in restraint. The restraining power can only be Rome in the exercise of her God-given function of government. Thus does Paul in a single passage delineate the ambiguous nature of Roman power. From one point of view the state was fulfilling its divinely-appointed office of restraining the evil-doer, but from another point of view its authority was so corrupt as to be constantly in danger of usurping the authority of God' (op. cit., p. 26f).

[15] 'The social degradation which results from sin is the most radical manifestation of "the Wrath", but also the retributive system of justice in a non-Christian society is also a manifestation of the same principle. The Christian order of society rests on a different and higher principle expounded in Chapter 12 and succinctly stated in 13^{8-10}' (Dodd, *Romans*, p. 204).

[16] Nygren, in *Romans*, shows how this tension and dualism faces us in Chapters 6–8 of the letter, e.g. Chapter 6: free from sin, yet having to battle against it; 7: free from the law, yet not yet righteous; 8: free from death, yet longing for the redemption of our bodies (pp. 295f).

[17] This is, as Nygren describes it, God's 'alien' work, but nevertheless, God's work (ibid., p. 431). The Christian should recognize this God-given function, therefore, in the ruler (Rom 13^7; 1 Pet 2^{17}).

have power to crucify thee?' The Roman Governor knows of the 'authority' he exerts under his appointment, giving him the right to order a man's execution, or to release him. It is 'authority' of this kind the Centurion in Matthew 8[9] and Luke 7[8] refers to. Under Caesar, he possesses delegated authority. In Pilate's case, this means power of life and death.

C. K. Barrett, commenting on these two verses,[18] remarks that what Pilate has is *potestas*, and that in verse 11 John is using one of his 'common literary reverses', here 'shown in reverse'. He instances 3[3-8] as an example of this. Jesus uses a word in a theological sense, which is misunderstood by his hearers and repeated in a purely literal manner. Here, he suggests, Pilate uses the word quite 'untheologically'; 'Jesus takes the word out of his mouth, and uses it absolutely, speaking of the authority not of Rome but of God.' What He is doing is to drive home still further Pilate's sense of delegated authority, and to remind this ruler, as Barrett himself phrases it, that 'all authority is derived from God's (cf. Rom 13[1])'. Like all other power and authority in the universe, civil power is only rightly used when it is in accordance with God's will.

We must not overpress these references, nor wrest from them too definite a theology of civil power, for in the New Testament one cannot escape the sense of a certain indifference to the State. It is as if Christ's people were exempted from overmuch concern about its ordering and its organization. Living in the new aeon, they are detached from such considerations, recognizing that their point of reference is not that of this world. In their community, among the people of God, the Lordship of Christ can be fully worked out and known.[19]

With this background in mind, it is impressive to examine our Lord's logion in Mark 12[17], which can now be seen not merely as an astute dealing with a difficult situation: it enshrines the same exhortation to loyalty as has been noted in the Pauline and Petrine passages.[20] We can then look at the story of Holy Week, as

[18] *Comm.*, pp. 451f.

[19] Cf. 1 Cor 6[1ff]. See Bultmann's *Essays*, pp. 204f: 'The peculiar dual existence of the Christian in Church and State with its problems' had 'not become a subject for reflection as yet in the New Testament'.

[20] See Chapter VIII of E. Stauffer's *Christ and the Caesars* (pp. 112ff) for an examination of the story of the Tribute Money and its implications. Jesus, says Stauffer, affirmed the symbolism of power (on the imperial coinage) but rejected the symbolism of worship (p. 132).

Stauffer suggests, as 'the existential exegesis of His words: submission to the dominion of Caesar, submission to the dominion of God—united in the acceptance of that monstrous judicial murder by which Caesar's most wretched creature fulfils *sub contrario* the work of God (Mt 26^{52ff}; Jn 19^{1f})'.[21]

The one thing not to be granted to the earthly ruler is worship;[22] and it is at that point that the Christian, prepared to follow the Christian code of loyalty and submission to the Emperor, and even to pray for him,[23] confronts the cult of Emperor worship with emphatic non-compliance. So, in the same New Testament,[24] Revelation 13 can follow Romans 13. Never must Caesar be given the things that belong to God.[25]

Since the ruler is himself a child of this age exercising power in this aeon, from the outset his fallibility must be reckoned with. Indeed, as Lord Acton's dictum reminds us, power itself corrupts, and 'absolute power corrupts absolutely'. We can expect, therefore, in terms of New Testament demonology, to see the ruler fall victim to the angelic forces that have themselves grasped at power.[26] Earlier, we have looked at the passages suggesting that power over this world (and this means, of course, especially political power) has been allowed to Satan, and that our Lord Himself faced, and rejected, the possibility of accepting his way as the price of world dominion.[27] As a 'servant of God to execute His wrath on the evildoer', the ruler must 'bear the sword', but the dangers of that weapon are everywhere spoken against in Scripture: it has a habit of turning upon the person who wields it.[28] In the exercise of rulership the inevitable point of corrupti-

[21] Ibid., p. 135.

[22] This is also Judaism's one proviso (see above, p. 37, and also Moore, *Judaism*, II.114).

[23] 1 Tim 2^{2}; cf. 1 Clem 60f. Sacrifices for foreign rulers seem to have been an ancient custom (see 1 Macc 7^{33}; Philo, *Legatio ad Gaium*, c. 33. 152f, *c.* 45. 355–7). Prayers doubtless accompanied these sacrifices (Yoma 69a, Josephus. *Jewish Wars*, ii, 10, 4, *Antiquities*, xii, 10. 5. etc.).

[24] Note the verbs in 1 Pet 2^{17}: 'Fear God, honour the King.' and cf. Rev 14^{7}, 15^{4}.

[25] Oscar Cullman's point about the 'apparent contradiction' of Rom 13 and Rev 13 vanishes when this point is clearly grasped. (As he himself says in his *State in the New Testament*, pp. 5, 70, 86, etc.)

[26] G. B. Caird in the book from which we have already quoted attempts a synthesis of St Paul's treatment of all the powers that exercise lordship in this world—the powers of the state, the powers of legalized religion (the Torah), the powers of nature. They are all agencies appointed in the economy of God; but each, through sin, has become corrupted, and instead of exercising divinely appointed authority are capable of showing themselves as demonic agencies.

[27] See above pp. 81, 170f; cf. Lk 4^{5f}; see Stauffer, *New Testament Theology*, p. 85.

[28] Mt 26^{52}; Rev 13^{10}.

bility centres in human pride and the tendency to self-glorification (e.g. Dan 5^{18ff}).[29] It is *then* that the ruler ceases to be the agent of God. Instead, he has succumbed to the forces of evil, and, as in the pictures of Daniel 8^{9ff} and Revelation 13, usurps God's prerogatives, demanding worship. Now, as the agent of the devil, his forces are used against God's purposes, and can be turned to persecute His Church. As surely, in the nemesis that overtakes those who follow this path, they finally engineer their own destruction.[30]

No wonder, with the perils of rulership so acutely unmasked, the New Testament exhorts that, first of all, 'supplications, prayers, intercessions, thanksgivings, be made for all men; for kings and all that are in high place' (1 Tim 2^{1f}). In human society, good rule is a necessity, and those exercising it need to be safeguarded from the perils resulting from human frailty.

[29] Stauffer has a fine paragraph illustrating this in his *New Testament Theology*, pp. 85f. Our prayers, for this very reason (1 Clem 61) must be directed to the end that the State will be kept from this temptation.

[30] For an exhibition of this principle at work in the widest of applications, see, e.g., Arnold Toynbee's *A Study of History*.

CHAPTER NINETEEN

THE NATURE OF THE FAITH THAT IS THE LINK WITH POWER

THE result of our study of both Testaments is an underlining of the fact with which we began: that the God of the Bible is the God of Power. This is axiomatic in both Old and New Testaments. The realm of power is not man's, but God's. The good news of the New Testament is based not on man's action, but on God's. The Kingdom has irrupted into our world. Victory over sin, death, and evil has been achieved by the Son. His Cross and Resurrection are facts of history, possessing ever-present power. Through Him, God's Spirit is now available universally. The fact is that all 'spiritual' power comes from God, and is shared with men at His volition.

There is, however, a factor of response that is part of the human situation; and this, also, is of God's ordination. In any study of 'power' this 'factor of response' must be examined. The New Testament word for this is 'faith': a word with a variety of meanings and many overtones. What needs to be carefully noted is the nuance given to it in central New Testament passages to do with God's working in power—in forgiveness, in healing, in establishing new relationships and living after new ways.

When, for example, Jesus makes His announcement (Mk 1^{15}) concerning the imminence of the Kingdom, the response asked for is faith. The good news is to be believed in, accepted, received.[1] The Kingdom is God's gift (Lk 12^{32}; Mt 16^{19}): faith is the way to welcome it (Mk $9^{27, 42}$, 10^{14f}; Lk 18^{17})[2]. Prayer, the expression of faith, is the means by which the Spirit—source of power—can be received (Lk 11^{13}). For *δυνάμεις* to occur, Christ looked for faith in others, and used it himself.[3] After the events of the Passion, the Resurrection, and Pentecost, the Apostles pointed to faith as the key to their new-found ability to work the works of their Master (Acts 3^{16}).[4] With the proclamation of the gospel it is also announced that this quality is required for its right reception (Acts

[1] Above, p. 80. [2] P. 86. [3] P. 114. [4] P. 136.

8^{37}, 13^{39}; cf. Rom 1^{16}, 10^{9}). By means of the identification it suggests and makes possible with Christ's Death and Resurrection, faith enables the Christian to die to sin and rise to newness of life and, as in baptism, enter the life of the Church (Rom 6^{3ff}; Col 2^{12}). When Peter sees and believes who Jesus is, the foundation for the Church is established; and for him, and all others in a like relationship with Jesus, faith becomes the means by which heaven and earth are joined in power.[5] It is by faith that the supreme possibility can occur—that Christ may dwell in our hearts (Eph 3^{17}).

In previous sections of this work, reference has been made to the place of trust and obedience in Hebrew religion, and to *Emunah* in its LXX translation as πίστις as a root idea and a root word leading directly toward the 'faith' of the New Testament.[6] We have also noted the connexion between Prayer and Power in the old literature.[7] But though these facts prepare for the emergence of New Testament πίστις, there is, at this very point to do with power, a great leap forward in the New Testament. The records themselves help to locate how and where this took place. Without doubt, it centred in our Lord's own life and ministry. Because He adventured in this way of joining heaven and earth in power, others in His company and by His example were induced to follow Him. A swift survey of the New Testament helps to reveal the common source of this new dynamism.

It becomes impressive when we discover that in no case recorded in the Synoptics does Jesus use the word πίστις otherwise than in a dynamic way. It is never used here of mere conviction or belief. The term occurs without explanation. Doubtless Jesus could rely on the popular understanding of it, but in His company the people of His day had to pour into it a content of trust, receptivity and adventurousness that made of it something altogether new.[8]

[5] Pp. 144ff. [6] Pp. 29, 57. [7] Pp. 32ff, 57f.

[8] Πίστις occurs 25 times in the Synoptics, as against 30 uses of the verb (35, if the cases in Mark's longer ending are included). 9 of these are in Matthew, 5 in Mark and 11 in Luke. Once the word is used in the passive sense of 'faithfulness' (Mt 23^{23}). In Mt 9^{29} the faith is in Christ's ability to heal—verse 28 makes this apparent. Mt 8^{10} (Lk 7^{9}), Mt. 9^{2}, (Mk 2^{5}; Lk 5^{20}), Mt 9^{22} (Mk 5^{34}; Lk 8^{48}), Mt 15^{28} Mk 10^{52} (Lk 18^{42}) and Lk 17^{19} use the word in somewhat similar fashion, though the faith is unspecified. It is 'faith' that saves these people. Similarly, in Lk 7^{50}, it saves the woman who was a sinner, not from bodily harm, but from guilt and sinfulness. Mk 4^{40} (Lk 8^{25}) Jesus asks His disciples how it is that they have no faith; in Lk 22^{32} He prays for Simon that his 'faith' fail not. Mt 17^{20} (Lk 17^{6}), 'faith as a grain of mustard seed'; Lk 17^{5}, 'increase our faith'; Lk 18^{8}, 'when the Son of Man cometh shall he find faith on the earth?'

Behind this usage, we discover certain governing ideas: (1) The basis of faith is an unswerving certainty concerning God's power, sovereignty and complete freedom of action. This is *His* world and He is in control. (This is Old Testament *Emunah* developed to the full, together with the trust in His goodness and providence expressed in such a root as b-t-h.)[9] (2) On man's part there must be an unhesitating obedience to promptings and intuitions coming from God. (3) Faith is not a 'surface' response. It involves the opening of one's inner nature to God. This 'total' response to what He is revealing and offering, provides a channel by which His power can enter a situation. Openness of heart and mind, the spirit of expectancy and receptivity, are all part of this. Stauffer refers to faith as Jesus used it as '*ein verwegenes Furmöglichhalten*', which might be translated as 'an adventurous conviction that something is possible'.[10] He grasped at the possibilities seen in God. 'All things are possible to him that believeth' is His own daring statement (Mk 9[23]; cf. Mt 17[20]). As Walter Grundmann comments, this is a clear pronouncement that the power of God is received through faith.[11]

It is an attractive idea that in the words of Mk 11[22f] we approach something like a 'definition of faith'.[12] The passage begins 'Have faith in God' (*Ἔχετε πίστιν θεοῦ*). In God were all the possibilities that Jesus used. Schlatter's comment on the objective genitive here, which he labels as an Aramaism, is that 'the trust directed to God belongs to God, and is His'.[13] It is both God-

With the possible exception of Mt 23[23], these provide dynamic uses of *πίστις*, in a stratum unique even in the New Testament.

The verb is used in various senses: e.g. such as 'giving credence to a statement', etc. Here we note its more 'dynamic' usages. Mk 5[36] (Lk 8[50]) gives the word without any object specified: 'Fear not, only *believe*' (i.e. 'have faith'); Mt 8[13], 'As thou hast *believed*, so be it done unto thee', Mk 9[23], 'All things are possible to him that *believeth*', Mk 9[24], 'Lord, I *believe*, help thou my unbelief', and the two references (Mk 11[23f], Mt 21[22]) to believing prayer, all have to do with a kind of 'believing' by means of which power is able to flow.

To refer, as Bultmann does in his *T.W.z.N.T.* article on *πίστις* (VI.206) to Synoptic uses of the word as denoting 'faith in Jesus' miraculous powers' begs the question. People in His presence were encouraged to an audacious faith. *The result was miracle.*

[9] A. Weiser, *T.W.z.N.T.*, VI. 190 points out that the roots *bth, hsh, qwh, yhl, hkh* were all ultimately affected by the meaning of *he'emin* and were used in various ways to express the personal relationship possible between man and God.

[10] *Die Theologie des Neuen Testaments*, p. 147. The English translation gives 'an audacious assertion of a possibility' (p. 768).

[11] *Der Begriff der Kraft*, p. 116.

[12] J. A. Findlay makes this suggestion in an early book of his, *Jesus as They saw Him*, 1921, p. 102.

[13] *Der Glaube im Neuen Testament*, p. 588.

inspired and God-directed. Faith of this kind, even if it be but a grain, possessing the power of life and growth of the mustard-seed (cf. 4^{31}), can remove mountains.[14] The stress in verse 23 falls upon the mountain-mover's concentration. There is an intense integration about his purpose and desire and his faith in God. There is to be no 'doubt in his heart' (cf. Jas 1^{6f}), as he enters upon his act of faith. He must be possessed (verse 24) of a confident assurance of the outcome.

All these are elements of the picture one gains of faith in the Synoptics. It is clear everywhere that it is based entirely upon God. Places where we can observe the component of concentrated purpose and desire are the story of Bartimaeus; the incident in Mark 2 (verse 5), where the word of forgiveness is first drawn from Jesus because of the ingenuity and determination of the four men (cf. Mk 7^{24ff}; Mt 15^{21ff}); and that of the woman in Mark 5, who, having sought cure for twelve years, determined to gain help from Jesus, making and carrying out her plans accordingly. The element of not being 'distracted', of 'not doubting in his heart' is illustrated in the Lord's swift move to counter the effect on Jairus of the announcement of his daughter's death: 'Be not afraid: only believe (go on believing).'

In the kind of faith for which He looked, confident assurance counted. 'Believest thou that I am able to do this?' He asks in Matthew 9^{28}. All the powers of the Kingdom are present in Him to help and to heal, but the one who asks must be certain of this, in order that the full relationship of faith be possible. With Mark 11^{24} ('All things whatsoever ye pray and ask for, believe that ye have received them, and ye shall have them')[15] is to be compared Matthew 11^{22} ('And all things whatsoever ye shall ask in prayer, believing, ye shall receive'.) This kind of believing is not only the attitude of confident assurance—it most certainly is that—but it is inspired first and last by God. It looks to God, both for power, and for guidance. It is *enlightened*, and therefore certain.

The Fourth Gospel is written, so its author declares (20^{31}), to induce faith in Jesus and enable its readers, thus, to find 'life'

[14] The repeated use of this logion (cf. Mt 17^{20}) points to its being a saying of Jesus. Its striking character would fix it in men's minds. Its use by Paul (1 Cor 13^{2}) corroborates this view. T. W. Manson (*Sayings*, p. 141) regards Lk 17^{6} (with the sycamine tree substituted for the mountain) not as a variant, but as a similar saying preserved in Q quite independently.

[15] An indication as to where Jesus found the source of His own power? Cf. Mk 9^{29}.

in Him. 'Look at the Gospel as a drama', says E. A. Abbott, 'and you will find that few of its leading characters are not placed at some time in such circumstances as to show us—or make us ask—what, or whom, and how, and why, they "believed", or why, and what, and whom, they were exhorted to believe.'[16] It is self-confessedly a book concerning the forging of this living link first with the incarnate, and now with the exalted Lord, through faith, and an exposition of what this is and how it operates.

The dynamic attitude of which it treats has thus, in John, a characteristic object. Directed towards Christ, it fulfils its mission when He is recognized and accepted as Son of God, uniting believers in the bond of His Love and the body of His Church, and linking mortals with the realm of everlasting life.

John's concern is not, as with other New Testament writers, to carry the thought of faith's consummation into the future. Eschatology for him has impinged upon the present (though none speaks in higher terms than he of all that the future holds for the believer; cf. 1 Jn 3^{2}). His interest is with 'sonship' now. We are made sons through the Son, and the way into this relation is through faith. A man may know the Life of God from the moment of believing (Jn 3^{26}; 1 Jn 5^{12}). Straightway he is partaking in the Spirit, granted now that Jesus has been 'glorified'. By means of faith, here and now, the 'believer' enters into what Bultmann calls 'eschatological existence'.[17] Redeemed from his merely worldly self, he is no more 'of the world' though still 'in the world' (17^{11}, 14^{16}).

It is argued sometimes that John's avoidance of the noun πίστις is because of its Gnostic associations. This may be so, but it is also symptomatic of his treatment of faith that it is portrayed in the active, verbal form. This also has a bearing on his use with the verb of the preposition εἰς. Thirty-seven out of the forty-five times in the New Testament this construction occurs are in the Johannine writings. The kind of belief in Christ with which John is concerned is a venturing of the personality, a commitment of one's inner self, which the phrase literally translated 'believing *into* Him' embodies and pictorializes.[18]

It is to be noted that, in John's account, during the Lord's

[16] *Johannine Voc.* (*Diatesserica*), para. 1,464.

[17] See para 50, pp. 75ff, Bultmann, *Theology of the New Testament*, II.

[18] In *T.W.z.N.T.*, Bultmann (VI.204) describes this construction as an 'abbreviation which became a formula in the language of the Christian Mission'. It is not in the

ministry, the disciples are mere ciphers in the realm of power. Their importance is that they are witnesses of God's acts through and in His Son. They are fully commissioned only after the Resurrection (20^{22f}) and are never expected, as in the Synoptics, to exercise faith themselves in a dynamic way and share either in prophetic preaching or in healing. This fact sets the promise of 14^{12} in even sharper relief, 'Verily, verily, I say unto you, He that believeth on me, the works that I do shall he do also; and greater (works) than these shall he do, because I go unto the Father.' This all-important relation of 'believing-into-Him' introduces the disciple, thenceforward, to the realm of power. The gospel, the vehicle of salvation, has now been forged. The 'believer' has this most powerful of weapons in his hands and in his heart; and together with this he has also the witnessing power of the Spirit. Christ, now 'gone to the Father' is guarantee of these possibilities. The context of the promise in 14^{12} speaks of this, and of the almost unlimited power accorded by the Lord to prayer now in His Name. The dividing point between the disciples' lack of power, and their accession to it, as elsewhere in the New Testament, is in the events of Christ's Death and Resurrection, and the coming of the Holy Spirit.

Turning to Paul, it is impressive to set out certain references from his Epistles, noticing how in them 'power' is in apposition to, and shown to be dependent upon, 'faith':

> For I am not ashamed of the gospel: for it is the power of God unto salvation to every one that believeth (Rom 1^{16}).
> . . . that your faith should not stand in the wisdom of men, but in the power of God (1 Cor 2^{5}).
> . . . and what the exceeding greatness of his power to usward who believe. . . . (Eph 1^{19}).
> To this end we also pray always for you, that our God may . . . fulfil every desire of goodness and (every) work of faith, with power (2 Thess 1^{11}).

(The list could be still further extended by including such texts as Gal 3^{5}; Phil 3^{9f}; Col 2^{12}, etc.)

H. J. Schoeps, in his book on Paul, says that in his use of the

LXX, and is comparatively rare in the Synoptic Gospels and Acts. E. de Witt Burton (*Galatians*, *I.C.C.*, pp. 475ff) thinks, rather, 'that it came into literary use in the Christian (perhaps Pauline) circles of the apostolic age, as being more exactly expressive of the Christian feeling respecting the relation of the believer to Christ, especially in its aspect of acceptance and adherence, than any previously current phraseology'.

word πίστις the Apostle is obviously referring to something different from the Biblical-Talmudic *Emunah.* The latter, as Professor Schoeps says, connotes trust in the sense of fidelity. Paul's 'faith alone' can introduce a man into the

membership of a community which the Pharisees from the standpoint of their faith would have to call a community of sinners. The Pauline faith is not trust in the Biblical God, but is faith in the sacral event of Christ-soteriology, which he assesses as a saving disposition of God.[19]

It is *this* because Paul has learned of πίστις as the way to the reception of God's gifts. All that happened in Christ's Death and Resurrection becomes powerful for the believer through faith.

In these urgent missionary letters of Paul a variety of strands can be disentangled concerning this conception. What needs to be safeguarded is this very aspect which is now under consideration.[20]

The essence of faith for Paul, we would say, is whole-hearted acceptance. In Ephesians 2[8f] faith is clearly indicated as the faculty by which we respond to what is there at the initiative of God alone: but the words immediately warn against regarding faith as in any measure the cause of our salvation. It is the agent on our side of the transaction, not the cause. *That* is in God's grace alone. So Paul, typically, would have us think of our faith itself as a gift of God. To regard it in this fashion destroys any risk of thinking of it meritoriously (cf. Rom 12[3, 6]; 2 Thess 2[13]). Thus faith, while the method of response to grace, is itself due to the Grace of God (Eph 1[19]; Phil 1[29]).[21]

[19] *Paul: The Theology of the Apostle in the Light of Jewish Religious History* (E.T.), London, 1961, p. 204.

[20] Bultmann states that for Paul faith is primarily obedience in reception of the Gospel. It is not an 'experience', but simply the condition of salvation, including not only this element of obedience, but also that of confession and a form of knowledge. (*Theology of the New Testament*, I.314ff). He writes similarly in his *T.W.z.N.T.* article. Wissmann (*Der Verhältnis von πίστις und Christusfrömmigheit bei Paulus*, v. 67), committed to the view that faith and Christ-mysticism represent two different strains in Paul's thinking, writes 'πίστις does not mean to trust, but to believe in the naked sober sense of affirmation, appropriation and agreement'. Martin Buber is influenced by views of New Testament scholars of this order in his thesis, *Two Types of Faith.* On p. 97 he quotes Wissmann as saying that Pauline faith 'is above all entirely believing [*fürwahrhaltender*] faith'.

[21] However, because of the factor of human free will, all do not respond to God's offer: the Grace of God can, indeed, be received in vain (2 Cor 6[1]). It is therefore at the point where faith begins to operate that the fusion comes between the work of God in the heart and the willingness of man to go forward. As over against what God does, this human factor is so unimportant that it scarcely counts in the picture. *All* is of God's grace.

Faith is the 'Amen', the whole personality saying 'Yes'[22] to what God is revealing. By means of our responsiveness we enter into all that God offers, and, supremely, receive what is revealed to us in Christ. Faith thus becomes the way of union with our Lord in spirit. By means of it we can identify ourselves with the powers released and manifested in His Death and Resurrection. This is the 'faith in the sacral event of Christ-Soteriology'.

It can be viewed in its various aspects of belief and acceptance; reliance, trust and confidence; fidelity and loyalty. The power it invokes and the truths with which it connects are, however, not in itself: all is of God and His Grace. Faith is the faculty in man by which contact is made with these spiritual realities: but even this faith is something in ourselves which we owe to Him. At the very same time it forms the contrast to law-righteousness, to any form of trust in personal merit to put one right with God, and to all forms of self-confidence and self-glorying (note Gal 6^{14}; Rom 3^{27}—'boasting' is excluded by faith).

Behind Paul's use of this concept there is much taking us back to Jesus and the Synoptic testimony concerning πίστις. It is, indeed, with this background in mind that Paul in Galatians $3^{23, 25}$ uses the phrases, 'before faith came . . . now that faith is come'. He is not implying that before the Christian era there was no faith, but that in Jesus it came uniquely to light, and in Him also it found its supreme object.[23] D. S. Cairns, after referring to the ascription of originality to Paul in the matter of 'faith', concludes:

original St Paul certainly is, but his originality comes in at a later stage. He seizes upon Christ's principle, and applies it with extraordinary freshness, boldness, and insight, to the new situation created by the death and resurrection of Jesus Christ, and the gift of His Spirit. But so far as I can see there is nothing said in his writings about the vital place of faith in the Christian life which his Master had not said before him.[24]

In Hebrews faith is also pictured as the means to the reception of power. Without faith, 4^2 indicates, we are in danger of having listened merely to words without making union with what lies behind them. Taking the alternative reading with χ, the Old

[22] This 'Amen' response of faith echoes something implicit by derivation in Old Testament *Emunah*; cf. 1 Cor 1^{20}.
[23] Jakob Jocz, *The Jewish People and Jesus Christ*, 1949, p. 289.
[24] *The Faith that Rebels*, 5th Ed., p. 252.

Latin, the Peshitto (ὁ λόγος τῆς ἀκοῆς μή συγκεκ(ε)ρα(σ)μένος τῇ πίστει τοῖς ἀκούσασιν), Moffatt translates: their good news did them no good, 'since it did not meet with faith in the hearers'. In his *Commentary*[25] he makes the further point that τῇ πίστει may be an instrumental dative: 'since it did not enter vividly into the hearers by means of the faith which it normally awakens in men'.

The definition of faith in Hebrews 11[1], 'Now faith is the assurance of (things) hoped for, the proving of things not seen' joins together many apparently diverse ideas. The author is a combination of Platonist and eschatological thinker; and this fact explains how to him faith is at once insight into and connexion with, the eternal, and also anticipation of what is to come. Käsemann in *Das wandernde Gottesvolk* refers to another regulative idea in Hebrews: that in this world God's people are all pilgrims. Faith is thus the bridge between the perishable and imperishable worlds, over which the Christian passes as pilgrim. 'As an echo of the objective divine Word, faith is an assurance which has an objective foundation which surpasses all earthly possibilities.'[26] Faith, thus, is the link between two worlds, this and the spiritual—the hand by which we grasp what God offers, and the power by which we go forward to prove what Christ is and can be to us. It is 'confident assurance' based on what is revealed by God, and it is a creative link by which what would otherwise not materialize in this world is brought into effect. In this sense, it stands for our 'title-deeds'[27] and it becomes our 'proof'. Even at its most daring, faith, which oscillates between creativity and obedience, is conformable to what is shown to be the will of God. It is like this with all the examples of faith shown in Chapter 11.

In Chapter 12, against the mighty examples quoted, and with a sense of kinship with these witnesses, the reader is brought back to his own times and admonished to show a like faith and steadfast patience. Even more especially, with eyes fixed on Jesus, origin and goal of faith, who Himself 'endured all that hostility from sinful men', we should hold fast and not fail. This verse, 12[2], is valuable in that alone of all the texts in the New Testament it speaks of the Lord Himself as exercising faith. The idea is implicit

[25] *I.C.C., Hebrews*, p. 50. [26] Ibid., p. 22.
[27] See Moulton and Milligan, *Vocabulary of the Greek New Testament illustrated from the Papyri and other Non-literary Sources*, for this meaning of ἔλεγχος in the papyri.

everywhere,[28] but here we are bidden to look at Jesus, as the Pioneer and Perfection of faith (ἀφορῶντες εἰς τὸν τῆς πίστεως ἀρχηγὸν καὶ τελειωτὴν Ἰησοῦν).[29] From Him, the Christian learns how to devote the whole will to God, as He did.

In spite of what is 'intellectual' in the treatment of faith in Hebrews, it can be said that this Epistle is equally concerned with faith as a dynamic force. Notice, as the letter ends, that its author asks for the prayers of his readers (13^{18}).

The General Epistle of James illustrates in a much more obvious manner two strains concerning faith. There is (1) the typical assent to items of belief. It is this at which James tilts in 2^{19}.[30] This 'intellectual' form of faith needs to be substantiated by works. Without the appropriate deeds following it is barren and dead ($2^{17, 20}$). What a man does should grow out of his beliefs. Then there is (2) the dynamic attitude, illustrated in 1^{5f}, 5^{15}. Concerning this kind of 'asking' and praying, James comments, 'The supplication of a righteous man availeth much in its working' (5^{16}).[31]

The controversy in James 2^{14ff} is often interpreted as levelled against the Pauline conception of justifying faith. That this should be so is due, in part, to the fact that Paul has merged the two elements shown separately in James. In the truly Pauline faith, the dynamism James thinks of in connexion with prayer and healing has interfused with the intellectual element; and this form of belief becomes so effective that it means a change of spiritual relationship and inward personality.[32] Those who misunderstood Paul left out the dynamic element, and thought he was teaching that mere belief, on the intellectual level, results in

[28] Note the πίστις Ἰησοῦ Χριστοῦ of the Pauline letters: this expression may, in certain instances, be subjective rather than objective. Faith has its spring, its origin in Him, as well as finding in Him its supreme object.

[29] Moffatt translates ἀρχηγὸν καὶ τελειωτὴν as 'pioneer and perfection' (*Comm.* p. 196). Here we are looking at the perfect exemplar, from whom most of all and best of all faith is to be understood. ἀρχηγός means a pathbreaker into uncharted lands. It also means 'the first', thus supplying the impetus for those who follow. (Bauer, p. 112 and C. K. Barrett, *Background to New Testament* and *Its Eschatology*, p. 390, n. 1.)

[30] The belief that God is one is the necessary basic belief common to Jew and Christian (cf. Deut 6^{4}; Mk 12^{29}).

[31] Is ἐνεργουμένη, placed at the end of this sentence, there for emphasis, and is it middle or passive? Mayor and others argue for a passive meaning (cf. the kind of prayer that Paul describes in Rom 8^{26}: see Alex. Ross, *Comm. ad loc.*). It may, however, as in Paul's usage, mean 'set in operation by Divine agency' (J. A. Robinson, *Ephesians*, p. 247).

[32] James's dynamic faith, it must be noted, also affects spiritual relationships too. He thinks of forgiveness as well as of healing in connexion with the 'prayer of faith' (5^{15}).

justification, whereas it is the inner committal alone that can have such an outcome. Committal of this kind issues in new conduct, so that here, too, faith and works cannot really be thought of as sundered: 'faith working through love' is Paul's ideal (Gal 5^{6}). His justified sinner declares his new state by acting in accord with the ethic Paul is always eager to enunciate.

By contrast the Pastoral Epistles exhibit most clearly the tendencies which are moving away from the kind of accent we have discovered elsewhere in the New Testament. Faith here is canalized completely into 'saving faith', and the usage with the definite article, '*the* faith' is general. In these letters, faith is no longer the vital link by which contact is made with God and all heaven's powers, but rather a matter of directing aright one's faculty for belief and keeping in the path of strict orthodoxy. In this, these letters are not typical of the New Testament in general. Faith is normally a dynamic attitude, the link with power.

We need, now, to return on our tracks to make one or two general observations. The first concerns a matter to which we have already alluded: the close connexion between faith and prayer. 'The "faith" of Mark 11^{23f} is a faith that prays (cf. Mk 9^{29}; Lk 18^{1}; Jn $11^{22f,\ 41}$)', comments Ethelbert Stauffer.[33] 'Prayer is the source of its power, and the means of its strength—God's omnipotence is its sole assurance, and God's sovereignty its only restriction.'

Men, said Jesus, should ask, seek ,and knock (Mt 7^{7ff}). They will be answered. Prayer is the expression and the vehicle of faith, by which we can command the powers of God. It moves, however, at the impulse of God within us. To pray, *πιστεύοντες*, in the sense of Matthew 21^{22} is not a matter of using the faculty of faith in praying—though that is of first importance: prayer, to be effective, must always be 'in faith'—what matters is that we pray in communion and in harmony with God. Then we are 'believing' rightly. Prayer of this kind will always be 'according to the will of God' (Rom 8^{27}, I Jn 5^{14}).

Paul thinks of this element in Christian prayer in such a way that he can view it as the Holy Spirit praying within us (Rom $8^{15f,\ 26f}$). In Hebrews Christ is the mediator of our prayers, and our heavenly intercessor. He is the ground of our confidence as we draw near to the Father through Him. John, in his Gospel,

[33] *New Testament Theology*, p. 169.

promises as much as do the Synoptics regarding prayer 'in faith'. His equivalent is that prayer shall be 'in His Name' ($15^{7, 16}$, 16^{23f}). This kind of praying is uttered within our discipleship, because of Him, and it is made, through Him, to the Father.

In the living communion of prayer man is 'admitted to a share in causality'.[34] What we desire deeply and express thus on earth is heard by our Father in heaven and answered. That is the simple New Testament statement. Small wonder, then, that prayer needs to be watchful, and the one who prays needs to guard against any attempt to use prayer 'magically'.

There is need, then, to note the distinction between 'true' and 'false' faith, which Adolf Schlatter makes.[35] Faith does not present us with special facilities for selfish use or exploitation. It is a 'false faith' which seeks to reverse the true relation between man and God. It would *use* God, instead of living at His disposal. The Temptation story shows Jesus making this distinction: the idea of throwing Himself from the pinnacle of the Temple providing an example of a spurious faith that would exploit God's protection. All our Lord's sayings concerning faith's mighty powers need to be set against the background of His devotion to the Will of God. Whoever in this realm is aiming at the fulfilment of His own wishes is thinking of God as servant, instead of living to fulfil His purposes. By his teaching on the severity of God, our Lord would keep the disciples' faith rightly balanced. Only he truly believes in God who is awed by His judgement and subdued to His Will, even while rejoicing in His goodness and mercy.

In this matter of faith, as in all else, Jesus is the Mediator. Faith as the link between heaven and earth receives in Him, who came to join these realms, its supreme manifestation. In His presence, faith in its lowest forms and weakest adumbrations received illumination and is shown to be the parent of great possibilities. In His presence, too, faith is augmented as well as illuminated. 'Help thou my unbelief,' cried a man who was making this discovery.

The key to our Lord's own attitude is that He identified Himself with the Father and the doing of His Will.[36] One of the things

[34] A Maillot, 'Prayer', *Vocabulary of the Bible* (ed. Atkinson), p. 329. Grundmann (*T.W.z.N.T.*, II.303) finely says: 'In the faith which resulted in miracle the believer has a part in the Lordship of God'.

[35] *Der Glaube im Neuen Testament*, pp. 165ff.

[36] This, in turn, is the key to the faith of a disciple, who now, in the hierarchy of faith, is to identify himself with his Lord, and to pray 'in His Name'; cf. the statements about prayer in Mt 21^{22} and Jn 16^{23f}.

that delighted Him concerning the Centurion (Mt 8^{5ff}; Lk 7^{1ff}) was that in his 'great faith' this man recognized the principle of delegated authority at work in Jesus. As the One 'under authority', Jesus could command the spiritual powers effectively. A further item that we can state categorically about Jesus is that He lived the life of trust in God that He advocated to others. He was sure of the Father's love, guidance, care, and providence (cf. Mk 4^{38}, 8^{14ff}, etc.). This confidence was reinforced by His sense of mission. He was in the Father's hands and lived to do His Will.

The faith with which Jesus met death is specially to be noted. It has much to reveal concerning 'power'. Notice, first, His certainty, as expressed at the Last Supper and at the Jewish trial, of His victorious return beyond death (Mk $14^{25, 62}$). Then there is the dual nature of faith shown (1) in the consciousness of power available to avert catastrophe, on the one hand, and (2) in the sense of guidance and obedience, on the other, leading Him at this time into the midst of apparent disaster. This tension makes His going to death the most impressive study of faith-in-action that we have. Matthew 25^{53} shows Him refusing the powers open to faith, after one kind, to avoid that to which His faith, after another kind, had brought Him. Nowhere is the intricate relation between faith as initative and faith as obedient response more perfectly illustrated. Jesus exercises the faith that is humble submission to God's will, even when it means that the powers of evil are to have their way. The faith which He has continuously proved as dynamic energy overthrowing these powers must rest in abeyance.

Because of what we see in Jesus, the prominence of this term, *πίστις*, can now be understood. It was demonstrated, in Him, as the link with the realm of God's Power. In turn, the experience of the Apostles was illumined and interpreted by the aid of this concept, which had flashed into newness of life. The era of power had dawned, and men had been presented with the key by which to enter it. Alone of all the New Testament writers, the author of 'Hebrews' makes apparent the indebtedness of all. For the understanding of what faith is, he looks to Jesus, its 'pioneer and perfection', and bids others look there, too (Heb 12^{2}). *He* demonstrated faith in its perfection, and pioneered into its possibilities. His type of faith, and His insistence on its importance, provides the explanation of what is to be discerned in Acts and Paul and John. Because of its high character, it can be understood as a point from which men will all too easily decline. Naturally, and rightly, it came to be specified into 'saving faith'. But the progression thus began by which faith came to be equated with the idea of 'sound doctrine' and intellectual 'belief'. The final step in the process occurred when it was transferred from a subjective to an objective use. Within the bounds of the New Testament itself one can travel from the *πίστις* of the Synoptics to 'the faith' of the Pastorals. The process of diminution points back to the time when it could be seen in full vigour.

When we claim faith as the link with power we have the stamp of the Lord's authority. 'All things are possible', He said, 'to him that believeth.'

WE referred in Chapter 1 to the great doxological statements and credos which formed the rallying-point of Old Testament religion. Repeated at the cultic festivals, they provided constant reminders of God's present power, and of His covenant with Israel. Hymns and psalms re-echoed these statements.

Within the New Testament we find, somewhat similarly, statements of the *kerygma* that have settled into a pattern. Snatches of early Christian confessional formulae are also to be found, affirming Christ's Lordship and referring to His Death, Resurrection and Exaltation. The Pastorals provide us with 'faithful sayings' that were in current use, and here and there we can detect quotations from early Christian hymnology. At the end of the great argument in Romans (11^{33-6}), and at the end of certain other letters, the writer breaks into doxology. But there is nothing as stereotyped about these statements as in the typical Old Testament references to God's might shown to Israel.

In the last book of the Bible there are numerous outbursts in the form of ascriptions of power and might to God (e.g. 7^{12}, 19^{1f}). The doxologies in Revelation 11^{17f} and 12^{10} especially concern the eschatological unfolding of His power and the resulting Satanic overthrow. God has 'taken His great power' and 'reigned'. In the great choric sections of the central chapters, the angelic hosts thunder their praises to God and to His Christ. With these we can fittingly bring this book to an end.

Worthy art thou, our Lord and our God, to receive the glory and the honour and the power: for thou didst create all things, and because of thy will they were, and were created (4^{11}).

God's might in creation is here in review. In the next chapter those who sing the 'new song' add their ascription to the One who has 'purchased unto God with his blood (men) of every tribe, and people, and nation', making them, too, to be kings and priests unto God, reigning upon the earth (5^{9ff}). This is the 'new song', the note added to all that the Old Testament can tell regarding God's love and power to Israel. This is the tribute to God's act in Christ, whereby His love and power have now been released for all time available to all, throughout all generations, who have faith in Him.

Worthy is the Lamb that hath been slain to receive the power, and riches, and wisdom, and might, and honour, and glory, and blessing.

And every created thing which is in the heaven, and on the earth, and under the earth, and all things that are in them, heard I saying, Unto him that sitteth on the throne, and unto the Lamb, (be) the blessing, and the honour, and the glory, and the dominion, for ever and ever. *Amen.*

BIBLIOGRAPHY

General

Articles in various Bible dictionaries: Hasting's *Dictionary of the Bible*, *Dictionary of Christ and the Gospels*, *Dictionary of the Apostolic Church*; *Theological Word Book of the Bible* (London, 1950); *Vocabulary of the Bible* (ed. von Allmen) (E.T.), London, 1958; and in Kittel's *Theologisches Wörterbuch zum Neuen Testament* (especially articles on *βασιλεία τοῦ θεοῦ*, K. L. Schmidt; on *δύναμις* and *ἰσχύς*, etc., W. Grundmann; *ἐξουσία*, W. Foerster; and *πίστις* A. Weiser and R. Bultmann).

Grundmann, W. *Der Begriff der Kraft in der Neutestamentlicher Gedankenwelt*, Stuttgart, 1932.
Bentzen, Aage. *King and Messiah* (E.T.), London, 1955.
Brunner, Emil. *Justice and the Social Order* (E.T.), London, 1945.
Bultmann, R. *Essays Philosophical and Theological*, London, 1956.
—— *Primitive Christianity in its Contemporary Setting* (E.T.), London, 1956.
Dodd, C. H. *The Bible and the Greeks*, London, 1935.
Eliade, Mircia. *Patterns in Comparative Religion* (E.T.), London, 1958.
Frazer, James. *The Golden Bough* (Abridged Ed.), London, 1932.
Guignebert, Ch. *The Jewish World in the Time of Jesus* (E.T.), London, 1939.
Hanson, A. T. *The Wrath of the Lamb*, London, 1957.
Heiler, Friedrich. *Prayer: A Study in the History and Psychology of Religion* (E.T.), New York, 1958.
Klausner, J. *The Messianic Idea in Israel* (E.T.), London, 1956.
Langton, E. *Essentials of Demonology*, London, 1949.
Manson, T. W. (ed.). *A Companion to the Bible*, London, 1939.
Moore, G. F. *Judaism in the First Centuries of the Christian Era*, Vols. 1 and 2, London, 1927. Vol. 3 (Notes), London, 1930.
Murray, G. *Five Stages of Greek Religion*, Oxford, 1925.
Schmidt, W. *The Origin and Growth of Religion* (E.T.), London, 1931.
Thackeray, H. St. J. *St Paul and Jewish Thought*, London, 1900.
Tillich, Paul. *Love, Power and Justice*, Oxford, 1954.
Wright, G. E. *Biblical Archaeology*, London, 1957.
Appropriate sections in Strack-Billerbeck, *Kommentar z. N.T.*; *Peake's Commentary on the Bible*, London, 1962.

Old Testament

Albright, W. F. *Archaeology and the Religion of Israel*, Baltimore, 1953.
——*The Archaeology of Palestine*, London, 1949.
Buber, M. *The Prophetic Faith* (E.T.), New York, 1949.
—— *Moses* (E.T.), London, 1946.
Bright, John. *A History of Israel*, London, 1960.
Cook, S. A. *The Old Testament: a Reinterpretation*, London, 1936.
—— *The 'Truth' of the Bible*, Cambridge, 1938.
Eerdmans, B. D. *The Religion of Israel*, Leiden, 1947.
Eichrodt, W. *The Theology of the Old Testament*, Vol. I (E.T.), London, 1961.
Elmslie, W. A. L. *How Came Our Faith*, Cambridge, 1950.
Heaton, E. W. *The Book of Daniel*, London, 1956.
Hebert, A. G. *The Throne of David*, London, 1941.
Hooke, S. H. *In The Beginning* (*Clarendon Bible, VI*), Oxford, 1947.
—— *Myth and Ritual*, London, 1933.
Jacob, Edmond. *Theology of the Old Testament* (E.T.), London, 1958.
James, E. O. *The Concept of Deity*, London, 1950.
—— *The Old Testament in the Light of Anthropology*, London, 1935.
Johnson, A. R. *Sacral Kingship in Ancient Israel*, Cardiff, 1955.
—— *The Vitality of the Individual in the Thought of Ancient Israel*, Cardiff, 1949.
Köhler, Ludwig. *Hebrew Man* (E.T.), London, 1956.
—— *Old Testament Theology* (E.T.), London, 1957.
Löhr, Max. *A History of Religion in the Old Testament*, London, 1936.
North, C. R. *The Old Testament Interpretation of History*, London, 1946.
—— *Isaiah 40–55*, London, 1952.
—— *The Thought of the Old Testament*, London, 1948.
Noth, M. *Exodus* (E.T.), London, 1962.
Oesterley, W. O. E., and Robinson, T. H. *Hebrew Religion: Its Origin and Development*, London, 1937.
—— *A History of Israel*, Oxford, 1932.
Otto, R. *The Idea of the Holy* (E.T.), London, 1923.
Pedersen, Johs. *Israel* (E.T.), Vols. I and II, Oxford, 1926.
Pfeiffer, R. H. *Introduction to the Old Testament*, London, 1948.
Procksch, Otto. *Theologie des Alten Testaments*, 1949–50.
Rad, D. Gerhard von. *Der Heilige Krieg im alten Israel*, Zürich, 1951.
—— *Old Testament Theology*, Vol. 1 (E.T.), London, 1962.
—— *Genesis*, (E.T.) London, 1961.
Richardson, Alan. *Genesis I–XI*, London, 1953.
Robinson, H. Wheeler. *Inspiration and Revelation in the Old Testament*, Oxford, 1946.

Robinson, H. Wheeler. *The Religious Ideas of the Old Testament*, London, 1913.
—— (ed.) *Record and Revelation*, Oxford, 1938.
Rowley, H. H. *The Biblical Doctrine of Election*, London, 1950.
—— *The Faith of Israel*, London, 1956.
—— *The Growth of the Old Testament*, London, 1950.
—— (ed.) *The Old Testament and Modern Study*, London, 1951.
Snaith, N. *Distinctive Ideas of the Old Testament*, London, 1944.
Wright, G. E. *The Old Testament against Its Environment*, London, 1950.
Vriezen, Th. C. *An Outline of Old Testament Theology* (E.T.), Oxford, 1958.
Weiser, A. *The Psalms* (E.T.), London, 1962.

Apocrypha and Pseudepigrapha

Charles, R. H. (ed.). *The Apocrypha and Pseudepigrapha of the Old Testament*, Vols. 1 and 2, Oxford, 1913.
Oesterley, W. O. E. *An Introduction to the Books of the Apocrypha*, London, 1935.
Pfeiffer, R. H. *A History of New Testament Times: with an Introduction to the Apocrypha*, London, 1949.
Torrey, C. C. *The Apocryphal Literature: A Brief Introduction*, Yale, 1945.
Walker, T. *Hebrew Religion between the Testaments*, London, 1937.
—— *The Teaching of Jesus and the Jewish Teaching of His Age*, London, 1923.
Wicks, H. J. *The Doctrine of God in the Jewish Apocryphal and Apocalyptic Literature*, London, 1915.

The Dead Sea Scrolls

Allegro, J. M. *The Dead Sea Scrolls*, London, 1956.
Bruce, F. F. *Second Thoughts on the Dead Sea Scrolls*, London, 1956.
Burrows, M. *The Dead Sea Scrolls*, London, 1956.
Dupont-Sommer, A. *The Dead Sea Scrolls* (E.T.), Oxford, 1952.
—— *The Jewish Sect of Qumran and the Essenes* (E.T.), London, 1954.
Gaster, T. H. *The Scriptures of the Dead Sea Sect*, London, 1957.
Vermes, G. *The Dead Sea Scrolls*, London, 1962.

Philo

Colson and Whitaker (ed.). *Works*, London, 1929.
Drummond, J. *Philo Judaeus*, London, 1888.
Wolfson, H. A. *Philo*, Harvard, 1948.

New Testament

Allen, E. L. *The Purpose of Jesus*, London, 1951.
Angus, S. *The Mystery Religions and Christianity*, London, 1925.

Aulén, G. *The Faith of the Christian Church* (E.T.), London, 1961.
Barrett, C. K. *The Gospel according to St. John*, London, 1955.
—— *The Holy Spirit and the Gospel Tradition*, London, 1947.
Beare, F. W. *The First Epistle of Peter*, London, 1947.
Bernard, J. H. *St John* (*I.C.C.*), Edinburgh, 1928.
Borchert, O. *The Original Jesus* (E.T.), London, 1933.
Brandon, S. G. F. *The Fall of Jerusalem and the Christian Church*, London, 1951.
Branscomb, B. H. *The Gospel of Mark* (*M.N.T.C.*), London, 1937.
Bruce, F. F. *The Acts of the Apostles: Greek Text with Introduction and Commentary*, London, 1951.
—— *Commentary on the Book of the Acts*, London, 1954.
Buber, M. *Two Types of Faith* (E.T.), London, 1951.
Bultmann, R. *Theology of the New Testament* (E.T.) Vol. 1, London, 1952. Vol. 2, London, 1955.
Burton, E. de Witt. *Galatians* (*I.C.C.*), Edinburgh, 1921.
Cadoux, A. T. *The Theology of Jesus*, London, 1940.
—— *The Thought of James*, London, 1944.
Caird, G. B. *The Apostolic Age*, London, 1955.
—— *Principalities and Powers: a Study in Pauline Theology*, Oxford, 1956.
Cairns, D. S. *A Faith that Rebels*, London, 1933.
Campbell, J. (ed.). *The Mysteries* (*Eranos Year Book*, 2), New York, 1953.
Carrington, P. *The Early Christian Church*, Cambridge, 1957.
Case, S. J. (ed.). *Studies in Early Christianity*, New York, 1923.
Charles, R. H. *Revelation of St. John* (*I.C.C.*), Edinburgh, 1920.
Conzelmann, H. *The Theology of St. Luke* (E.T.), London, 1960.
Creed, J. M. *Gospel according to St Luke*, London, 1930.
Cullmann, O. *Christ and Time* (E.T.), London, 1951.
—— *The Early Church* (E.T.), London, 1956.
—— *The State in the New Testament* (E.T.), London, 1957.
Cumont, Franz. *The Oriental Religions in Roman Paganism*, Chicago, 1911.
Dalman, G. *The Words of Jesus* (E.T.), Edinburgh, 1902.
Davies, W. D. *Paul and Rabbinic Judaism*, London, 1948.
Deissmann, A. *Bible Studies* (E.T.), Edinburgh, 1903.
—— *Paul* (E.T.), London, 1926.
Dibelius, M. *Der Brief des Jacobus*, Göttingen, 1921.
—— *Studies in the Acts of the Apostles* (E.T.), London, 1956.
Dix, Gregory, *Jew and Greek: a Study in the Primitive Church*, London, 1953.
Dodd, C. H. *The Johannine Epistles* (*M.N.T.C.*), London, 1946.
—— *The Interpretation of the Fourth Gospel*, Cambridge, 1954.
—— *The Parables of the Kingdom*, London, 1935.
Duncan, G. S. *Galatians* (*M.N.T.C.*), London, 1934.

Duncan, G. S. *Jesus, Son of Man*, London, 1948.
Durrwell, F. X. *The Resurrection* (E.T.), London, 1960.
Easton, B. S. *The Pastoral Epistles*, London, 1947.
Farrer, A. *A Study in St Mark*, London, 1951.
Findlay, G. C. *Fellowship in the Life Eternal*, London, n.d.
Findlay, J. A. *The Fourth Gospel: an Expository Commentary*, London, 1956.
—— *The Way, the Truth, and the Life*, London, 1940.
Flew, R. N. *Jesus and His Church*, London, 1938.
Foakes-Jackson, F. J. *Acts of the Apostles* (*M.N.T.C.*), London, 1931.
Geldenhuys, J. N. *Supreme Authority*, London, 1953.
—— *The Gospel of Luke*, London, 1953.
Goguel, Maurice. *Jesus the Nazarene* (E.T.), London, 1926.
Goodspeed, E. J. *Introduction to the New Testament*, Chicago, 1937.
Grosheide, F. W. *The First Epistle to the Corinthians*, London, 1954.
Guignebert, Ch. *Jesus* (E.T.), London, 1935.
Guy, H. A. *The Origin of the Gospel of Mark*, London, 1954.
Harrison, P. N. *The Problem of the Pastoral Epistles*, London, 1921.
Hatch, W. H. P. *The Pauline Idea of Faith*, Harvard, 1917.
Heim, Karl. *The New Divine Order* (E.T.), London, 1930.
Hopwood, P. G. S. *The Religious Experience of the Primitive Church*, Edinburgh, 1936.
Hort, F. J. A. *The Christian Ecclesia*, London, 1897.
Hoskyns, E. C. *The Fourth Gospel*, Edinburgh, 1940.
—— and Davey, F. N. *The Riddle of the New Testament*, London, 1936.
Howard, W. F. *Christianity according to St John*, London, 1943.
Hunter, A. M. *Paul and His Predecessors*, London, 1940.
—— *Interpreting Paul's Gospel*, London, 1954.
—— *The Work and Words of Jesus*, London, 1950.
Jeremias, J. *The Parables of Jesus* (E.T.), London, 1954.
Jocz, Jacob. *The Jewish People and Jesus Christ*, London, 1949.
Käsemann, E. *Das wanderdne Gottesvolk, Eine Untersuchung zum Hebräerbrief*, Münster, 1939.
Kennedy, H. A. A. *The Theology of the Epistles*, London, 1919.
Kiddle, M. *Revelation of St John* (*M.N.T.C.*), London, 1940.
Kirk, K. E. (ed.). *The Apostolic Ministry*, London, 1947.
Klausner, J. *Jesus of Nazareth: His Life, Times, and Teaching* (E.T.), London, 1925.
Knox, John. *Chapters in a Life of Paul*, London, 1954.
Knox, W. L. *The Acts of the Apostles*, Cambridge, 1948.
—— *Paul and the Church of the Gentiles*, Cambridge, 1939.
—— *Some Hellenistic Elements in Primitive Christianity*, London, 1944.
Kümmel, W. G. *Promise and Fulfilment: the Eschatological Message of Jesus*, London, 1957.

Lagrange, M. J. *Evangile selon Saint Marc*, Paris, 1947.
—— *Evangile selon Saint Jean*, Paris, 1948.
Lake, K., and Foakes-Jackson, F. J. *The Beginnings of Christianity*, London, 1933.
Lake, K. *The Earlier Epistles of St Paul*, London, 1930.
Lampe, G. W. H. *The Seal of the Spirit*, London, 1951.
Langton, E. *The Angel Teaching of the New Testament*, London, 1936.
Lightfoot, J. B. *Galatians*, London, 1887.
—— *Colossians and Philemon*, London, 1879.
Lightfoot, R. H. *Gospel Message of St Mark*, Oxford, 1950.
—— *Locality and Doctrine in the Gospels*, Oxford, 1938.
—— (ed. C. F. Evans). *St John's Gospel: a Commentary*, Oxford, 1956.
Lietzmann, Hans. *The Beginnings of the Christian Church* (E.T.), London, 1937.
Lofthouse, W. F. *The Father and the Son*, London, 1934.
Loisy, A. *The Origins of the New Testament* (E.T.), London, 1950.
Macgregor, G. H. C. *Gospel of John* (*M.N.T.C.*), London, 1928.
Manson, T. W. *Beginning of the Gospel*, London, 1950.
—— *The Church's Ministry*, London, 1948.
—— *Sayings of Jesus*, London, 1949.
—— *The Teaching of Jesus*, Cambridge, 1931.
Manson, W. *The Epistle to the Hebrews*, London, 1951.
—— *Gospel of Luke* (*M.N.T.C.*), London, 1930.
—— *Jesus the Messiah*, London, 1943.
McNeile, A. H. *The Gospel according to St Matthew*, London, 1915.
—— *Introduction to the Study of the New Testament* (2nd ed. revised by G. S. C. Williams), Oxford, 1953.
Micklem, E. R. *Miracles and the New Psychology*, Oxford, 1922.
Milligan, G. *Thessalonians*, London, 1908.
Moffatt, J. *First Epistle of Paul to the Corinthians*, London, 1938.
Morris, Leon, *The Apostolic Preaching of the Cross*, London, 1955.
Müller, J. J. *Epistles of Paul to the Philippians and to Philemon*, London, 1955.
Murray, J. O. F. *Jesus, according to St John*, London, 1936.
Neil, W. *Thessalonians* (*M.N.T.C.*), London, 1950.
Nelson, J. R. *The Realm of Redemption*, London, 1951.
Nineham, D. (ed.). *Studies in the Gospels*, Oxford, 1955.
Nygren, A. *Commentary on Romans* (E.T.), London, 1952.
Otto, R. *The Kingdom of God and the Son of Man* (E.T.), London, 1938.
Plummer, A. *An Exegetical Commentary on the Gospels according to St Matthew*, London, 1911.
—— *St Luke* (*I.C.C.*), Edinburgh, 1901.

Ramsay, W. M. *The Bearing of Recent Discovery on the Trustworthiness of the New Testament*, London, 1915.
—— *The Teaching of Paul in terms of the Present Day*, London, 1913.
Ramsey, A. M. *The Resurrection of Christ*, London, 1945.
Rawlinson, A. E. J. *The Gospel according to St Mark*, London, 1925.
Richardson, A. *The Miracle Stories of the Gospels*, London, 1941.
—— *An Introduction to the Theology of the New Testament*, London, 1958.
Ridderbos, H. N. *Galatians* (*M.N.T.C.*), London, 1934.
Robinson, J. Armitage. *Ephesians*, London, 1909.
Robinson, T. H. *Matthew* (*M.N.T.C.*), London, 1928.
—— *Hebrews* (*M.N.T.C.*), London, 1933.
Sanday, W., and Headlam, A. C. *Romans* (*I.C.C.*), Edinburgh, 1902.
Sanders, J. N. *Foundations of the Christian Faith*, London, 1950.
Schlatter, A. *Der Glaube im Neuen Testament* (3rd ed.), Stuttgart, 1905.
—— *The Church in the New Testament Period* (E.T.), London, 1955.
Schmiedel, P. W. *The Johannine Writings* (E.T.), London, 1908.
Schoeps, H. J. *Paul: The Theology of the Apostle in the Light of Jewish Religious History* (E.T.), London, 1961.
Schweitzer, A. *The Mystery of the Kingdom of God* (E.T.), London, 1901.
—— *The Mysticism of St Paul* (E.T.), London, 1931.
—— *The Quest of the Historical Jesus* (E.T.), London, 1911.
Schweizer, E. *Church Order in the New Testament* (E.T.), London, 1961.
Scott, C. A. *Christianity according to St Paul*, Cambridge, 1932.
Scott, E. F. *The Book of Revelation*, London, 1940.
—— *Epistles to Colossians, Philemon and Ephesians* (*M.N.T.C.*), London, 1936.
—— *Pastoral Epistles* (*M.N.T.C.*), London, 1936.
Selwyn, E. G. *The First Epistle of St Peter*, London, 1947.
Stanton, H. U. W. *The Gospel according to St Matthew*, Madras, 1919.
Stauffer, E. *Christ and the Caesars* (E.T.), London, 1953.
—— *New Testament Theology* (E.T.), London, 1955.
Strachan, R. H. *The Fourth Gospel; Its Significance and Environment* (3rd ed.), London, 1941.
—— 2 *Corinthians* (*M.N.T.C.*), London, 1935.
Streeter, B. W. *The Four Gospels*, London, 1924.
—— *The Primitive Church*, London, 1930.
Swete, H. B. *The Holy Spirit in the New Testament*, London, 1909.
Taylor, V. *The Atonement in New Testament Teaching*, London, 1940.
—— *The Formation of the Gospel Tradition*, London, 1933.
—— *Gospel according to St Mark*, London, 1952.
—— *Jesus and His Sacrifice*, London, 1937.
—— *The Life and Ministry of Jesus*, London, 1954.
—— *The Names of Jesus*, London, 1953.

Taylor, V. *The Person of Christ in New Testament Teaching*, London, 1958.

Turner, H. E. W. *Jesus, Master and Lord*, London, 1953.

Westcott, B. F. *The Epistles of St John*, London, 1883.

—— *The Epistle to the Hebrews*, London, 1909.

Williams, C. S. C. *A Commentary on the Acts of the Apostles*, London, 1957.

Windisch, H. *Der Hebräerbrief*, Tübingen, 1931.

—— *Die Katholischen Briefe*, Tübingen, 1930.

Wissmann, E. *Das Verhältnis von πίστις and Christusfrömmigkeit bei Paulus*, Göttingen, 1926.

INDEX OF NAMES

INDEX OF SUBJECTS

TEXTUAL INDEX

1. OLD TESTAMENT

2. NEW TESTAMENT

3. THE APOCRYPHA

4. THE PSEUDEPIGRAPHA

5. QUMRAN DOCUMENTS